BLACK CHRISTIAN NATIONALISM

New Directions for the Black Church

BOOKS BY ALBERT B. CLEAGE, JR.:

The Black Messiah
Black Christian Nationalism

BLACK CHRISTIAN NATIONALISM

New Directions for the Black Church
Albert B. Cleage, Jr.

Including papers presented to the
First Black Christian Nationalist Convention,
edited by George Bell, National Co-ordinator

First Printing Morrow Quill Paperbacks, New York 1972

Second Printing:

Luxor Publishers of the Pan-African Orthodox
Christian Church, Detroit, MI 1987

The Introduction, "Authority and the Black Revolution," is reprinted by permission from *Erosion of Authority*, edited by Clyde L. Manschreck. Copyright © 1971 by Abingdon Press. Original title: "A Black Man's View of Authority."

Chapter 2, "The Black Church," is reprinted by permission from *Quest for a Black Theology*, edited by James J. Gardiner and J. Deotis Roberts, Sr. (Philadelphia, Pilgrim Press, 1971). Copyright © 1971 by Albert B. Cleage, Jr. Original title: "The Black Messiah and the Black Revolution."

Library of Congress Cataloging in Publication Data

Cleage, Albert B
  Black Christian nationalism.

  Bibliography: p.
  1. Black power—United States. 2. Afro-Americans—Religion.
I. Title.
E185.615.C62   1980   322.4′2′0973   80-14648
Luxor Publishers   ISBN 0–941205–01–0

Printed in the United States of America

Library of Congress Card Number: 74-151929

To my mother
Pearl Reed Cleage
who listened to me "preach" from the time I was four,
and told me that my New Testament professor was wrong
because Jesus was Black . . . *with love.*

ACKNOWLEDGMENT

During the past two years Black student groups at colleges, universities, and graduate schools of religion across the country have invited me to their campuses to lecture and to conduct seminars on the new Black theology.

The growing student interest in restructuring the Black church to make it relevant to the Black Revolution offers the only real hope for the future of an emerging Black Nation. Black Christian Nationalism challenges young Black people to devote their lives to the task of building an institutional power base on the foundation of a restructured Black church capable of spinning off all the other institutions which are necessary for Black survival.

Last summer BCN announced a ten-week ministerial training program for twenty college students interested in entering the BCN ministry. Hundreds of students responded and were disappointed because the program could not be immediately expanded. I express sincere appreciation to Black students who have invited me to speak and have persuaded college administrators to finance my visits adequately. Much of the material in this book was tried out on students at the following schools and has passed the test of frank and honest Black discussion:

Ball State University (Muncie, Indiana)
Chicago Theological Seminary (Chicago)
University of Chicago (Chicago)
City College of New York (New York)

Claremont School of Theology (Claremont, Calif.)

Colgate-Rochester Divinity School (Rochester, N.Y.)

Defiance College (Defiance, Ohio)

University of Detroit (Detroit)

Duke University (Durham, N.C.)

Elmhurst College (Elmhurst, Ill.)

Fisk University (Nashville)

Georgetown University (Washington, D.C.)

Goucher College (Towson, Md.)

Grinnell College (Grinnell, Iowa)

Heidelberg College (Tiffin, Ohio)

Howard University (Washington, D.C.)

Indiana University (Bloomington, Ind.)

Interdenominational Theological Center (Atlanta)

Kellogg Community College (Battle Creek, Mich.)

Macomb Community College (Warren, Mich.)

Malcolm X Liberation University (Durham, N.C.)

Michigan State University (East Lansing, Mich.)

University of Maryland (College Park, Md.)

University of Michigan (Ann Arbor, Mich.)

Morehouse College (Atlanta)

State University of New York at Buffalo (Buffalo, N.Y.)

Nirobi College (East Palo Alto, Calif.)

Norfolk State College (Norfolk, Va.)

North Carolina Central University (Durham, N.C.)

Ohio State University (Columbus, Ohio)

University of Pittsburgh (Pittsburgh)

Princeton Theological Seminary (Princeton, N.J.)

Ripon College (Ripon, Wis.)

Seattle University (Seattle)
Syracuse University (Syracuse, N.Y.)
Union Theological Seminary (New York)
Wayne State University (Detroit)
Western Maryland College (Westminster, Md.)
Western Michigan University (Kalamazoo,
   Mich.)
University of Wisconsin (Madison, Wis.)
College of Wooster (Wooster, Ohio)
Yale University Divinity School (New Haven,
   Conn.)

CONTENTS

The Black Christian Nationalist Creed

I Believe that human society stands under the judgment of one God, revealed to all, and known by many names. His creative power is visible in the mysteries of the universe, in the revolutionary Holy Spirit which will not long permit men to endure injustice nor to wear the shackles of bondage, in the rage of the powerless when they struggle to be free, and in the violence and conflict which even now threaten to level the hills and the mountains.

I Believe that Jesus, the Black Messiah, was a revolutionary leader, sent by God to rebuild the Black Nation Israel and to liberate Black people from powerlessness and from the oppression, brutality, and exploitation of the white gentile world.

I Believe that the revolutionary spirit of God, embodied in the Black Messiah, is born anew in each generation and that Black Christian Nationalists constitute the living remnant of God's Chosen People in this day, and are charged by Him with responsibility for the Liberation of Black people.

I Believe that both my survival and my salvation depend upon my willingness to reject INDIVIDUALISM and so I commit my life to the Liberation Struggle of Black people and accept the values, ethics, morals, and program of the Black Nation defined by that struggle, and taught by the Black Christian Nationalist Movement.

Authority and the
Black Revolution

Since the publication of *The Black Messiah* * in November, 1968, all efforts to construct a Black theology have been compelled to deal with the Blackness of Jesus (and of God). For the most part, Black theologians have been willing to assert the relevance of the Black experience without coming to grips with the historic fact that Jesus was a Black man. In a *Christian Century* issue dealing with Black theology, Miles J. Jones, Dean of Virginia Union University's school of theology, as though facing the issue, makes a classic irrelevant statement: "We need not color God or the Christ Black in order to appreciate Blackness as an instrument of the Divine." What then do we do, leave them white in defiance of the facts of history? Black schoolmen's theology is written for white acceptance. For the Black man their theology is sterile and stillborn because it is content to *declare* and *assert* with no feeling of

* Albert B. Cleage, Jr., *The Black Messiah* (New York: Sheed and Ward, 1968).

urgency or involvement in the Black man's struggle for existence.

We are not dealing with a matter of "appreciating Blackness" but with Black survival. Black theology is not a matter of putting together a pleasant jigsaw puzzle, making sure to use all the traditional white pieces, but of enabling the Black church to become relevant to the Black Liberation Struggle. We want to know:

1. How does God work in the world?

2. What was the meaning of the *life* of Jesus? What did *He* try to do?

3. What is the nature of man as affected by white racism and the Black experience? Is the white man a devil or a beast? If not, how can we explain his bestial behavior?

4. How does God relate to the Black Liberation Struggle? Does He join us in the faith that nothing is more sacred than the liberation of Black people?

5. Is either God or Jesus really relevant to the Black Man's Liberation Struggle?

6. What is the nature of salvation for the Black Man in terms of the realities of the modern world?

7. What should be the role of the Black church in the Black Liberation Struggle?

The Black theologian must ask himself *not only*, Are God and Jesus Black? but also, Are they relevant in terms of whether or not they make sense to Black brothers and sisters who are fighting with their backs against the wall? I am now convinced that Black theologians cannot move beyond the basic theological statement outlined in *The Black Messiah*. Therefore I feel compelled to move on to the essential restructuring of the Black church implicit in that theology. Black theology is much more important to Black people than Black theologians suspect. The existence of Black people in America depends entirely upon whether or not it is possible to change the Black man's theology. Unless we can discard the white man's individualistic slave theology and accept a Black theology which emphasizes the Black Nation and a communal way of life in a Promised Land here on earth, making it possible for the Black church to become relevant to our Liberation Struggle, Black people are doomed to genocide or an eternal hell on earth.*

I have chosen to introduce this study of the Black church with a basic consideration of *authority* because few people understand the relativity of all "truth." Truth is that which serves the interests of a people. Two groups of people locked in combat cannot be expected to have the same truth. Members of each group will look at the world from a different perspective. What is truth for one will be a lie for the other. I discard the possibility of any individual or group ever possessing objective truth. We are all liars because we are permitted to see only through one pair of eyes in terms of one experience. This fact is so obviously true that the emotional response which the assertion elicits from most people can. be judged only in light of the old proverb, "The man who says he never masturbated still does." The man who claims to be dealing with objective truth is not only lying, but knows that he is lying! There is only one authority for a Black man and that is the Black experience as it is influenced by the never-ending Black Liberation Struggle. This is equally true for

* My very good friend Dr. James H. Cone is undoubtedly a most interesting and meaningful Black theologian. His task is certainly not an easy one. He is our apostle to the Gentiles. He drags white Christians as far as they are able to go (and then some) in interpreting Black theology within the established framework which they can accept and understand.

white people in their struggle to perpetuate white supremacy. I am speaking to Black people who share the same Black experience and are engaged in the same Black struggle. They may not agree with my conclusions, but they will understand my position. White people will find it difficult to accept either my position or my conclusion because I am Black and an enemy, and "ought not" understand them so completely and "ought not" presume to build a realistic position for Black people which may some day threaten their position of white supremacy. I am not greatly concerned about how white people will react to my analysis, but I am tremendously concerned that Black people understand and critically evaluate my total position, because time is running out for the Black man. It is Black-Nation building time!

We are in the midst of a gigantic social upheaval, and the continuation of American society as it now exists is an impossibility. We are in the midst of change. As a Black man I am anxious that change proceed as rapidly as possible and that the society that now exists be radically altered as quickly and as completely as possible. So I approach the question of authority differently from the way I would if I considered myself a part of this society and accepted the continuation of existing authority as basic to its continued existence. I reject all authority which does not support the Black Liberation Struggle. By the yardstick of that struggle all things must be judged, evaluated, maintained, or discarded.

A determining aspect of the Black experience in the Western world is the continuing Black Liberation Struggle. Even the dream of integration constituted a phase of that Struggle by which all things must be judged. If it supports the Liberation Struggle of Black people, then it is good. If it is in opposition to the Liberation Struggle of Black people, then it is bad. If it supports the Liberation Struggle of Black people, then it is moral. If it opposes the

Liberation Struggle, then it is immoral. If it supports the Liberation Struggle of Black people, then it is the will of God. If it opposes the Liberation Struggle of Black people, then it is satanic. With this simple key to the mysteries of life both events and institutions can be judged.

We cannot discuss authority without considering power, because in the final analysis authority depends on power for its existence. The power or sanction by which authority is maintained may be more apparent than real, as is true of the police power of a state or of the Godpower of an ecclesiastical institution. The authority of a state cannot be maintained by police power alone for the simple reason that no state has sufficient police power. This becomes increasingly obvious as a society in the midst of chaos and conflict tries to maintain itself. Remember the Detroit rebellion of 1967 (which you may still call a riot) and the rebellions which swept the country in '65, '66, and '67? If in any five or six cities rebellions comparable to the rebellion in Detroit had broken out, it would have been utterly impossible for the police power of America to have maintained the authority of the state without calling home front-line troops from Vietnam, and whether they could have been brought back in time is questionable.

During the Detroit Freedom March in 1963, approximately two hundred thousand Black people walked down Woodward Avenue with Dr. Martin Luther King, and I will never forget the pathetic sight of police officers assigned to keep order and the policemen on motorcycles who were expected to keep the marchers in an orderly procession. Their frightened faces as they tried to stay out of the way revealed their knowledge that a crowd of two hundred thousand Black people could have walked them into the asphalt of the street without even striking a blow. The preponderance of sheer people power reduced to absurdity the thought that a few thousand police officers could keep order. And so I say that the authority of the state cannot be maintained by police power alone. The citizens of a state must be programmed to believe that the authority of the state ought to be accepted because it is right and that the power of the state is invincible, even though it is not. So actually the power of the state is a myth. The state can exist only so long as the people permit it to exist. This is the compact theory of society. The Declaration of Independence declares that governments exist by the consent of the governed. This is true, and yet the police power of a state is important because during ordinary times most of the people in a state believe in the rightness of the things it protects and are prepared to accept the authority of the state. They believe that police power ought to be used when necessary to maintain the state against attacks by disgruntled minorities who would subvert the rights of the majority.

The authority of an ecclesiastical institution is founded upon its mythological Godpower, and this can be most embarrassing when it cannot produce its Godpower in time of crisis. When a society needs the Godpower for which it has paid by the building of churches, the payment of salaries, and the training of experts in the art of God-power manipulation, ecclesiastical institutions are expected to make immediate delivery. And people in a society which is in the process of change find their churches irrelevant and meaningless when those churches cannot do the thing for which they were created. The church must maintain the stability of the social order, put down the unwashed legions who declare the society evil and unjust, and thwart all attacks upon the *status quo*. The authority of any ecclesiastical institution rests on its ability to program its followers to believe that it actually has the Godpower to do these things. Services of worship are designed to keep people conscious of this power made available for them. Here again we can see the mythological nature of the power on which the authority of the state is presumed to rest.

During a period of social upheaval and general insecurity, people begin to question the Godpower of the church because of its obvious inability to alter the course of events. Gallup polls will indicate that most people feel that the church is no longer a satisfactory institution and that the church has failed. And so people in many ways vote against ecclesiastical institutions—by not attending services regularly, by not contributing, by being hostile and unco-operative to indicate their general displeasure. This is both reasonable and justifiable because the church, like all social institutions, exists to help maintain the *status quo*. It is a power institution, and its function is essentially to maintain the stability of society by warding off threatening evil spirits that might tend to corrupt sinful men by making them dissatisfied with the existing social order. Its authority is the power of God and the earthly power establishment of which it is a part. People expect it to do the things for which it was created. When it cannot do these things people are dissatisfied.

This is true in any situation in which authority must be maintained by actual power. In inner-city high schools across the country the authority of school administrators has been destroyed. School authorities do not have the power to maintain authority. And so an extralegal student authority has come into being which maintains *de facto* control of the schools. On many college campuses the administration has been challenged and large numbers of students have supported the challenge. College administrators have lacked the power to maintain authority. They have been forced to turn to either the city police or the state police for the power to maintain authority. This public admission of their inability to maintain authority without outside power has forced a totally new readjustment of the relationship between college administrator and student body on the American college campus. A new concept of authority is emerging.

In short, authority depends upon power for its existence, but rarely possesses more than the illusion of power and depends in large measure upon passive acceptance. In fact, much of the talk about authority deals with illusion rather than with reality. A Biblical scholar will maintain in all seriousness that the "authority of the Old Testament" is much less than the "authority of the New Testament" —because much of the Old Testament does not measure up to the high ethical and spiritual standards revealed by Jesus in the New Testament. To prove this point he will completely misinterpret the revolutionary message of Jesus in the New Testament and completely overlook the fact that the actual teachings of Jesus are but an extension of the Old Testament. He is not dealing with "authority," but with an ecclesiastical illusion which is necessary to enable the church to serve its social function in the world.

A group, any group of any color and in any geographic part of the world, comes together only upon the basis of power and self-interest. A mob of individuals coalesces because self-interest dictates that only through coming together can they increase their individual power. For no other reason will individuals subordinate their desire for status and recognition and their individualistic seeking after power. The individual coalesces with a group because through the group he can satisfy his individual lust for power by seeing the group as an extension of himself and his self-interest.

A mob becomes a group (or a nation) when it recognizes the simple fact that by necessity it must accept the authority of leaders and institutions created to serve its power interests. Each individual gives up something of his individualistic lust for power in order that he can merge with a group and share a larger vision of power with a far greater possibility of success. He accepts the necessity for the authority of leaders and institutions which he helps create to serve his power interests by serving the power interests of the group of which he is a part. Once established, however, institutions take on a kind of independent existence. Even though we forget the circumstances out of which they came into being, they are necessary to the power of the group and automatic mechanisms exist to protect these power institutions. When any of them are threatened, the individuals who make up the group experience a spontaneous emotional reaction of discomfort and of being *personally* threatened. The group reacts with protective hostility to anything which threatens its power institutions, and as an individual, you will react with a hostility which you cannot explain on a personal basis when the institutions which are an extension of your power hunger are threatened by outside forces.

Just as a group comes together, sets up institutions, delegates authority, and accepts authority, those who are excluded from power eventually coalesce in order to attack the power establishment. They seek to destroy the authority of the power establishment and to structure the transference of power to themselves. This attack can be either within the existing rules, as is largely the case with the Black Revolution (attacking within the rules established by the dominant white power group), or within a completely new framework established by the creation of a completely new set of rules, as is true of a communist revolution. Eventually every revolution must repudiate the authority of the rules established by the dominant power group as the basis of its attack.

Today's repressive measures are the typical reaction of any society as it begins to collapse under attack. Repression can be seen in the increase of police brutality across the country, in the shooting down of Black Panthers in northern urban ghettos, and in the general increase of repression and brutality in schools and universities across the country. The general repression of all kinds of dissent in America reflects the general insecurity which has resulted from a multiple attack upon the white power institutions of the Western world. There has to be this kind of repression; there has to be this kind of hostile emotional reaction. The white group is under attack. Its institutions have to be protected. The silent majority of white Americans begin to feel hostile because they realize that they are being attacked on every front by Black people who are demanding a restructuring of society and by young people who are questioning all the values on which the power of their group depends. Feeling themselves attacked from every side, the silent majority are moving to fortify and protect the institutions which are basic to the preservation of the power and authority of white America.

It is not accidental that Nixon is in the White House at this time; that Middle America is front-page news at this time; that repression is growing at this time; and that the so-called liberal white establishment has begun to feel that it must stop this polarization that is exposing its failure to absorb conflict. And so all across the country the liberal establishment is calling for peace and integration: the anti-defamation leagues, the urban coalitions, and the liberal wings of the Protestant denominations—which have no power but represent the human-relations fronts of the churches and cannot act on a policy-making level, but serve as buffers between those who are alienated and those who are in power. These groups are coming together to issue joint statements. The repressive measures are as necessary for the preservation of white power as the joint liberal statements are futile. Some naive Christians dare to wonder why there can still be reactionaries and conservatives in the churches after all the years of preaching. After all the years of preaching! That's what the churches are for! That is the purpose of the churches! We can only wonder that for so many years the authority of the power establishment was so secure that it was unnecessary for the churches to voice the conservatism that is essential to protect the overall institutionalization of white supremacy. But now authority is being challenged upon every hand, and the challenge is to white supremacy.

The Black man is engaged in a revolution to restructure American society; and so we—as Black people—have a very clear-cut position. Nixon's silent majority insists that his white churches either defend white American institutions or go out of existence. No white minister in America will be permitted to preach liberalism. He will either defend the white power establishment or he will be driven out of the church, because the church is too important an institution to be left in the hands of irresponsible white liberals who had their chance and failed to keep the peace. Middle America will take control of the church as it has taken control of the government, and as it will take control of all other white institutions in America. White polarization will gradually become complete.

Black people in America have been programmed for inferiority deliberately, consistently, exquisitely. The white man's *declaration of Black inferiority* is basic to all American life. There is no institution in America, no aspect of American life that does not basically reflect the declared inferiority of all Black people. Not poor Black people, not ignorant Black people, not uncouth Black people, but *all* Black people have been declared inferior. This *declaration of Black inferiority* is the foundation on which American history has been built. From the time Black people were brought to these shores as slaves, the *declaration of Black inferiority* was the framework within which the Black man was forced to build his existence. In the slave ship, on the slave block, on the plantation, fleeing from the lynch mob, fleeing north into slum ghettos, the Black man was not only "declared" inferior but everything possible was done to make that "declaration" a statement of fact. The Black man could accept this declaration of inferiority or he could reject it; and for the early part of his existence in America, the Black man accepted the white man's *declaration of Black inferiority*. As a slave, systematically separated from people who spoke his language, living in a country about which he knew nothing, not even the simple geography necessary to attempt escape, he was forced to accept the authority of the white slave master to define his person and the conditions of his existence.

The Black man had no alternative to an acceptance of the white man's declaration of his inferiority. His freedom had been taken from him, his culture had been taken from him, his history had been taken from him, his language had been taken from him, his dignity had been taken from him—he had nothing left but his physical being and the will to survive. The Black man learned to live with this *declaration of Black inferiority*, and self-hate became a basic characteristic of the Black man's life in America. In the words of John O. Killens, "The white man brought Black men to America and made Niggers out of them."

Integration is the name given to the Black man's slave philosophy of self-hate. The dream of integration is the Black man's response to the white man's *declaration of Black inferiority*. The dream of ultimate escape from Blackness has motivated Black people from the days of slavery through the brutal period of Reconstruction down to the present. "Integration Now" was the heroic battle cry of Dr. Martin Luther King. "We Shall Overcome" our separation was the anguished cry of the Black man's faith that escape from Blackness was possible. The dream of integration is the Black man's acceptance of the white man's declaration of his inferiority and is a mechanism that perpetuates his enslavement.

This is not easy for white people to understand. For the white oppressor who has declared Black people inferior to say, "I believe in integration," is one thing. But for a Black man, after all the suffering, oppression, brutality, and inhumanity which he has suffered at the hands of white people to say, "I believe in the possibility of integration," or, "I dream of integration," "I work for integration," "I would accept integration," is obviously a sign of insanity. No Black man in his right mind, in a healthy, normal state of mind, could possibly dream of integration with his enemy. So the dream of integration that has motivated

Black people has been the mechanism by which our enslavement has been perpetuated. To dream of integration, a Black man must believe in the goodness of white people. He must believe that for some reason what is being done to him is his own fault and that he must persuade white people to accept him in spite of his shortcomings and that he must work to measure up to white people. Self-hatred is the inevitable corollary of the dream of integration. Obviously there is something wrong with me—because the white man is superior; he has everything, he is good, and if he won't accept me, there must be something wrong with me. For the Black integrationist self-hate is inescapable.

The Black man's final fantasy is to believe that the white man will accept him as an *individual* of superior merit, even if he won't accept other Black people. This means that Black people in the final analysis are reduced to an individualistic struggle against one another. Not only does the Black man then hate himself, in terms of this overall declaration of Black inferiority, but he hates all other Black people, on the simple theory that if it were not for all those obnoxious Black people, white people would not hate him. The Black man then begins to hate everything about his community, everything about his culture, everything about his imitation institutions which he has patterned after white institutions, believing that all of these things are inferior because he is inferior. For the Black man to permit the white man to define his being as well as his condition by a *declaration of Black inferiority* which he accepts is to accept the Black world of self-hatred from which there is no possible escape. The dream of integration then becomes the mechanism of his continuing enslavement.

Everything in the Black community is contaminated by the Black man's efforts to identify with the enemy world of the oppressor. The Black church received its God, its Jesus, and its interpretation of the Bible from the white master. Obviously, the white master was not concerned with giving Black people a revolutionary religion which could liberate them. Naturally, the kind of religion which met the needs of the white master could not possibly meet the needs of the Black slave.

The religion which the master gave to his slave was designed for pacification and to support the authority of white supremacy. He said, "This is a picture of God. This is a picture of Jesus. They are both white as you can plainly see. Here are Biblical characters. They are all white. But they love you in spite of your evil Blackness, and they offer you salvation in the great beyond! You have to live such a life here on earth, that after death, when you cross over Jordan, there will be a reward for you. Sometimes you think that all the suffering that you are doing down here is passing unnoticed by God, but it is not! God is watching everything, every minute of every day. And every bit of suffering you have down here is written down in God's big book and eventually on the other side of Jordan there will be a reward, milk and honey and golden streets." So Black people had only to accept the authority of the white world to inherit a glorious reward in heaven.

Black people live in a world in which there is no possibility for dignity or decency of life here on earth. Life is only a testing and a preparation for death and some mystical existence that follows death. It is a beautiful myth, an application of the pagan distortion which the Apostle Paul took to the white gentile world in the name of Jesus following his conversion on the road to Damascus. His fanciful interpretation had nothing to do with anything that Jesus ever said or did. Through the slave master's distorted interpretation of Christianity the authority of the white power establishment was assured. Little physical power was needed to perpetuate the Black man's enslavement. Everything that could be done to liberate the Black man had already been accomplished on Calvary two thousand years ago. The Black man need do nothing himself but accept his lot and be washed in the blood of the Lamb and he would be made white like snow (in preparation for the life to come).

So if you are Black you can be poverty-stricken, you can be brutalized, and you can still be saved. Your children can be discriminated against and denied a decent education and you can still be saved. You can live in a neighborhood from which all the decencies of life have been taken and you can still be saved. This kind of primitive Christianity the Black slaves received from their white slave masters. And for many years this helped Black people survive situations in which there were few real possibilities of escape from total powerlessness here on earth. The dream that in some mysterious afterlife things would be different at least helped to maintain sanity. Suffering Black people brought to a mystical escapist religion the emotional fervor and soul necessary to make it vital and beautiful. We had been programmed for inferiority and the Black church as an institution contributed to this process. The authority of the Black church was the authority of the white man, of the white slave master, and of the white church with its white God and white Jesus. As Black people we tried to do the things that they said were right because we accepted the white man's definitions and his power.

This was also true of all other institutions in the Black community. A Black businessman with a little store didn't work too hard in his little store because he wanted to be a part of the great economic thing that the white man had. He wanted to become a part of the white establishment. Black colleges and universities were established as control mechanisms for Black people. White Christians put money into Fisk, Talladega, Atlanta, and other Black schools to teach Black people how to act as white people and to despise everything Black. These so-called Black institutions are still controlled by white people and exist to serve the interests of white people. Why else would they ignore the history and culture of Black people and teach that Black music is inferior, Black art is inferior, Black poetry is inferior, Black literature is inferior, and the totality of the Black experience is something of which Black people must be ashamed and from which they should seek speedy deliverance through education.

When young Black people enter a college, a "negro" college, kindly, well-intentioned white people and brain-washed Black people teach them how to act like white people and take on the refinements of white civilization. This is what a "negro" college is supposed to do and this is the process by which the white power establishment perpetuates its authority. This is the structure which white people maintain, even though they claim to have no knowl-edge of the reason for their actions. If a Black church moves out of the beaten path of white identification, white people feel disturbed. If a professor on a Black college campus begins to teach anything other than accommoda-tion to the white *declaration of Black inferiority*, white people feel immediately threatened and money is cut off from that institution. All institutions in the Black com-munity were established as mechanisms for control of Black people and to perpetuate the authority of the white power establishment. "Integration" is the name given to the Black man's philosophy of self-hate, and the dream of integration is the mechanism by which Black people per-mit themselves to be controlled.

Black people in America are united by a bond of com-mon Black experience. We are not Americans in the sense that white people are Americans. We fight in their wars. Their astronauts go to the moon. The wealth of America belongs to them. We are not Americans. We are an Afri-can people who against our will were brought to America. We are a people because here in America common expe-riences have welded us together. We share a common background and a common cultural heritage. Our cultural heritage has been confused and modified by our experience in America, but it binds us together even when we would break apart. In one respect the white man was very kind. He said, "Any person who has any Black blood at all is Black!" So we don't have to worry about whether or not we are all Black or just a little bit Black. If we're Black at all, we are all Black and so psychologically we share a common cultural heritage. The agony of being Black in America unites all Blacks with bonds which even self-hatred cannot break. The white man's oppression drives us together even as we dream of integration with him. All Black people experience the same dehumanizing oppression, brutality, and second-class citizenship. No matter how learned a Black man may be, his children find it difficult to get a decent education in a public school. No matter how well-mannered he may be, he finds it difficult to secure a decent house to live in. These are the things which make a people, and so the Black experience has made us a people. Only a Black fool can believe that he is not discriminated against in America. The white man's *declaration of Black inferiority* has served to provide for Black people a unique experience. Our lives are the result of this Black experience. We have been shaped and molded by it. We are a separate people. We can sit in the same room, we can live in the same town, we can be neighbors on the same street, but we are a separate people because our experience has been different.

For a Black person, authority is a much different thing than it is for a white person. The very institutions they wish to preserve we wish to destroy. When they react with hostility because their institutions have been attacked, we react with glee and with the desire to participate in their speedy destruction. When young white people march on the Pentagon, we cheer because they are attacking one of the institutions which oppress us. When hippies cry out that Western civilization must be restructured because it is destroying mankind, we say amen. The

Black man is not a part of white America. He has been placed outside by the white man's *declaration of Black inferiority*. The Black Liberation Struggle has become the dominant expression of the Black experience and it affects all aspects of our life. More and more, all Black people are being caught up in the Struggle.

It is very difficult to find a Black person who is totally outside the Liberation Struggle in which Black people are engaged. The Black church is moving slowly into the Struggle and it is my hope and prayer that it will soon become its heart and center, bringing new stability, dynamics, and sense of direction. This will not be accomplished, however, without confrontation and conflict. Every Black institution must fight its way out of bondage to the white power establishment. Every Black college is being torn asunder by the efforts of Black students to bring it into the Liberation Struggle. The ultimatum is simple: Come into the Struggle or die. In every Black community Black people are insisting that everything become a part of the Black Liberation Struggle, that there be no element in the community which is separate and apart from the Struggle. No businesses are to be permitted to remain in the community that are not a part of the Black community and controlled by the Black community. We are engaged in an all-out Struggle for Black Liberation and more and more *this* determines the Black man's life.

The Struggle is coming to determine everything about our existence. And this makes the Black man different and strange and difficult to understand. We are no longer a part of the things that trouble white people, or that they believe in. For us the church must become an institution which serves the interests of the Black community and the Liberation Struggle of Black people. We reject the mythology by which white people have kept us enslaved with their faith in the authority of their pronouncements, their institutions, and their white power establishment.

We believe that Jesus is a revelation of God, but not the only revelation. We believe that we have a revelation in Marcus Garvey, who looked at the world in which Black men lived and asked, "Where is the Black man's government?" and called Black men to build a Black Nation in Africa. We have a revelation in Brother Malcolm, who taught Black people that the white man is an enemy and that you can't deal with an enemy in terms of persuasion. Because that's what Black people were doing when Brother Malcolm began to talk. Dr. King was organizing mass demonstrations across the South and white people were showing day after day that in any situation in which the Black man appears to threaten white institutions, all white people will come together. But we needed Brother Malcolm to interpret the simple truth that the white man is an enemy. He revealed to us the fact that we are dealing with an enemy structure, and that even when white people say that they are liberal they still hate Black people because they are partners in the white *declaration of Black inferiority*. Even though a white man lives in a community without a single Black person, he still shares in the benefits of a white society that derives much of its wealth from the exploitation of Black people. So all white people are a part of the exploitation, are a part of the process; and so it was very important for Brother Malcolm to tell Black people, "You're dealing with an enemy, and you deal with an enemy in a different way than you deal with a friend." And that is where Black people find the demands of the Liberation Struggle difficult; because the authority of old master's pronouncements about turning the other cheek and going the second mile are being challenged.

Black people must understand that only within the Black Nation do we turn the other cheek. We turn the other cheek only to a Black brother or a Black sister. We do not turn the other cheek in any other situation. This is what Jesus was telling Israel, because Israel was engaged in the same kind of liberation struggle against the white gentile world. The teachings of the Bible must be reinterpreted for the benefit of Black people so that the church can become useful in the Liberation Struggle. If the Black church cannot free itself from the white church, then the Black church must be destroyed by Black people and we will have to find a new religion and build a new independent church resting on the authority of the Black experience. Only if we can rediscover the historic roots of Christianity and strip from them the mystical distortions that are not basic to the concept of nation as revealed in the Old Testament and in the revolutionary teachings of Jesus, will we be able to bring the Black Christian Church into the Liberation Struggle and make it relevant to the lives of Black people.

In the pews of Black churches across America we have the same kind of unrest that you find in the white pews— but for different reasons. In the white pews white people are saying to white preachers, "Defend our institution." And Black people are saying to Black preachers, "Build new Black institutions for us. Stop catering to white authority. Free yourself from the domination of white institutionalism." So the church is being forced to change. The white church must change because white people in the pews are demanding that it defend the white institutional structure that has declared Black people inferior. The Black church must change because Black people are demanding that it become a part of the Struggle to liberate Black people from this declaration; that it become the heart, the soul, and the brain of the Black man's Struggle; that it become a teaching church in the sense that it teaches Black people what is necessary if they are to participate intelligently in the Liberation Struggle; that it organize Black people effectively for participation in the Liberation Struggle; that it give Black people a sense of dignity as God's Chosen People.

It's becoming impossible for Black people to use Sunday-school literature from white publishing houses. Literature from Black publishing houses is just as bad because it is a copy of the same material. Such is the persistence of white authority. When white publishing houses began to put Black pictures in every quarterly to make it "respectable," this did not change the basic white orientation of the literature. Black church-school literature must teach Black children at all age levels that there is nothing more sacred than the liberation of Black people. This message can be conveyed in terms of the heroic Biblical stories of the Old Testament, the heroism of Jesus, the heroism of Black men and women who have served the continuing Struggle. The emphasis must be on the hero motif in the continuing Struggle for the liberation of Black people. Individualism must be rejected, and this must be emphasized again and again. There is no justification for a church-school lesson in a Black church that does not combat the individualism of the white world. Black children must be taught that the communal life of Africa is essential for the survival of Black people. The individualism of the white man's society means death and destruction for Black people. Black people must learn to bury their individualism in the life of the Black Nation. Children must be taught that sacrifice for the Black Nation is the highest good.

The Black church must undertake a total restructuring of the church and its educational functions. We must develop techniques which do not depend on trained teachers. We must learn to use the mechanical techniques of tape recorders, filmstrips, and movies that can be sent out to small churches everywhere. Without trained teachers every church can convey the same basic message to Black people everywhere. We must become a people like the Black children of Israel as they stood on the plains of Moab ready to enter the Promised Land. They had wandered for forty years in the wilderness and had learned to find authority in their own experience. No longer did they bear the mark of slavery and dream of returning to bondage in Egypt. The king of Moab looked out upon the Nation Israel and said, "A people has come out of Egypt." Only if the Black church can build a Black people in America with the courage to stand against the repressions that are rising everywhere will Black people be able to survive.

If, then, we are moving toward black-white polarization, the Black church is moving toward Black nationhood, and the white church is moving to defend institutional white supremacy and repression, what hope do Black people have? White people have more power, numbers, armies, and munitions. What hope is there for Black people? It is a complex question and one which cannot be decided simply in terms of whether or not Black people can win an armed conflict. We have no choice. Having decided to be free, a man cannot then decide how free he wants to be. He knows that he is either free or he is a slave.

White people also face a very real problem. How dangerous can a minority of thirty-five million people be? In Germany it was difficult to kill six million Jews, and they were docile and nonviolent. In America it would be very difficult to kill thirty-five million Black people without also destroying America.

There is, however, a state of human society that depends on a balance between opposing forces. Black people seek to establish such a balance of power. Even the power of a minority might be sufficient to protect Black people against the oppression, exploitation, and brutality which the totally powerless cannot escape in a white society that has declared all non-white people inferior. The Black man must fight to escape from total powerlessness even though he die in the attempt.

The most that an intelligent white man can hope for in America is that this balance-of-power equilibrium come into being as quickly as possible. Rational white people should be aiding in the building of this equilibrium for reasons of self-interest. If Black people must remain totally powerless, anger and frustration will be a constant source of conflict. If Black people could secure sufficient power to maintain a balance it might be possible for Black people and white people to live together as two separate peoples in one country. Black people must remain separate using the separateness that already exists as a basis for political power, for economic power, and for the transmission of cultural values. On the basis of this separateness the Black church must seek to program itself, seeking always to build and maintain a protective balance of power. The only hope for peace in America depends upon the possibility of building this kind of Black power. Black people will not again passively accept slavery. A Black Nation within a nation must come into being if we are to survive. For the Black man everything must be judged in terms of Black liberation. There is but one authority and that is the Black experience.

PART 1

We Define Our Faith

CHAPTER 1

The Black Nation

Generations of Black Christians have found inspiration in the tale of Israel's escape from bondage in Egypt without realizing that the Biblical Nation Israel was a Black Nation.* As Black Christian Nationalists in the twentieth century, we do not debate this historic fact, we merely assert it, because it serves to explain the African origins of the basic religious myths and concepts of ancient Israel, and also makes it possible to determine the historicity of specific teachings attributed to the Black Messiah, Jesus, in the Synoptic Gospels.

The New Testament reflects the primitive pagan distortions that the Apostle Paul foisted upon the early church as a self-appointed apostle to the white gentile world. Jesus was a revolutionary Black·religious leader fighting for the liberation of Israel. We can understand Jesus more fully by looking at Moses and the Maccabees than by looking at the Apostle Paul with his pagan concept of blood redemption. The teachings of Jesus and of Israel

---

* Present-day white Jews were converted to Judaism in Europe and Asia following the fall of Jerusalem in A.D. 70.

reflect the deep spirituality of Black people. The religious ideas of Israel that shaped the ministry of Jesus can only be understood in the light of the history and culture of Africa. Moses gave form and shape to the religion of Israel by borrowing from the ancient religions and culture of Black Africa. The story of Creation harked back millions of years to that moment when God created the first man in His own image in the heart of Black Africa.

Black Christian Nationalism finds a pattern for today's Black Liberation Struggle in the efforts of Moses to create a Black Nation anchored to the Black man's historic past and to move Black men from oppression and powerlessness to a Promised Land here on earth where Black people could live together with dignity. The religion of Israel began with Moses, who was an African. Having killed an Egyptian and fearing the anger of Pharaoh in whose palace he had been reared, Moses fled, leaving his people in bondage. He settled among the Black people of Midian, who thought him an Egyptian, and married the daughter of Jethro, the Midianite high priest. He sat at the feet of Jethro and was taught the religion and culture of Black Africa. Watching his father-in-law's flock, he pondered the oppression of Israel and, almost against his will, committed his life to a liberation struggle which he must create and to which he must call the Nation Israel.*

He was awe-stricken and humble as knowledge of the ancient civilizations and cultures of Black Africa were unfolded to him. Using the ancient mythology, cultures, and religions of Black Africa which had been handed down

---

* See Part 5, We Define Our History, in which both Rabbi Hilu Paris and Dr. Yosef ben-Jochannan correctly locate Midian and describe the Black African people among whom Moses settled. Rabbi Paris states, "Moses married a Kushite woman [Numbers 12:1] . . . the Kushites did not recognize any difference between a Hebrew and an Egyptian. Again we have evidence that the Hebrews, the Egyptians, the Midianites, and the Ethiopians were of one racial stock and background . . . the Ethiopian empire was situated in those days on both sides of the Red Sea."

for more than a million years, he began slowly to put together the Yahweh religion, borrowing the Black man's ancient stories of the Creation, the Fall of Man, and the Negative Confessions of the Egyptians from which he derived the Ten Commandments. He thanked the Black Man's God who had been revealed to him by Jethro for bringing him to Black Africa, the source of all life and knowledge. By comparison the religion and culture of the Mediterranean Africans seemed primitive. Abraham had covenanted with an ancient God whom he did not know, and the Nation Israel had little right to consider itself a "chosen people" while it still followed pagan gods.

Moses understood the magnitude of his mission. He must present the Yahweh religion which he had learned in Midian as the religion of Abraham, Isaac, and Jacob. He must define the God of Midian as the God of Israel. He must use religion and the myth of a Promised Land to separate Israel from the Egyptians and to create an institutional power base for Israel's liberation struggle.

The story of the burning bush recounts the inner struggle that Moses experienced in bringing himself to undertake this difficult task. He recognized the fact that he was poorly equipped. He was not a fluent, charismatic leader. He was not entirely clear about the nature of the God he was to represent nor of the religion he was to preach. But he knew the enemy. He had grown up an Egyptian in Pharaoh's palace. He understood the Egyptian mind. So Moses returned to Egypt armed with the wisdom of Black Africa to free the Black Nation Israel from bondage.

It is no exaggeration to say that Israel was in fact an African Nation. When Israel went down into Africa the Nation consisted only of Jacob, his sons, and their households, including wives, children, servants, and slaves.*

---

* The Africanization of Israel had begun many years before, when Abraham had gone into Egypt and left with servants and slaves, including his Egyptian mistress, Hagar, by whom he had a son, Ishmael.

They numbered in all no more than a hundred or a hundred and fifty people. This was Israel. Israel as a Nation came into being in Africa, in intimate association and intermingling with the Black people of Africa. Joseph was already there, married to an African woman. His brothers had sold him into slavery and he had risen to become an important person in Egypt. They went into Africa as beggars seeking food. It is important to remember how many people went down into Africa because when they crossed the Red Sea with Moses some seven hundred years later, they numbered more than two million people, "six hundred thousand men on foot, besides women and children." * For some strange reason little emphasis is placed on the tremendous number of people who escaped bondage in Egypt. The movement of well over two million people would present something of a problem in logistics to a modern mechanized army. How long would it take more than two million men, women, and children to come together at the Red Sea from all parts of Egypt? How would their movements be co-ordinated so that they could arrive in an orderly fashion at the proper time? Obviously some would be forced to leave home days or even weeks before others. How could the problems of food, sanitation, and water have been dealt with? How long would it have taken more than two million people to walk across the

---

* White Biblical scholars attempt to maintain the fiction that Israel remained in Egypt for approximately four hundred years to substantiate God's promise recorded in Genesis 15:13. Actually there is no way to determine when the first Hebrews entered Africa or how long they remained. Some were brought into Africa as prisoners of war, as the thirty-six hundred who were enslaved by Amenophia II (*c.* 1435-1414). Others came of their own free will, as Abraham did. Others, like Joseph, came as slaves. Even the Biblical story in Exodus 12:40 gives four hundred and thirty years as the time Israel spent in Africa. The time must have been at least seven hundred years to account for the years of freedom and the four hundred years of bondage. No shorter period of time can explain the tremendous population increase (not including the "mixed multitude" accompanying them).

Red Sea at a single point? I can remember the Detroit Freedom March in 1963, when two hundred thousand Black people took more than five hours to walk fifteen blocks to the Cobo Arena. Bayard Rustin is still considered an organizational genius in some quarters because he got two hundred thousand Black people into Washington, D.C., and out again on the same day, using buses, airplanes, and trains. Moses took more than two million disorganized Black people out of Africa, kept them together for more than forty years in the wilderness, and finally brought them to the Promised Land. The king of Moab looked down in fear at the Nation Israel and said, "A people has come out of Egypt." No greater feat of sheer organization has been achieved anywhere in the annals of human history.

Israel lived in Africa for at least 350 years as a free people. Then there came a pharaoh who knew not Joseph, and he looked around and said, "These people are multiplying and they are dangerous. We don't know what they would do if an enemy attacked. Perhaps they would try to take over the country because they are still not a part of us." A group in power always has this sense of separateness. And a group in power is very reluctant to include anyone else within the sacred confines of its group structure. Israel had lived in Africa 350 years but the Egyptians still thought of them as outsiders. They had intermarried and felt that they belonged in Egypt. But Pharaoh said, "They are not a part of us and if the enemy comes they will join the enemy and take our country." After 350 years they were still visitors in someone else's land.

Sometimes we forget this simple fact and feel that if we live in a country for a long time it gradually comes to belong to us. But here in America we could stay for five thousand years and the Black folks who were our descendants would still be visitors in a white man's land. The white man will not accept us because we have been here for a long time. He will not accept us because we have been trying to be good and identify with him. Like Pharaoh he will say, "These Black people are not a part of us." All his institutions will be structured to keep us out just as they were in Egypt. The Israelites had been there so long that they had begun to feel like Egyptians, but we are not dealing with feelings but with power. No people will include an outside group within its power establishment because no group is willing to share power. The Egyptians were not bad. The Israelites and the Egyptians were all Black people, but they comprised two separate groups. Egypt had power. Israel was powerless. Egypt used Israel to serve its interests. This is a simple fact of human existence: those with power exploit the powerless. The powerless cry to be included in the name of morality, and the dream of integration becomes the mechanism of their continued enslavement. Relationships between groups change only in response to shifts of power.

Most Black people in this country feel that they are a part of the white man's structure. Because their lives are built on this misconception they act in peculiar ways. They do things that appear strange because they do not realize that they are on the outside because they have been deliberately excluded. American white people do not consider Black people a part of American society. We would be destroyed in a moment if it served the interests of the white group. Every white leader this country has had has said it as clearly as he could, "If I must destroy all Blacks to save the white American nation, I will do it." We find this difficult to understand only because we want so badly to become a part of white America. We dream that someday we are going to be accepted. It is just a matter of time. We shall overcome. But we will never become a part of the white man's institutional structure unless we are able to take it from him. If we are unable to take it from him, we had better be about the job of building institutions of our own that belong to us.

Israel had been living in Egypt for 350 years when Egypt said, "These people are not a part of us and we are going to make slaves of them." This did not constitute a basic change in their condition because they had always been outsiders. Outsiders exist to be exploited. The degree of exploitation is only a matter of the exploiters' choice. Slavery is a condition which makes it easier to keep a powerless people on the outside and to exploit them more fully. To keep a people on the outside, as Black people in America are, requires skill. We could not be exploited, brutalized, and oppressed unless we had been conditioned to accept slavery.

We were not always slaves. The white man came to Africa with guns, and he subjugated us. Naked and in chains we were brought across the ocean and told that we were slaves. We had a cultural tradition superior to that of our new white master but we were powerless and we learned to be slaves. We experienced the same conditioning that the Black Israelites experienced in Egypt. We learned to be slaves. To learn to be a slave you have only to concentrate upon individual survival. You take care of yourself and yourself alone. You reduce yourself to a physical being who is determined to survive at any cost. "Take my wife and rape her, take my children and sell them, I will survive! Whip my brothers and sisters to death before me, I will survive!" This is the process by which a human being becomes a slave.

Black Christian Nationalism is designed to deal with the Black man's conditioning in America and throughout the world. Believing that nothing is more sacred than the liberation of Black people, we are a revolutionary Pan-African movement dedicated to the building of a heaven on earth in the here and now for all Black people everywhere. Black Christian Nationalism recognizes the effects of slavery, oppression, and brutality upon a people. We are pragmatic realists. We understand our own people and we understand the enemy. We understand the psychology of individualism and the effects of social fragmentation. We deduce from the history of the Black Nation, Israel, and the life and teachings of the Black Messiah, Jesus, basic principles which give form and direction to our leadership. We are sensitive to the revelations which God has given to Black men since the beginning of time, and we seek a deepening spirituality in order that we may receive continuing revelations and new insights. We treasure our history because it holds the key to our identity and to our future. We will not permit the oppressor to define either our person, our condition, or our struggle. As we see God in Jesus and in the Black Nation Israel, we also see God in Nat Turner, Marcus Garvey, and Brother Malcolm. We are confident that in today's world God speaks to Black people through us.

Black Christian Nationalism calls Black people to an understanding of reality. We must face the fact that we live in a world in which power is in the hands of enemies who have declared us inferior and now seek to destroy us because we have challenged that declaration. The white man feels that his privileged position is being threatened and he fights to preserve white supremacy at any cost. The white *declaration of Black inferiority* dominates every aspect of the white man's world. It is both cause and effect of his insanity. Every institution in the Western world is built upon the assumption of white superiority and Black inferiority. Every institution exists to serve the interests of white supremacy. The schools teach it. The churches preach it. The police power of the state enforces it. And the economic system perpetuates it by creating conditions out of which only Black inferiority can emerge! To the white man all nonwhite people are subhuman, having no rights that the white man must respect. A white chaplain who served on the Japanese front during the Second World War tells of the insanity which characterized the daily behavior of American soldiers dealing with Japanese prisoners. The total depravity of white men dealing with powerless nonwhites defies description. The fiendish tortures and the sexual orgies of mutilation could only have been conceived by deranged minds. More recently, a young white soldier tried to explain the massacres and atrocities in Vietnam. He said it in the only way he could. "We don't consider them human. We think of them as animals." So to rape a Vietnamese girl in a rice paddy and then shoot her is not unreasonable. To shoot thirty or forty defenseless women and children in a ditch or two hundred in a village can be a justifiable activity.

This same white insanity is reflected in official government policy. The United States fights a different kind of war against a nonwhite people, because all nonwhite peoples have been declared inferior. The United States dropped the atom bomb on Japan. It would not have used the atom bomb in fighting a white nation. The United States drops napalm on defenseless villages in Vietnam. It would not use napalm on nonmilitary targets when fighting a white nation. The United States supplies napalm to white Israel for indiscriminate use against nonwhite Arab nations. It would not supply napalm for use against white people.* This is the same white insanity which killed more than one hundred million Black people during the slave trade and did not hesitate to use smallpox to subjugate the American Indians.

In the area of race the thinking of white people is nonrational, as evidenced by the things American spokesmen say as well as by the things America does to nonwhite people. The United States has opposed the seating of the People's Republic of China in the United Nations because "China has not yet learned to live as a responsible member of the family of nations." A nation engaged in an

---

* The fact that the Arabs are "nonwhite" can be visually verified anywhere in the Arab world if anything more than a picture of Anwar el-Sadat or a Cairo street scene is necessary. So-called European racial classifications reflect only the white man's racial insanity.

indefensible and unspeakably inhuman war in Southeast Asia; a nation which still refuses to ratify the Genocide Convention of the United Nations; a nation which only recently undertook an adventurous invasion of Cuba and an unnecessary intervention in the internal affairs of the Dominican Republic; a nation which is engaged in systematic efforts to subvert the independent Black governments of Africa; a nation which has launched a police-state program of genocide against Black Panthers in America— this nation can stand before the world and oppose the seating of China in the United Nations because China "has not yet learned to act as a responsible member of the family of nations."

Black people have been excluded from real participation in American society by firmly entrenched white institutional racism. Even so, we have been corrupted by an individualistic and materialistic white value system because we have tried to identify. But white hatred and hostility have saved us. White people would not let us in when we demanded integration so, in a sense, we have preserved our soul. A unique Black experience makes us different from white people. The separateness which the white man has forced on us is now our basic hope for the future. On the one hand it has preserved our African heritage, and on the other it has provided a basis for the power which is essential to our survival. Black Christian Nationalism seeks to build upon this black separateness.

Across America Black people are beginning to realize that only Black Christian Nationalism can offer a new sense of direction, institutional stability, and a trained leadership totally committed to the Black Liberation Struggle. For the first time we are beginning to put together a structure that can serve Black people because it is rooted in the Black experience. For the most part Black people in the Western world have produced neither genuine leadership nor genuine institutions. We have been content to ape the white man and pretend that institutions and leaders could serve him and belong to us. So in a most ridiculous sense we have been "integrated." Everything in the Black community belongs to the white man and serves his interests. We have not permitted anything all Black to thrive and grow. A people without institutions that serve their interests are powerless. They are a non-people, and for all practical purposes they do not exist.

Neither have we created genuine Black leadership. Only a few Black men have seriously attempted to lead Black people. Marcus Garvey tried to lead Black people away from integration and toward separatism. He offered a program designed to serve the basic needs of Black people by re-establishing the Black man's African homeland. The Honorable Elijah Muhammad has tried to lead Black people toward the establishment of a separate Black Nation in the Western Hemisphere. Brother Malcolm tried to lead Black people to understand their true relationship with white people and with the Black people of Africa. Black Christian Nationalism joins this select company of Black men who have realized that integration is death and separatism is life. Trying to help a group of people cease to exist, to disappear, to become a nonpeople, is not leadership. Dr. Du Bois was trying to integrate, he was not offering leadership. He offered a very sophisticated, "Let's disappear" philosophy. In his controversy with Booker T. Washington he was basically wrong. He did not offer leadership. Adam Clayton Powell did not offer leadership. He fought white people only until he got into a position where he seemed to be personally integrated, then he was content to go through the motions of being a race man. Dr. Martin Luther King did not offer leadership. He was a charismatic, articulate spokesman, and he said all the mixed-up things that Black people wanted to hear. We said amen, because he was speaking the same confused philosophy we already believed.

Genuine Black leadership cannot lead in the direction of integration because integration is asking Black people to become a nonpeople. Anyone who asks us to become a nonpeople asks to destroy ourselves. We look at our children and say, "Don't you worry, in a few years nobody will notice the fact that you are Black." That is a terrible thing to say to a child. It would be better to say, "In a few years everyone will look up to you and respect you because you are Black," or even, "Everyone will be afraid of you because you are Black." Tell him anything, but don't tell him that in a few years his blackness will be of no consequence. You are lying to him in the first place, and in the second place you are destroying his self-image.

We have no institutions and we have no leaders. Consider the individuals who presume to be our leaders today. Ralph Abernathy and the Southern Christian Leadership Conference cannot possibly offer leadership to Black people. They are committed to integration and the creation of a nonpeople. Even if Dr. Abernathy wanted to assume leadership he could not escape the withering hands of Coretta King and Dr. Martin Luther King, Sr., and their obsession with integration and Kennedy-like memorials of brick and stone. All top SCLC leaders are integrationists working to create a nonpeople. Andy Young has everything but a commitment to Black separatism. Jesse Jackson in Chicago remains a confused integrationist. His Black Santa Claus is still a white Santa Claus who painted his face Black. Santa Claus is a white thing and Black people cannot deal with it. We do not need to create more copycat Black celebrations. You can take anything and paint it Black, but that does not make it Black if it is still serving white interests and if it still comes out of the white experience. A Klansman in a Black sheet would still be a Klansman. A thing is not Black because it is painted Black. If it is not building a Black institution it is not Black. We have the kind of pseudo-leadership we deserve. We deserve Ralph Abernathy, Jesse Jackson, Adam Clayton Powell, and Dr. Martin Luther King. We deserve them because as a people we have been trying to disappear and become a nonpeople.

The thing that sets us apart as Black Christian Nationalists and gives our movement an importance out of proportion to our numerical membership is the fact that we are unashamedly separatists. We do not want to disappear. We do not want to become a nonpeople. In fact, we would rather die than become a nonpeople. The white man cannot intimidate us and confuse us into becoming a nonpeople. If he shoots Black people down in the streets, that does not make us run to him promising to integrate if he will only stop. If he can shoot, so can we. Black Christian Nationalism rejects nonviolence both practically and philosophically. We do not wish to become a nonpeople. We want to stay Black. We are an African people and we are not ashamed of it. But here again we must face reality. Black people in Africa are just as mixed up as Black folks here in America. The white man is controlling Black people everywhere in the world. An article in *U.S. News & World Report* stated that Christianity is the fastest-growing religion in Africa. When Black people come into town they put down Black religions and are converted to white Christianity. There are now more Christians in Africa below the Sahara than there are Moslems. But after they become Christian, they move toward Black Christian Nationalism incorporating African elements into the services of worship and picturing a Black Messiah and a Black Madonna.

We must send representatives to Africa. We must join with our African brothers in redefining the revolutionary religion of the Black Messiah. Teachers being sent to Africa must include anthropologists, historians, and theologians. These are as important to the Black Liberation Struggle as doctors, engineers, plumbers, and electricians. A people cannot seriously engage in a Liberation Struggle until they have developed a revolutionary theology. Black people cannot worship a white God and a white Jesus and fight white people for Black liberation.

The Black Christian Nationalist Movement looks to the establishment of Shrines of the Black Madonna, Black training-action centers, Black cultural centers, and Black economic development programs throughout the world. We reject the traditional concept of church. In its place we will build a Black Liberation movement which derives its basic religious insights from African spirituality, its character from African communalism, and its revolutionary direction from Jesus, the Black Messiah. We will make Black Christian Nationalism the cornerstone of the Black man's struggle for power and survival. We will build a Black communal society which can protect the minds and bodies of Black men, women, and children everywhere. We deliberately reject the individualistic and materialistic value system of the Western world and find in the Black experience the values necessary for our survival.

When a movement becomes a church its meaning and dynamics usually die. Jesus headed a movement. The Apostle Paul established churches. People who came together to do something with Jesus became, with the Apostle Paul, a group of people waiting for God to do something for them. With our emphasis on building a movement, much of the nonsense which characterizes the traditional Black-church program will be discarded. Nothing will be considered important unless it contributes to the liberation of Black people. Black churches as they now exist are mechanisms of pacification designed to divert our attention from the everyday problems of the world. We are taught to consider heaven more important than life on earth. Most Black people have been programmed to self-destruct when they hear the key words "salvation" or "integration." They are afraid to change the slave-church structure, theology, and program of the Black church for fear that any change will endanger their salvation in the afterlife.

Black Christian Nationalism calls Black people to a new commitment with full realization that many who are outside the organized church will respond more quickly than those on the inside who mistakenly think that they are following a risen Christ. Students and young adults who have rejected the traditional church because of its irrelevance and counterrevolutionary effects in the Black community will follow a Black revolutionary Messiah who is concerned about the here and now. Black Christian Nationalism seeks to build counterinstitutions outside the hostile white institutional structures that have been created by the enemy to serve his interests. As an oppressed people we have been systematically structured out of the power establishment. This is the mechanism of our enslavement. Only the transference of power can help us. Established institutional structures cannot serve the needs of the people they were created to enslave. If we are serious about liberation, whatever we do as Black people must be seen in terms of building counterstructures. Our first counterstructure is being built in opposition to the otherworldly, white-oriented, Black slave church, and we do it openly. We see the existing Black church as an integral part of the white man's institutionalized control of Black people. If we are going to follow in the footsteps of the Black Messiah, we must transform this institution which is dominated by an individualistic integrationist mentality. The existing Black Church is trivial, irrelevant, divisive, and counter-revolutionary.

Because of the nature of our task we demand total commitment. The traditional church requests only that you drop in and contribute to support vaguely defined "good works." It is difficult to take "church people" and teach them to function in a movement. Participation in the church has failed to prepare them for serious revolutionary commitment and involvement. They cannot even conceive of total commitment in the name of Jesus. They can only picture Jesus meek and mild, with his blond curls, piously going about doing good. Even when Jesus carried on his personal ministry, the people who came to him were not prepared for total commitment. With brutal honesty he could say, "Let the dead bury their dead," to a young man whose father had just died. Let's be honest. What could he have accomplished by going home with the man to bury his father? His father was dead. Jesus could have shown respect. Jesus had a great capacity for respect, but in this instance he was dealing with a very simple problem. The young man with the dead father was not ready to give total commitment. Burying his father was just one of the many excuses he could have used. He could have said anything. "I must go home and cut the grass." "My child is graduating and I must attend the ceremonies." It could have been anything.

He was not offering total commitment and Jesus would not accept less. He responded in the same way when his own mother came to take him home to his sisters and brothers. He was preaching and healing. She wanted to bring him home so that he would stop making a fool of himself. She did not have the slightest understanding of what he was about. He said, "Tell her that my mother and my brothers and sisters are in here. Whatever family I have are these people who are committed totally to the struggle in which I am engaged. If she is my mother and those are my brothers and sisters, they ought to be in here, not out there." Most church Christians do not believe in that kind of total commitment. It irritates us because it makes us feel guilty. Few of us are ready to give that kind of total commitment. Yet that is what Jesus demanded of his followers. In describing discipleship he said, "You must hate your mother and your father and your brothers and your sisters." He said it that way because we can best understand commitment in terms of our commitment to other human relationships and to our material wealth. He told the rich young ruler who had obeyed the commandments all his life and wanted to be a disciple to give his riches to the poor. The young ruler turned sadly away.

Black Christian Nationalism calls Black people to total

commitment to the Black Liberation Struggle. Total commitment requires the submergence of individualism in the Black Nation and the acceptance of the discipline of the movement. We do not demand commitment to your program of Black liberation or to your philosophy of Black liberation, or to your theology of Black liberation, or to your psychology of Black liberation, or to your sociology of Black liberation, but *to the Black Christian Nationalist theology, ideology, program, and leadership.* This is especially difficult for Black people because the dream of integration and self-hatred has blocked the development of both Black leadership and Black institutions. We have been unwilling to delegate authority to either a Black leader or a Black institution. While we dreamed of integration, both Black leaders and Black institutions were logical impossibilities. The acceptance of the white man's *declaration of Black inferiority* made the delegation of real authority and power to Black leaders and institutions impossible. Our condition of Blackness was an unpleasant and temporary state from which we sought speedy deliverance. The basic inferiority of Black leaders was an accepted fact. A Black leader existed only as a transitional powerless figure pointing the way to integration. Black people did not follow him, they only permitted him to speak their thoughts and to act out their fantasies.

Successful Black "leaders" have understood their role and have played it with skill and style. They have not sought to lead but to inspire. Organizations such as the National Association for the Advancement of Colored People (NAACP), the Urban League, the negro College, and the negro Church have always been white institutions serving the integration dream of Black people. They were the only institutions that Black people wanted in an interim while they patiently waited for integration. Even though accepted by Black people, these pseudo-institutions were never delegated power and authority by Black people. They were never permitted to act for Black people.

They were never really "institutions" any more than Black leaders were ever really "leaders." A powerless people dreaming of integration is incapable of producing either leadership or institutions. It would rather pretend that the leaders and institutions of the enemy actually served its interests.

Black Christian Nationalism demands that Black people accept Black leadership and Black institutions and delegate to them power and authority. This requires a basic change in the thinking of Black people. We would move Black people from the dream of integration to an acceptance of the necessity for separatism. Although many Black people are momentarily alienated by our separatist position, we emphasize it and spell it out in detail because it is the Black man's only hope for the future. We ask Black people to look at the world in which we live and make a decision. If you honestly think that white people will eventually integrate with you and give you power and equality, then obviously you don't need Black Christian Nationalism. All you need is some kind of public-relations machinery to let white folks know that you are waiting to be received.

There is no real Black liberation movement in America today apart from Black Christian Nationalism. Black people are confused, fragmented, and totally disorganized. No movement brings together a majority of Black people. BCN is beginning to put together that kind of movement. Today we represent only a small minority of Black people, but a minority that is disciplined and totally committed. Black individuals are going to be destroyed. Only Black people who are willing to accept total commitment to a philosophy, a program, and a discipline, and come into the Black Nation can hope to survive.

CHAPTER 2

The Black Church

In 1954, the United States Supreme Court ended its "separate but equal" doctrine and declared that inherent in the legal segregation of Black people was a white *declaration of Black inferiority*, which automatically rendered any education received by a Black child within this framework psychologically damaging and consequently inferior. The schools of America were ordered to desegregate "with all deliberate speed" in order that Black people could develop a positive new self-image.

The effects of the court order upon Black people were instantaneous and profound. Desegregation has not yet been accomplished but interpreting the court's decision as a basic legal revocation of the white man's *declaration of Black inferiority*, Black people began a frantic struggle to realize instant integration in all areas of life. Although segregation remains, participation in the Black struggle has enabled the Black man to reject the white man's *declaration of Black inferiority* and has actually served to bring into being the positive self-image which the Supreme Court decision implied could only come with the ending of segregation, signaling the white man's rejection of his own *declaration of Black inferiority*. A white court naturally assumed that the initiative in the long, slow, and difficult process of changing the relationship between white people and Black people must come from white people. This assumption was reflected in the nonlegal determination that desegregation should proceed "with all deliberate speed." Segregation in public education was declared illegal and unconstitutional, but it would be ended only as speedily as white people could be persuaded to permit it to be ended. Few people then realized that if white people were not willing to change their definition of Black people then Black people could force a new relationship by changing their definition of themselves and forcing white people to deal with them on a new basis. Let us trace the steps by which this strange revolution in the thinking of an oppressed people came to pass.

In its 1954 decision the Court lay a foundation for social change of which it could not then have been aware and for which it cannot now be held responsible. The lives of Black people in America were grounded in a dream of integration. African culture had been uprooted and destroyed, and even language and religion had been forgotten. Africans of the diaspora had become a people without a past. With the will to survive they adjusted to a new reality and the demands of their powerlessness. They identified with the white slave master, his white institutions, and his white culture. Each Black man struggled to survive by aping his white master and seeking his approval. The only escape from powerlessness and the indignities of inferiority here on earth appeared to be integration with the powerful and therefore superior white master. The effects of the 1954 Supreme Court decision upon Black people can be understood only in this light. The integration of which an enslaved Black people had dreamed now seemed possible. The nation's highest tribunal had declared that integration was now the law of the land and segregation was no longer legally acceptable. Black people took the Supreme Court decision and made of it a heroic declaration of equality.

The Supreme Court had not intended to say as much as Black people read into the decision. But the decision did say that segregation in public education was no longer legal and that with all deliberate speed changes had to be made so that Black people could have an integrated education. Black people drew the rather logical conclusion that if segregation in education is wrong because there are inequities in the fact of segregation, then segregation itself is wrong and must be abolished everywhere immediately. So the beginning of the Black Revolution was the dream of integration. Black people took the Supreme Court decision seriously and began the struggle to realize instant integration. Black college students in the South proceeded to try to implement the Supreme Court's decision by protesting against all kinds of segregation. Black people wanted immediate integration in all areas of life. So we had the sit-ins, the wade-ins, the kneel-ins, and the freedom rides all over the South. Militant young Black people and older Black people were united in a common effort to realize total and complete integration. So the movement came into being, as a struggle, to realize immediate integration. Today's militant Black leaders were yesterday's integrationists. Stokely Carmichael was an integrationist and co-operated with Dr. King, the messiah of the integrationist movement. Rap Brown was a part of the integrationist Student Nonviolent Co-ordinating Committee.

The integration movement dominated the scene in America following the 1954 Supreme Court decision. Today it seems strange that in 1954 Black people took seriously the possibility of integration. It can only be understood if we remember that Black people had believed in the possibility of integration through all the misery of their American bondage. Always there was the hope that integration would offer an escape from powerlessness and oppression. More than one hundred million Black people were killed during the slave trade (being captured in Africa, being taken to the slave ships, on board the slave ships, on the slave block, and on the plantations). Yet during all of this horror and brutality, Black people still looked forward to the time when they would be integrated with their oppressors. The dream of integration was a basic part of the Black experience in America.

During this whole period Black people felt that the reason integration was so slow in coming was really the fault of Black people themselves. White people were good, they were kindly, they were well-intentioned, and their apparent brutality was necessary to prepare Black people for integration. Even when millions of Black people were being killed, they still felt that they were wrong, and that they were engaged in a mysterious process of trying to become as much like their white oppressors as possible. Self-hatred was a part of the Black man's desire for integration. The Black man's life in America constituted a process by which a proud African people were "niggerized." The end of slavery and the rise of the Klan, with the thousands of public lynchings which were condoned by the total community, did not change the Black man's faith in the goodness of white people. The little book, *One Hundred Years of Lynching*, with documented accounts of five thousand lynchings from newspapers and other public documents, indicates the exquisite conditioning by which Black men were psychologically destroyed. Counties would come together for a lynching party with advance notices and press releases. People would meet at an appointed time and place and a Black man would be lynched. The lynchings were of the most brutal kind. The Black man would be mutilated, killed slowly, and his body destroyed. Yet through all of this, even when Black people were forced to watch the brutality, they still believed that white people were good and that Black people were bad and that the only reason white people did these things was because of the badness of Black people, and still they longed for integration.

Against the background of this kind of total identification with white people and the desire to be accepted by them and to become a part of their white world and its white institutions, the 1954 Supreme Court decision called into being a movement designed to accomplish instant integration. Black people really expected to see the walls of Jericho come tumbling down. The mobilization of white people to prevent integration was at first assumed to be the work of a few bad white people who did not represent the white community. Only gradually did it become obvious to Black people that their interpretation of reality was false. The white man was not good. He had not been waiting for the Black man to achieve a degree of perfection which would enable him to be accepted for integration. Actually the white man hated and despised Black people. The white man was an enemy and all his institutions were enemy institutions. This was not an immediate revelation for Black people. They didn't just wake up one morning realizing that they lived in a hostile land surrounded by enemies who were determined to destroy them psychologically, and physically if necessary. But gradually over a period of time—through personal experiences or vicariously through television—Black people came to the realization that white America is built on a basic contradiction which excludes all Black people from the American Dream. White people hate Black people and are committed to their oppression and exploitation.

On television Black people would see a Black mother taking a little Black child through a howling, savage white mob into a school that had been integrated by law. The howling mob of white people organized to prevent this integration was a part of the revelation which came to Black people. These were not white people who had been released from insane asylums and penitentiaries for participation in a mob scene. They were the ordinary white people of the community, the deacons of the church, the Boy Scout leaders, the Girl Scout leaders, YMCA people—together they made up the mob. For Black people it was a new experience. It was seeing suddenly that white people were united in the exclusion and total oppression of Black people. The sit-in demonstrations where Black people asked only for the privilege of eating a ten-cent hot dog at a lunch counter aroused a community-wide defense of white supremacy. The television scene showing a huge white man knocking a black girl from a counter stool, kicking her, throwing mustard and ketchup on her, to the obvious glee of the white people who were present, was part of the educational experience of Black people. Only gradually did Black people begin to loosen their identification and to realize that white people do not want integration, will not accept it, and will do anything to prevent it.

Black people began to seek a new reality on which to build their lives. Obviously they had been living a lie and now somewhere in their Black experience they had to find something on which they could build a life that was real. So Black people began the painful search for a new Black reality. Dr. King's integration movement had taken Black people as far as he was equipped to go and that had been a long, long way indeed. Dr. King took Black people who were still stepping off the sidewalk in the presence of white people and set up face-to-face confrontations with white power across the South. Through the absurd nonviolent and redemptive-love tactics that Dr. King used, Black people learned that they could stand up against white people and white power and that white people were not invincible. Dr. King moved across the South from one confrontation to another, preaching love but actually exposing the white man as he had never been exposed before. Black people began to see that there is no possibility of integration with white people because the white man is the Black man's enemy.

Black people, with their tremendous capacity for forgiveness and love, still tried to rationalize away the fact that all white people were in fact a part of the same white system of oppression. They said bad white people were in the South, and good white people were in the North. Then Dr. King, as his last great contribution before his assassination, went to Chicago and proved conclusively that there is no such thing as good white people and bad white people and that white people make up one system of oppression and brutality. In Chicago there was exactly the same reaction as in the South: the total mobilization of the white community to block integration and the Black man's freedom struggle. When some of the brothers marched into Cicero they found exactly the same face of white hatred, the same drooling, idiotic, violent response to the Black man's demands for equality. Obviously the march into Cicero was a symbolic march. Nobody wants to live in Cicero. The revelation was complete. Even the white people who didn't want to live in Cicero themselves didn't want any Black people living there with them. And so the whole dramatic period of Dr. King's confrontations had come to a close. White people had finally revealed themselves to Black people. Black people had finally gotten the message.

Today when Black people talk about separatism, Black pride, and doing their own thing, white people are shocked, and they ask, "Why do you Black people hate us so? Why do you want to separate yourselves instead of being a part of the body of Christ [if they are Christians, or "of the nation," if they are politicians]? Why do you Black people want to do this thing? You are destroying America." It took us a long time to accept reality. Now we understand that there are two Americas, one white and one Black. White America has power, it controls the economics, the politics, the religion, and all the rest of the institutional structures of America. Then there is Black America, which is powerless, in which the people control nothing, in which Black people are en-slaved. Black people do not control the politics of the communities in which they live. They do not control the culture, the education, the libraries. They do not control any of the institutions upon which their communities depend. They are a powerless, exploited, oppressed, and brutalized people. Two Americas. One Black and one white. This then is the emerging reality for Black people. We had to learn that our problem does not grow out of the fact that some white people believe one thing and some believe another. It makes no difference; a white middle-class suburbanite, a white alcoholic on Skid Row, and a poor-white farmer have no real ideological difference insofar as Black people are concerned.

Black people are oppressed because they are powerless and they are identifiable. They are oppressed by white people who have power and who control a system. It is necessary to understand that a white person is a part of this system of oppression whether he engages in face-to-face brutality or not. You don't have to beat a Black man to death to be involved in the destruction of Black people. Teachers in schools, even those who think that they love little Black children and drive in from the suburbs because they want to teach little Black children, are a part of the psychological destruction of Black people. A white teacher who teaches in a Black school is a power symbol for a Black child. And whatever love she has in her heart cannot in any way compensate for the effects of her presence. She teaches a little Black child by her very presence that power in America is in the hands of white people. That even in a school the power symbols—the white teacher, the white principal, the white administration—indicate the basic and pervasive nature of white power.

Apart from the questions of motivation and power symbols, Black schools are inferior because money is withheld from the education of Black children in order that the education of white children may be improved. So if you live in a suburban community and there are no Black children there, your little white child gets a better education because a little Black child in a ghetto school receives a poorer education. If you are white, no matter where you work, you have greater job security because you don't have to worry about real competition from Black people because there is a ceiling on how far a Black man can go. So wherever you are, even in the church, a Black minister has a certain limited area in which he can function. A white minister does not have to worry about the competition of a Black preacher. The white man has a privileged position. It is a power position. It is difficult for white people to recognize this because they take power for granted, and because he who has power feels that his power has been divinely bestowed. He who is powerless also takes his powerlessness for granted and tends to feel that his powerlessness has been divinely bestowed as punishment for some mystical sin committed in the past. Black people have much to learn; we have only begun the difficult struggle involved in facing reality.

The truths which are basic to our new position sound strange when we say them aloud. First, and inescapable, is the simple fact that the white man is our enemy. This is important to the Black church, because Black theology must deal with this reality if it is going to be a theology which Black people can accept. To survive we must break our identification with the enemy. We must escape from powerlessness if we are to deal with a white enemy. To survive we must reject the dream of integration which serves as the mechanism of our continuing enslavement. A Black businessman feels that his business has very little significance because he is living in a mythical never-never land of integration that can never be. It is from this suspended animation that Black people are now in the process of reviving. To escape from powerlessness we must reject the dreams of integration.

So everywhere today Black people are enraged and

white people are resentful. These are the two faces of America which we see everywhere: a Black America which is powerless, in which Black people are enraged and struggling to escape from identification with white people, struggling for economic power, political power, and the power to control Black communities; and a white America in which white people feel threatened and resentful. "Good liberal" white people who have given so much for Black people are the most outraged and resentful. They are the most afraid and they feel the most threatened. In a sense they built their lives on a lie just as Black people did. To have that lie exploded shakes the foundation of their lives and destroys their reason for being. "Liberal Christian" white people are the most threatened by the new emerging Black man who wants to stand alone, to be a person, to be a Black man, and to think as a Black man and to live in terms of his struggle for power. White America and Black America are locked in a never-ending power struggle. This is the reality in which we all must live.

In the midst of a Black Revolution in which Black people are struggling for power, slave Christianity no longer meets the Black man's needs. Slave Christianity is the Christianity that old master gave Black people back on the plantation. He defined Jesus with pictures of a white man with flowing golden locks and blue eyes. The obvious absurdity was not immediately apparent to Black people. Jesus could not have looked like the pictures in the Bible, having been born in a part of the world reserved for Black people by God. But the whiteness of Jesus and Israel was basic to slave Christianity. Old master taught Black people that God was primarily concerned with petty sins (you don't fornicate, you don't smoke, you don't play cards, you don't drink). A petty morality too trivial for God's concern was the basic element of slave Christianity. Slave Christianity had to do with individualistic salvation. Two thousand years ago on Calvary a mystic event took place.

Jesus was crucified and somehow he rose from the dead. In this redemptive act, God made salvation possible for individuals in all generations who believe. This meant then that each individual must fight for his own little individual salvation.

Black people took this slave Christianity and made of it an instrument for survival. They put into it a vitality which the white man did not have in his own church. They believed fervently because they needed to believe, they needed a dream of escape from a world in which there was no real possibility of escape. They could conceive of no way to end their oppression so they used this slave theology as one way of maintaining sanity. Slave Christianity made it possible for Black people to survive. The slaves took the idea of going to heaven seriously. They took their pain and suffering to Jesus. The slave could stand anything that the white man did, saying, "The white man can beat me, he can rob me, he can cheat me, he can rape my wife and my daughters, he can do anything, but I can take it all to Jesus and I know that ultimately Jesus will triumph because through his sacrifice God has already redeemed me. So whatever the white man does I can accept." He went to church on Sunday and shouted with joy, running up and down the aisles in sheer ecstasy. The most effective Christian preaching in America was done in Black pulpits with ignorant Black preachers preaching slave Christianity as no one in the world had ever preached it before, to people who had to believe because they had no alternative to this mystical religious escape.

The Black slave church was also destroying Black people. Black people suffered discrimination because they were Black. They were persecuted, they were brutalized, they were discriminated against, they were exploited—solely because they were Black. And then in church on Sunday morning, the Black slave preacher would say, "God is concerned about each one of you. You think that all week He hasn't been looking at you, but He's been watching everything that the white man has been doing to you. God knows what white people have done to you and someday He is going to shake them over hell-fire. One of these days God is going to do for you what you can't do yourself. So get along with these white people as best you can because soon you are going to be taken up yonder to God and then you can sit at His right hand and look down into hell where white people are roasting over hellfire." That was a beautiful message with simple basic eloquence and power about it. I only wish that it were true! But then you remember that Black people had been working all week for nothing, being beaten up by policemen and exploited in every possible way. The preacher helped them to forget by telling them how beautiful it was going to be up there. Pretty soon they would be running up and down the aisles shouting and screaming, and for the moment each individual escaped from his everyday problems and for the moment was completely out of this world.

The church and slave Christianity has perpetuated our individualism. We don't have any sense of being a people fighting our problems together. We're waiting for God to save us individually. We're running up and down the aisle shouting and singing and hoping that Jesus will speak to our individual needs, not the needs of Black people. We do not really ask God to help us change the basic conditions under which Black people live. This is the weakness of the Black church. It was a survival instrument. It helped maintain sanity, but it destroyed the possibility of a united Black Liberation Struggle. The Black preacher preached escapism and individualism. He destroyed the possibility of Black people's fighting together to change oppressive conditions.

There were exceptions. There was Nat Turner, who was a Black preacher who understood that the lynching of Jesus on Calvary two thousand years ago did not stop him from trying to kill white people who were oppressing his people. He was a Black preacher who somehow saw the inadequacies and the contradictions of slave Christianity. But his revolt failed because a Black Christian brother betrayed him along the way to guarantee his salvation in glory. As long as Black people could see no possibility of changing the world, escapism was good old religion. It was all that a Black preacher could preach to a Black congregation. As long as there was no way for Black people to change their condition, it was natural to concentrate on the possibility of a good life after death.

As soon as Black people began to see realistically the world in which they lived, they began to see white people as they really were: corrupt, brutal, and oppressive. When Black people began to look at white people and see them as they were, they said, "We can change this world ourselves, we don't have to wait for Jesus." And that marked the beginning of a whole new way of life for Black people. Black people began to try to change the world day by day, not waiting either for Jesus or for the redemption of white people. This new attitude could not fit into the slave church. The new Black militant talked about people working together to change the Black man's condition. The slave preacher still talked about sending individuals to heaven one by one. The two can't mix. In Harlem half a million Black people crowd into thousands of little churches every Sunday and nothing is done to change the Black man's condition in New York City. The ineffectiveness of the Black church is reflected in the condition of Harlem. The Black church could change Harlem any day it offered Black people leadership here on earth by bringing Black people together. The white power structure has a vested interest in keeping slave Christianity alive. No one will ever organize a Black community for a united action as long as Black preachers are standing up on Sunday morning taking people to heaven one by one. As soon as Black people began to conceive of the possibility of changing the world, the absolute necessity for a new interpretation of the Bible and a new Black theology became obvious. There were other possible solutions. Black people could just leave the church—and I think many white people would rather that we did just that. But Christianity belongs to us. We are not going to give it up just because white people have messed it up.

So when we began to see that we could change the world, we began to see that the church offered a broad potential power base that could be useful in the Black Revolution. We have too much money tied up in Black churches to just turn and leave them. We need them in the Liberation Struggle. Which means that we must change the church radically. We must make the church relevant to the Black Revolution. The Black Revolution consists from day to day of those people who have severed their identification with white people, who realize that white people are the enemy and are engaged in a struggle for power to control Black communities. Black Christian Nationalism seeks to chart new directions for the Black church because the Black Revolution needs institutional power and stability. Many young Black militants think that restructuring the Black church is too much trouble. They say that it is more trouble than it is worth. They would rather just leave it. But Black Christian Nationalism is determined to take it along with the revolution. We are convinced that it can serve a valuable purpose if we will take the time to restructure it.

Everything must be restructured: its historical analysis, its Biblical interpretation, its theology, its ritual, its preaching, everything. We can't just say we're going to change it a little bit, we're going to patch it up a little here and a little there. The whole Pauline interpretation of Christianity is historically false. The theology built on it has no relationship at all to the teachings of Jesus. You can ask, "How do you know?" I can reply, "That's a good question, because none of us knows very much about what Jesus taught." All that we know about Jesus was filtered through the eyes of the early Church after it had already been corrupted by the Apostle Paul, who was an Uncle Tom who wanted to identify with his white gentile oppressors. Paul was very proud of his Roman citizenship, even though he was an oppressed Black Jew. He was just like a Black man today talking about his American citizenship. And I daresay that Paul's Roman citizenship did him just about as much good as a Black man's American citizenship does him today. But that doesn't have anything to do with the way a man feels. Paul wanted to feel like a Roman. He wanted to be a part of the pagan Roman world, so he took something that happened, the history and the person of Jesus, and distorted it to make it acceptable to a heathen world. There was some controversy about it. The Disciples who remained in Jerusalem knew that he was preaching a false doctrine that had nothing at all to do with Jesus with whom they had walked and talked. They tried to hold him accountable for his white corruptions. He tricked them just as people do today. He raised money from the churches he had organized and went back to Jerusalem with enough money to persuade the original Disciples to overlook the fact that what he was teaching was a false doctrine. Paul does not follow in the footsteps of Jesus, who derived his teachings from those of the Black Nation Israel.

The Black church must seek to rediscover the original teachings of Jesus and the Nation Israel. There is very little history in the Gospels and in the rest of the New Testament. In the Old Testament we have a little history intermingled with much fantasy and myth. Let's admit that we don't have much, except insofar as we can understand the conditions out of which Jesus came and the role which he played in his day. We can find a few historical fragments in the Synoptic Gospels. We must depend on the Old Testament to validate the New Testament.

Preachers don't quite know what to do with the Old Testament except to go back at Christmastime and find passages which prove that Jesus was the Messiah—all of which have nothing to do with Jesus. Essentially the Old Testament contradicts the new. The easy way to get around that, of course, is to say that the New Testament is an expansion and development and takes the Old Testament to new heights, which we also know is a lie. It says something entirely different. The New Testament does not take the Old Testament to new heights. It is a complete contradiction of the Old Testament, and Jesus came to fulfill the Old Testament.

We go back to the beginning of the Old Testament and we find mythology, of course. Moses did not write the first five books of the Old Testament. At some point Israel became a nation. At some point the process began. We like to begin with Abraham, who from the region of the Tigris and Euphrates rivers went down into Africa, where his wife had an affair with Pharaoh to save Abraham's life. Pharaoh finally discovered the deception and ordered Abraham and Sarah out of Egypt. To avoid God's displeasure Pharaoh gave him gifts, including animals, slaves, and concubines. Abraham continued his wandering. Sarah was unable to have a child, and so she suggested that he have a child by Hagar, an Egyptian servant girl.

So Ishmael, Abraham's heir, was born of an Egyptian slave, Hagar. Obviously the relationships were close and friendly. Later they tried to get rid of Hagar and Ishmael. But the Jews did not have any racial prejudice in the sense that they held themselves apart from other peoples. Wherever they went they tended to mingle, to intermarry, to become a part of the people. So as Israel wandered in Africa, Israel became Blacker and Blacker. Some of you may want to argue that the Egyptians were not Black. This is a ridiculous argument which could only arise in America. Studies have been made which prove beyond a doubt that most of the pharaohs were Black. I am not saying "nonwhite," I am saying Black. That most of the pharaohs were Black can be determined by X-rays of the mummies of the pharaohs. The percentage of pharaohs who obviously were Black was markedly high in a study done by the University of Michigan Dental School. Studies of poor Egyptians indicate an even higher percentage, as would be expected. The Egyptians were Black. The intermingling of the Egyptians with Israel in the building of the National Israel was a historic fact from the very beginning. Finally Israel went back into Egypt to escape from famine and settled there and became a part of the people. The constant mingling and intermixture are obvious. Then there were four hundred years of slavery. The Arabs were the great slave traders of the ancient world. And so in Egypt there were Black Egyptians, Black African slaves from the interior, and Black Israelites. For four hundred years they lived together and intermingled. When Israel fled from Egypt they were accompanied by a *mixed multitude* of other African slaves who also became a part of the Black Nation Israel. The Old Testament is the history of the development of a Black African Nation.

Black Jews, as they became a people in their wandering, developed basic ideas which were important to them. The history and religion of Israel are dominated by the concept of nation. God was concerned not with individuals but with the Black Nation Israel. God supported the efforts of the Black Nation Israel. The Black Nation Israel made up the Chosen People of God. God had a relationship with the Nation Israel, and the Nation Israel was to be saved or the Nation Israel was to be punished. God spoke to a prophet that he might bring a message to the Nation Israel. It is this concept of nation which Christianity loses entirely because of the Apostle Paul's identification with the pagan white world. Black people of the Nation Israel depended on God to support them in every struggle. The Old Testament is a Black-power document which no modern book can equal. God would even hold the sun still while the Black Nation Israel killed its enemies. God would do anything necessary to help the Black Nation Israel find the Promised Land and keep it.

Jesus, the Black Messiah, lived in the midst of this kind of Black Liberation Struggle. The Maccabean revolt freed Israel from white gentile oppression for a period, but by the time of Jesus the Jews had again become an enslaved people who had lost much of their sense of nationhood. Jesus was born into a situation comparable to that in which Black people in America live today, a situation in which Black people were oppressed by a white gentile oppressor and were exploited in every way possible. Jesus found an underground revolutionary movement led by the Zealot extremists. The baptism of Jesus obviously marked his introduction into this revolutionary Zealot movement. When John the Baptist was arrested and about to be killed, he sent disciples to talk to Jesus to find out whether or not he was the new leader who was to take over the movement. The terse reply of Jesus indicated quite clearly that he considered himself to be the new leader and that he was willing to be judged in terms of the things he was doing. "Tell John and let him decide whether or not I am the Messiah."

Following the death of John the Baptist, Jesus became the visible head of the revolutionary Zealot movement. Certain radical phases of the movement remained underground and certainly Jesus was forced to walk a tightrope in his relationship with an oppressed people who were fighting for liberation by any means necessary, and with those who were in collaboration with the white oppressors and who exacted certain benefits from this relationship. It is this kind of situation which is revealed in the little incident in which Jesus was asked about paying taxes to Caesar. The revolutionaries advocated paying no taxes to Caesar. They argued that this was one way of ending oppression. Jesus could have replied, "No, don't pay taxes

to Caesar." That would have led to his immediate arrest
by the government. On the other hand, he could have
said, "Pay taxes to Caesar." Then he would have alienated
the movement and endangered his life, but Rome would
have been satisfied. He said neither. He pointed to Caesar's
picture on the coin and said, "Give unto Caesar the things
that are Caesar's and unto God the things that are God's."
This is the kind of double talk that preachers still use
whenever they do not wish to answer a question.

One of the most confusing teachings of Jesus has to
do with the love ethic which the Apostle Paul attempted
to universalize. Jesus was defining a tribal ethic for the
Black Nation Israel. He was trying to bring together a
people who were oppressed and who had been fragmented
by their oppression. Any oppressed people are filled with
self-hate and tend to identify with their oppressors. Psychological studies of modern Jews in concentration camps
under Hitler indicate that the greater the oppression, the
greater the identification. In concentration camps the Jews
identified totally with their guards who exercised the
power of life and death. They were not even permitted
to take care of their bodily needs without the guard's
permission. So the guard became for them a kind of God
with whom they identified completely. This is true for
any oppressed people. Jesus understood the many forces
which separate an oppressed people from one another and
make them betray brothers to serve the interests of their
oppressors. So in dealing with his own people he had to
talk much about love. And in this sense, many of the
things that Jesus said sound remarkably like the things
that I've heard Stokely Carmichael say in talking to a
Black group.

Stokely Carmichael could come into a meeting jammed
with thousands of people and his first reaction would be
to the people's relationships with one another. If there
were brothers sitting down and sisters standing along the

wall, Stokely would ask the brothers to please get up and let the sisters have their seats, saying that a people must learn to respect their women. That might have sounded like hate to white people, but to Black people it pointed out a whole new approach to the possibilities of Black people living together. Most of his talk would be in terms of how Black people must love one another and build whatever they were going to build in terms of new human relationships, which could protect Black people from white people's materialism and selfishness. Listening to Stokely I understood the kind of thing that Jesus had to do to unite the Black people of Israel. He had to talk to them about the transforming and redemptive power of love within the Black Nation. If a Black brother strikes you upon one cheek, turn to him the other cheek, because we must save every Black brother for the nation if we are to survive. We can't say that this group of Black people is not important or that group of Black people is not important. Every Black brother and sister must be saved and brought into the Black Nation. This is what Jesus was talking about. Turn the other cheek, go the second mile, go a hundred miles if necessary, if in this way you can save a Black brother.

In the parable of the good Samaritan, Jesus is trying to make the same emphasis. The Samaritans were Jews. They were a lost tribe, despised because they rejected the Temple in Jerusalem. Jesus said this, too, was a part of the Jewish nation and it must be saved. Jews could no longer look down on any part of the Black Nation. The parable of the good Samaritan was merely an effort to show Israel that these people could no longer be despised. Jesus said it straight out when the brother came and asked what he ought to do if a brother refused to treat him properly. Jesus said, "Take another brother and go talk to him. If he still refuses to do right take another brother and talk to him again. If he refuses, put him out of the nation and treat him like a Gentile." We try to forget that Jesus talked about white Gentiles in this way. Put him outside the nation. Treat him like a Gentile. If Jesus had been preaching universal love when he said, "Go the second mile and turn the other cheek," he would not possibly have understood that the Black Nation Israel was separate and apart from its white gentile enemies. He labored to bring together a people who could stand against their oppressors.

We could say that this doesn't sound very revolutionary. Jesus engaged in little physical combat except in the almost symbolic act of driving the moneychangers out of the Temple. He didn't use a sword. Even in Gethsemane, when the soldiers came to arrest him and Peter drew his sword, Jesus stopped him in a very practical way. A battle would have been futile. The disciples were neither equipped nor trained for battle. If he had planned to fight, Jesus would have been putting together an army all the way to Jerusalem. But to turn what he had been trying to do for the nation into a military struggle at the last moment would have been ridiculous. Jesus was primarily concerned with building a people, bringing them together, and forming a nation. And this task to which Jesus gave his full commitment was profoundly revolutionary. Everything that Jesus taught, everything that he said is relevant to the Liberation Struggle in which Black people are engaged.

Instead of telling Black people about escaping from the world and going home to God on high, the Black church must begin to involve Black people in the Black Liberation Struggle by using the teachings of Jesus in the Synoptic Gospels, and the Old Testament concept of nation, to show Black people how coming together with Black pride and Black power is basic to survival. The Black church must become central in the Black Revolution. Jesus was a Black Messiah not in terms of his death on Calvary, but in terms of his dedication to the struggle of Black people here on earth.

In the Black church the sacraments can take on a new meaning. At the Shrine of the Black Madonna we baptize "into the nation." We die to the old Uncle Tom life. We die to the old identification with white people. To be baptized into a Black church must symbolize a complete rejection of the values of a hostile white world and a complete commitment to the struggle of Black people. When we take the sacrament of Holy Communion it symbolizes our total rededication to personal participation in the struggle of Black people and total rededication to the Black Nation. The sacraments and ritual of the church then become for Black people an intrinsic part of the revolutionary struggle.

Since all of the great religions of the world derive from the Black experience, we could turn to another religion if we wished. They all belong to us. Or we could put together a new religion suitable to our present needs and true to our historic revelations of God. But for Black people in America, Christianity is a part of our past. Its reinterpretation in terms of its historic Black roots is a joyful task which we have undertaken. To realize finally that Jesus is a Black Messiah, that the things he taught are still relevant to us, and that the distortions which we have learned are deliberately perpetrated by the white man for his own benefit and convenience is to realize that the restoration of the original Christianity taught by Jesus is a task that we cannot put aside. We can restructure theology, making it something that Black people can understand and appreciate. In many places young Black people are honestly ashamed to be seen going in or coming out of a church—and understandably so, because the Black church has been an Uncle Tom institution, committed to the preservation of the white *status quo* and the pacification of Black people. A revolutionary Black church must be a place to which Black people come with pride, knowing that Jesus was Black, that the Nation Israel was Black, and that we are following in the footsteps of a Black Messiah. Even now we are restructuring the Black church that it may become the foundation on which we can build the Black Christian Nationalist Liberation Struggle and the emerging Black Nation.

CHAPTER 3

Black Christian Nationalism

As Black Christian Nationalists, we seek to change society in order to accomplish the liberation of Black people; and we realize that we are engaged in a struggle for power and for survival. We believe that nothing is more sacred than the liberation of Black people. We must transform the minds of Black people by freeing them from dependence on white cultural values and from their unconscious acceptance of the white man's *declaration of Black inferiority*. We must restructure our relationships within the Black Nation toward unity and love in preparation for a realistic power struggle against our white oppressors. We must control all the basic institutions which dominate the Black community. Self-determination and community control must become realities in every area of ghetto life.

The white man's *declaration of Black inferiority* and the oppression that has been a natural result of this declaration have served to provide us with a unique Black experience that has separated us from white America. Our lives have been molded by this experience. Our minds have been shaped by it. The Black church is an expression of the totality of this Black experience. Efforts to copy the white church, which is the product of a totally different experience, have been futile. An emerging new revolutionary Black church will bring Black brothers and sisters together in one joyous experience of worship, commitment, unity, and struggle.

The officers and members of the Shrine of the Black Madonna believe that the Black church can become relevant to the Black Revolution. Upon the foundation of this faith we have undertaken to build a "Black Nation within a nation," following the teachings of the Black Messiah, Jesus of Nazareth. We are separatist, convinced that we need not be poor, disadvantaged, or exploited if we will but use our separation as a power base for political and economic self-determination, rather than permit it to be used as an instrument and symbol of our enslavement. The Black church must free the minds of Black people from psychological identification with a white society which seeks in every way to destroy them. Black people who dream of integration perpetuate the mechanism of their enslavement. They have been programmed to destroy themselves. The Black church must fight to free the Black man's mind so that he can fight to restructure or destroy the institutions which perpetuate his enslavement.

At the Shrine of the Black Madonna, we recognize and admit the betrayal of the Black church even as we struggle to redeem and transform it for the survival struggle that lies ahead. If the Black church is to commit its resources to the Black Revolution, we must develop a new Black theology founded upon a critical re-examination of the historic foundation of the Christian faith. We know that the Israel of the Old Testament was a Black Nation. We know that Mary and Joseph and Jesus were Black. So Christianity is founded upon the life and teachings of a Black Messiah.

As important as the fact that Israel and Jesus were Black is the fact that Jesus was a revolutionary leader engaged in a Liberation Struggle against the white gentile world.

In the light of these facts, the meaning of the Bible is dramatically changed, and Christianity is a Black man's religion, relevant to the Black Revolution. The Black church must build on this foundation.

The Shrine of the Black Madonna seeks to bring the Black church back to its historic roots through the BLACK CHRISTIAN NATIONALIST MOVEMENT, established in March of 1967, and through the organization of Shrines wherever Black people are.

The old Black church, grounded in the traditional neo-primitive individualist theology, defined its basic task as that of calling sinners to repentance. This was a clear-cut objective. Every Sunday morning the church was open for this express purpose. The message from the pulpit was designed to call sinners to repentance. The entire program was based on the sound theory that even those converted last Sunday needed to be called to repentance again by the following Sunday, if not sooner. The church evolved a very simple mode of operation involving little more than the calling of sinners to repentance and the ritualistic mediation of the free gift of God's salvation. The Black preacher understood his task and did it well. He was to convict men of sin, call sinners to repentance, and mediate God's salvation. A member was required to come down front, confess his sins and his faith in Jesus Christ, be baptized—dying to sin and rising in the newness of life—partake regularly of the Lord's Supper, and participate in the financial support of the church. The purpose and program of the church were simple and clear.

The Black church accepted the neo-primitive individualism of the white church. The more highly developed, African, communal conception of man's relationship with God had been lost when the Black man was uprooted and his history and culture stripped from him. Black men taken in chains from Africa were taught an unrecognizable distortion of a religion originally created by the religious genius of Black men. It is not strange that they did not recognize the African teachings of the Nation Israel and the Black Messiah, Jesus, in the neo-primitive individualism of Western Christianity. Even Black Israelites snatched from their homeland did not recognize the white man's golden-haired redemption symbol. Other Africans to whom the small Nation Israel had been virtually unknown on the great Black continent saw no trace of African communalism in Jesus, the Lamb of God slain for the sins of the world. They accepted Jesus as the white man's God who might in some mysterious way mitigate the violence and brutality of the white man on earth and transport them to heaven when they died. This new white man's religion had little relationship with the Black man's everyday problems. It was a complete process, separate and apart. Even today the Black church sees little relationship between the salvation it preaches and unemployment, bad housing, slums, exploitation, and war. The old Black theology has little real concern for these problems. They are the problems of a sinful world from which we seek escape through faith. The church does not worry about these mundane things. If the food in ghetto stores is rotten and we pay too much for it, if we must go to Vietnam and die, if we must crowd ten children into a two-room apartment—this is the cross that God has put upon us and we will receive our reward in heaven.

Old Black theology holds that worldly problems are not relevant to man's basic struggle for his soul's salvation. So the church constitutes a process separate and apart from the everyday process of living. Black people then are involved in two separate processes. One is the religious process of preparing for death and the hereafter, which is completely unrelated to the other, which is the process of trying to survive here on earth. Two-thirds of the wealth, resources, and leadership of the Black community are devoted to the religious process of preparing Black people for heaven. On the other hand, the survival process is almost without organization, resources, or leadership.

Black people do not know what to do about their real problems and generally have no place to turn for help. Most Black leadership is either tied up in the heaven process or is subservient to it for reasons of political expediency. Few so-called Black leaders accepted by the Black community are willing to deal with problems, confrontations, and conflict with the white oppressor. When four policemen beat you up in an alley or you are discriminated against on your job, take your problem to the Black church and receive a firsthand lesson in Black religious concerns. The Black preacher will tell you that he cannot deal with that kind of problem, after he checks you out in terms of membership and contributions. He clearly understands his process and you are bringing him a problem which is unrelated to it, except insofar as he may be forced to accept a very limited involvement in it in order to maintain your membership in the household of faith.

As a pseudo-institution the Black church has financial resources, buildings, and everything else that a movement needs, but it is completely cut off from the common life of the Black community. So Black people exist from day to day on an individualistic basis. The community in which we live is a jungle because it has no institutional stability. People are almost afraid to go to church because someone may move out their furniture while they are away. Even the most heaven-bent Christian realizes that faith is no answer to these very real everyday problems. As Black people we live in communities in which there exists a leadership vacuum.

Because we have no Black institutions (the Black church is not a Black institution because it does not exist to serve the power interests of Black people), only Black Christian Nationalism is working to develop a program and methodology by which Black people can deal with their powerlessness. A few people in every city are working to build relevant Black programs. This is a first step—but doomed to failure because we have no real institutional foundation.

No little organization in a single Black community can tackle the problems of Black people. You can set up your own little block club or your own little neighborhood organization but you are powerless. Real Black power is engaged in a counter-process dedicated to taking Black people to heaven. Even if you could organize your block or your neighborhood you might get a new streetlight or an extra garbage pickup, but you could not touch the real problem of Black powerlessness. Your block and your neighborhood suffer as a part of the institutional racism that oppresses all Black people everywhere. We are oppressed by impersonal white institutions with power.

The smallest problem of which you could conceive would require the total institutional power of the Black community for solution, and the only potential institutional power in the Black community is being wasted preparing Black people for heaven. Your corner grocer sells inferior produce at exploitative prices. You would like to deal with that problem. Where do you start? The store is just a small part of an international process that somehow puts a can of beans on the shelf of your corner store and makes Black people pay five cents more for it than white people pay. Who do you fight—the farmer? the canner? the wholesaler? the trucker? The process is beyond the ability of a handful of Black people in one community to change significantly. You can tell the owner that you are tired of rotten meat and that you are tired of high prices. Tell him that the store stinks (most stores in Black communities stink). Tell him that you are tired of the whole thing, and then burn it down. What have you done? You feel better. Grab a couple of cans of beans as you go, and you may feel better for a week or two, if you don't get shot. The process remains. The owner will take the insurance from the store you burned down and put up another store. It will be larger this time and he can rob you more efficiently. The process is too big for one little Black group in one little Black neighborhood to handle.

If we are going to deal with our oppression and exploitation we must build the institutions and mechanisms that will enable us to move from power rather than from weakness. As wrong and as irrelevant as the Black church has been, we need it. We need its potential institutional strength, and we must begin the task of reorganizing and restructuring it for Black liberation. It offers a workable basis for the establishment of a national Black institution, and without it Black liberation and even Black survival are impossible. It exists everywhere Black people are. It is accepted by the Black community. It alone can mobilize the institutional power necessary for our battle against oppression. Somehow we must merge the two separate processes present in the Black community. The task of deliverance must become a single process including the totality of life.

How are we to deal with the complex problems which make up so large a part of the Black man's life? Some methods are obviously ineffective. The method used by the anti-war demonstrators following the invasion of Cambodia was ineffective. It lacked institutional power, and without institutional power only violence commands attention and indicates seriousness. In a pragmatic sense the demonstrators would have been more effective if they had burned down the White House. When we had our Freedom March in Detroit in 1963, we were very careful. We did not break a window and nobody paid any attention to two hundred thousand Black people walking down Woodward Avenue with Dr. Martin Luther King. In 1967, a few brothers tried to burn the city down and everybody paid attention. The power establishment has an understandable psychology. It responds only when it is confronted by either power or violence. It does not believe that you are serious if you can engage in calm, dispassionate dialogue. Because Black people lack power, we constantly are being driven to insane violence as a means of communicating our seriousness. The institutional strength of the Black church would give us a greater choice of methods in confronting our enemies. In a sense, then, the irrelevance of the Black church drives Black men seriously protesting and legitimately aggrieved to insane violence as the only method open to them. It is not by accident that the Palestinian Arabs have chosen to hijack and destroy transcontinental jet airliners and to hold innocent passengers as hostages in their demands for the release of their comrades. It is not by accident that South American political parties kidnap foreign diplomats as hostages in their demands for the release of their persecuted comrades. It is not by accident that Canadian separatists have kidnapped government officials as hostages in their demands for the release of captured comrades. All are moving from weakness and lack sufficient institutional strength to make other methods of confrontation practical. The seriousness of their dedication to their cause makes insane violence the only method open to them. With the exception of the Black Panthers and a few isolated individuals, Black revolutionaries in America have not yet moved toward the planned and systematic use of insane violence. This could indicate either (1) that The Last Poets are right, and "Niggers *are* scared of Revolution"; (2) the absence of a serious Black revolutionary cadre; or (3) a prevailing absurd conviction that the Black man is actually moving toward integration as the result of interracial dialogue.

In Detroit's Black community unemployment is, at this writing, already approaching 25 percent and the recession is not yet officially under way. The Black church ought to be moving to meet this problem. We have survived depressions before but this one will be different. This time our survival will be at stake. Conditions have changed basically. We have few friends and many enemies. What could the church do? We could be dealing with community organization in terms of program. We could organize Black people to become a part of something in which they believed, and to support a program designed to enable them to work together. We could develop methods and techniques for the total mobilization of the Black community in the realization that our common Blackness is the most important single fact of our existence. We are immobilized by trivial differences. We would be helpless to defend Black people in a real survival situation.

I find it difficult to believe that the church can be helpless in dealing with our everyday problems and can be effective in dealing with God. The old Black church must be lying about its effectiveness in dealing with God, if we cannot confront the white enemy who is oppressing and exploiting Black brothers and sisters everywhere. If the white man announced that he was invading any urban inner city on Monday morning at 8 A.M. to wipe out Black people, the Black churches could not get together in time to be of any assistance. This is pathetic. A Black church which is so otherworldly that it has no relevance to the problems of the Black man's everyday life cannot become a significant institution until we learn how to breathe into it the power of institutional commitment to serve the total interests of all Black people everywhere. Black Christian Nationalism is a direct response to this need. We have undertaken to restructure the Black church with a new Black theology and a new revolutionary program.

As Black Christian Nationalists we follow a Black Messiah, Jesus. This is very confusing to white Christians and to many Black Christians. They cannot understand why we insist upon talking about the color of Jesus. We have a creed that proclaims the basic tenets of our faith, and we have developed our own theology, rituals, and program reflecting our total involvement in the Liberation Struggle of Black people.

Our development of a Black theology separates us from Christians who do not accept a theology of liberation.

Our theology determines the nature of our commitment. Their theology determines the nature of their commitment. We both say that we are followers of Jesus, but obviously we are not following the same Jesus. We follow a Black Jesus who was a revolutionary leader fighting for the liberation of the Black Nation, Israel. They follow a white Jesus who was used by God to wash mankind in the blood of the Lamb to accomplish individual salvation. When we say "committed to Christ," we do not both mean the same thing.

We live in a world in which people are believing less and less. Beneath all the talk of ecumenism, the new possibility of people all coming together under one great umbrella of faith, is the unspoken fact that the great religious problems have not been solved—though in the context of today's world they appear insignificant. We can all come together now in one great Christian family because few of us really believe anything. It makes little difference whether we are Catholic or Protestant. Catholics are moving as fast as they can toward the Protestant position and Protestants are moving as fast as they can toward the Catholic position. At some point they will pass and not know which side they are on. Great consultations on church unity are going on, and basic issues for which people were once willing to die no longer seem important.

Eventually the struggle for survival will force the white Western world to face realistically its repressed convictions, because what we really believe determines what we do. Ideological confusion (the American dilemma) has created the kind of world in which most people are by necessity egocentric and indifferent to all needs but their own. We are alienated from one another by the irrational nature of our behavior. Our actions do not stem from our beliefs but from the manipulation of mass media by semiautonomous power institutions blindly committed to the preservation of white supremacy. People see no contradiction between what they think they believe and what they do, because they do not understand either what they are doing or what they believe.

At the Shrine of the Black Madonna, Black Christian Nationalists have seriously put together a body of knowledge on which we are willing to stand. Our total program stems naturally and logically from the things we believe. We cannot afford the luxury of a "dilemma" that permits us to say one thing and do another. In a sense, then, we are separating ourselves from the confusions and contradictions of both white Christianity and white civilization. Both religiously and socially we accept the separate existence which has been forced upon us by our white oppressors.

We are separate, and our separation is maintained by the white man's *declaration of Black inferiority*. The mechanism for our continued enslavement and powerlessness lies in the futile dream of integration. An honest recognition of the fact of Black separation and its implications is the necessary first step toward Black sanity and programmatic realism. Black theology must accept this basic fact of existence without any childish equivocation about our "oneness in Christ." Black people and white people have never been "one in Christ" and never will be. The white church has never questioned the white man's *declaration of Black inferiority*. It has accepted the declaration even while with condescending paternalism it has sought to minister to the superficial needs of Black people without disturbing the power base on which white supremacy depends. Any ministry to Black people which is not designed to effect their empowerment is designed to perpetuate their enslavement. No serious program for the empowerment of Black people can be administered by white people (the mission boards of all of the white Christian churches and the national and world councils of churches notwithstanding).

This bothers many white Christians who would like to

pretend that they are color-blind. White Christians are not color-blind and they deliberately fight to keep power in white hands. They are willing to grant token representation if it does not involve a shift of power. They use the word "Christian" and we use the word "Christian," but when you put "Black" in front of one and "white" in front of the other, they become totally different things. The difference does not depend on whether or not you say the words "Black" and "white" aloud. We are separate. White Christians make up a major part of the white establishment that holds us powerless and enslaved. White Christians control the system that corrupts our minds and destroys our bodies. This fact we know and it separates us even when as Black people we maintain ties with a predominantly white denomination. Black separatism does not mean that we are afraid to associate with white people when it suits our interests to associate with them. It merely means that we recognize that our concerns are different and our objectives are different. Whenever we are dealing with serious matters relating to our Liberation Struggle, white people are automatically excluded from our war council because they are the enemy. This is not a matter of fear but of tactics. Within the system in which we live, we are not only separate, we are in conflict. We seek our freedom in a power struggle against them, and in the context of this struggle they are the enemy. We are not ashamed to call white people the enemy, and they ought not to resent it, because it is merely an honest way of defining our relationship.

The fact that Black people and white people are separate is obvious. But to say it makes you a separatist. "Separatists" stand in opposition to "integrationists" who believe that we are "one in Christ," and so "separatists" are bad and "integrationists" are good. Black Christian Nationalists are separatists in that we recognize the reality of the Black man's powerlessness, and we seek to use the fact of our separateness as a power base to end white exploitation.

White racist Christians who systematically oppose the smallest token empowerment of Black people bitterly denounce the Shrine of the Black Madonna for its "evil separatist philosophy." White ministers pastoring white UCC churches located in the lily-white, racist Detroit suburbs of Grosse Pointe and Dearborn have fought to have the Detroit UCC Association censor our "separatist teachings." Detroit's white Bushnell Church invited the Shrine minister and choir to visit on Brotherhood Sunday a few years ago. We were met by white pickets protesting the presence of Blacks in a white church. More recently the pastor of Bushnell Church publicly denounced the denomination for supporting our "evil separatist teachings." In some strange way the recognition of existing separation between white and Black people is interpreted as an evil racist act. It would be easy to assume that white people strike this self-righteous posture deliberately and hypocritically to block the empowerment of Black people. But Black people dreaming of integration are equally outraged at the suggestion that Black people and white people are actually separate, as though the statement brings into being something which does not already exist!

Many Black Christians do not realize that Christianity is the religion of a revolutionary Black Messiah. We have little more in common with them and their white Jesus than we do with suburban white Christians. To us everything they do as Christians is futile and unreal. Walk up and down the streets of any ghetto, visit the churches, and you will find few willing to admit that the Black church in a Black ghetto is separate. As Black people we share the same problems, the same oppression, and the same brutality, but we hesitate to admit that we are separate and outside the basic institutional structures of American life. We are on the outside, and the structure has been designed to keep us outside and powerless.

Black Christian Nationalism accepts the reality of our enforced separation and builds a philosophy of separatism to exploit it for our benefit. To deny reality diverts our energies into nonproductive channels. Black people who refuse to accept the fact of our separateness and the white man's *declaration of Black inferiority* on which it depends actually oppose the things we struggle for in the same way that the white man opposes them, because they feel that integration is being thwarted by our acceptance of separation as a basis for Black empowerment. Their commitment to an impossible "oneness in Christ" blinds them to reality. They do not understand their innocent unsophisticated complicity in the white man's oppression. So we find it difficult to communicate with many Black Christians who do not yet understand the nature of the struggle in which we are engaged.

We see every aspect of worship in a traditional Black church contributing to Black enslavement. Many Black Christians accept baptism as a mystery by which they are changed in their relationship with God so that they can escape from sin and the problems of life and fly away home. They die to the old sinful life, putting aside petty personal sins such as card playing, drinking, and fornicating. The entire experience has no meaning in terms of the Black Liberation Struggle. In a world in which color determines every aspect of their daily lives, conversion and salvation are considered colorless. They are still going to buy from white stores, vote for white candidates, and straighten their hair in order to look like their oppressor. They do not conceive of the Christian church involved in a revolutionary struggle to liberate Black people from the oppression of white people.

Dr. W. Hazaiah Williams, director of the Center for Urban Black Studies in San Francisco, contends that the Black church only appears to be otherworldly because it defines worldly objectives in heavenly terminology easily translated and understood by Black congregations. I wish that this were true, but a Black congregation hears what a Black preacher says, and only when the framework has been clearly defined in terms of individual salvation are they willing to ride the waves of sheer emotion with him, in an ecstatic orgy of spirit in which coherent words only serve to obscure rather than to clarify the message of a personal salvation through Jesus. This kind of worship is unquestionably a product of the Black experience, but totally unrelated to the Black Liberation Struggle. Because it diverts the Black man's attention from present ills and serves as an emotional safety valve, it is not merely irrelevant, it is counterrevolutionary.

For Black Christian Nationalists, baptism symbolizes dying to the old Uncle Tom ways and coming into a new birth of understanding and commitment. It is to say in all honesty, "I die to the old way, I will try not to be an Uncle Tom again. I will try not to be an individualist again." We say that we will "try" because "niggerization" and individualism are hard to stamp out. We can't die to the old individualism all at once and put our arms around Black people everywhere and not worry about self anymore. We can see and understand that individualism has been corrupting our lives, and that we have participated in the destruction of our people. We want to change and we want the church to help us, because we are not going to be strong enough to do it alone. We are going to need the church to walk with us and to chastise us when we go astray. Ours is a different kind of baptism. We rise in the newness of life committed to a revolutionary struggle for the liberation of Black people.

Many old-time Christians must have the sacrament of communion when they are sick. Even though they haven't been to church in years they must have communion. "Stop everything and bring me communion," they scream. They cannot die without stepping back into the charmed circle to be saved. For them the sacrament of Holy Communion is a ticket to glory. God looks down, Jesus smiles, turns to his angels, and says, "He's getting ready to take off. Watch him, he belongs to us now. Take good care of him." In today's world that is a beautiful unrealistic religion for simple people. You can pretty it up and call it High Mass and have bells ringing, but it is the same thing. The church is handing out tickets to glory. Black Christian Nationalists don't believe that. We believe that Holy Communion is a sacrament of commitment for a fellowship of people who have committed themselves to a revolutionary struggle for the liberation of Black people. It is not a ticket to glory, but a ticket to hard work, struggle, sacrifice, and danger. When you take communion with us you know that Jesus is saying, "I've got a liberation army down there that keeps fighting and is getting bigger and bigger all the time."

The act of joining itself is different for us. Traditional Christians feel that their name on the book validates their ticket to glory. They want to keep it there even though they never come to church. They are "members" and they do not want their names removed. They act as if God had computerized salvation. We write a name in magnetic ink on a church roll, and immediately it is inscribed upon the memory bank in God's great computer. If we take it off the church roll down here, it is automatically deleted from God's memory bank. There is nothing magic about a name on a church roll. If you die tonight, you will not be transported to heaven because your name is on the roll. Nor will you be sent to hell because your name has been removed. A few years ago the Abyssinian Baptist Church in New York dropped nearly five thousand names. People were upset from coast to coast. Why were they upset? They wanted to be buried from the church. Again we are dealing with the ticket to glory. For many people the church is little more than a very special kind of funeral parlor with a direct line to glory and jet service every hour on the hour.

Black Christian Nationalists come into the church when they decide to commit their lives to the Black Liberation Struggle as defined by the life and teachings of Jesus, the Black Messiah. They join the Black Nation. For us, then, worship is the coming together of a committed people. We seek direction, power, and inspiration as the Chosen People of God, and we see the power of God revealed daily in the life of the Black Nation. As Black Christian Nationalists we understand power and human nature. We are oppressed by a group whose power depends on its ability to maintain its cohesion. A group with power can oppress individuals, but over a period of time it begins to take its power for granted and to fragment. Its members, individuals who have sacrificed individualism to take power, revert to individualism, and the group disintegrates. On the other hand, the oppressed tend to come together because they have no alternative. Either they come together or they die. So gradually Black people are being driven together, just as white people are being driven apart. The process is irreversible. Even though the white man can see what is happening, he cannot prevent it. His very efforts to block it accelerate the fragmentation through increased alienation and force Black people together in response to increased hostility and repression.

The question of power cannot be considered apart from the question of human nature. People talk about human behavior as if they had never met a human being. They talk glibly of "oneness in Christ" as if this concept is compatible with human nature as we know it. Jesus died on Calvary, but human nature did not change. On Calvary they cast lots for his garments. He was betrayed by individuals who were afraid to come near the cross. Jesus was lynched. How then do we think that on Calvary we became "one in Christ"? Universal love and "oneness in Christ" are totally outside human experience. Can you forget what the white man has done to you any more than the white man can forget what you have permitted him to do? Then how can we all be one? The only world we will ever know will be a world of tension, confrontation, and conflict, in which those who have power fight to keep it, and those who are powerless fight to get it. A world of tension is a natural, normal world. Only fools sit around and pray for peace and tranquillity, because peace and tranquillity are synonymous with death.

In a world of constant tension and conflict, what are we to do? Black Christian Nationalists try to secure enough power to maintain a real tension. The absence of real tension produces power for and oppression by one group, and powerlessness and rage for the other group. Individuals are doomed to powerlessness. Power is an aspect of *group existence*. Black people can only seek escape from oppression, powerlessness, and the white man's *declaration of Black inferiority* through Black unity!

Let us, then, deal with human nature the way it is. We must somehow create a balance in which Black people and white people are not forced to kill each other daily. Black people must secure enough power to protect themselves. A helpless people provoke oppression and brutality by their very powerlessness. There is no known process by which a group with power can be redeemed into giving their power to the powerless. The only kind of world in which overt violence could be reduced to a minimum would be a world in which power was so equitably distributed that no one group dared to move against another.

White people say, "Niggers are trying to take over the world" (which isn't a bad idea, but somewhat impractical at the moment). If we took over the world we couldn't hold it, because we would become overly confident, just as white people have. We would relax, and white people would be driven together by their oppression. So for practical reasons of self-interest we seek to create a world in which there is a reasonable balance, in which we have enough power to protect ourselves, to control our own lives, and to build a Black Nation in which we can establish and maintain our own value system. That is Black Christian Nationalism's separatism, and it offers the only possible hope for racial peace. We understand that the power struggle is inescapable. The other day a beautiful Black sister committed suicide because she had grown tired of the struggle. She had worked for ten years and victory was not yet in sight. She couldn't stand the failure. If she could only have realized that we are engaged in a glorious struggle in which we plan, organize, build, and work together, she would not have killed herself. She sought a speedy solution and there is none. She thought that she was alone and she was not.

Black Christian Nationalism is pragmatic realism. The solution to our problem depends upon our ability to escape from powerlessness, so we evaluate everything in terms of power. Does it get power for us? Does it create a base from which we can move toward power? We struggle against oppression, and therefore we define the enemy in terms of visible realities. The power responsible for our powerlessness, exploitation, and brutalization is the enemy against whom we must do battle. If white people could change (and we do not think that possible unless our analysis of human nature is incorrect) and begin to love Black people, we would note the change. We would then begin to react in terms of a new reality, because reality would have changed. If they change and intensify repression and the present program of genocide, we will react accordingly because reality will have changed. We are not concerned with polite social amenities but with power and oppression. The only way in which we can deal with white people the way they are now is to recognize the fact that they are enemies. As Black Christian Nationalists we are committed to a total struggle for Black liberation by any means necessary. Our position is the will of God as revealed to the Black Nation Israel by Jesus, the Black Messiah.

If the Black church is to deal with specific everyday problems, it will need a total reorganization designed to recognize a new definition of function and providing leadership status to individuals with a wide variety of new skills. The church must be able to mobilize the manpower, the trained leadership, and the financial resources necessary to restructure the total Black community. The effectiveness of the Black church is destroyed by the simple fact that Black people do not accept the process of organization, the necessity of shared power, or the value of trained leadership. We expect to accomplish difficult long-term objectives by proclamation. We are afraid to bring organizations together for the accomplishment of a common purpose for fear of losing control to an outsider. We do not trust trained leadership because we fear that it will too easily identify with the enemy and betray us. One hundred Black churches in Detroit could buy fifty super-trucks and bring into Detroit all the food that Black people could eat. We could build a cannery and can the surplus. But we really do not believe that that is the way the church ought to function. New directions for the Black church depend upon a total re-evaluation of what the church ought to be doing. If going to heaven is our main concern, then certainly we will not worry about problems of everyday community life. But most Black people have mixed feelings about going to heaven. They want to go, but not soon. At least in the meantime we ought to be dealing with problems such as poverty, housing, clothing, and education. The church offers the institutional framework, if we dare to restructure and re-direct it.

We have not yet clearly defined the problem. We talk about new directions for the Black church, but we continue to do the same old things as though rhetoric is the answer to our problem. Black people talk more revolution and do less than any people in the history of the world. We have created a new kind of talk-revolution which really requires no action. We have made a new other-worldly religion out of a do-nothing revolutionary mysticism. There are two groups of irrelevant people in the

Black community. One group is headed for heaven and the other group is talking violent-revolution nonsense. We have reached a position in which almost all Black people have completely short-circuited the energies which ought to be mobilized to free Black people from white oppression and exploitation. We must recognize the reality of the white *declaration of Black inferiority* and its implications. The time has come for us to break our psychological identification with the white man, his world, and his Western values. We must teach Black people to substitute communalism for white individualism. We must do it, not talk about it. This must be the basic task of the Black church.

There can be no new directions for the Black church until we know what we believe. This is why Black Christian Nationalism is so important to Black people. We can state simply what we believe and what we are trying to do. We are engaged in a Liberation Struggle and we believe that nothing is more sacred than the liberation of Black people. And for us, "liberation" is more than just a catchword. How does the Black church engage in a Liberation Struggle? BCN is putting together the necessary ingredients so that any Black church can join us in the Struggle. First, we are putting together a new theology built on the Black Nation Israel's conception of nation and God's Chosen People, and the revolutionary teachings of the Black Messiah, Jesus. This alone transforms the entire thought pattern of a people. Second, we are developing a new program of education and evangelism. The Sunday-morning service of worship must be relegated to a functional position of secondary importance in the church program. The gospel of Black liberation must be taken to the people. People cannot come to church just on Sunday morning and think that they are engaged in the program of the new church. The Sunday service is a festival of liberation for those who are otherwise engaged in the

Struggle—a celebration. The burden of teaching is placed upon the church school, which is reorganized as a school of Black studies and an audio-visual information and training center, with regular weekday classes, lectures, and seminars. Third, a special cadre of community organizers and communication experts are trained to teach and to mobilize the Black community behind specific aspects of the Liberation Struggle. In short, the Black church will no longer wait for people to come in to worship but will educate, train, recruit, mobilize, and confront out in the community. The church involved in Black liberation will go where Black people are and bring them where they ought to be.

Fourth, the Black church must support United Front organizations, youth and community groups that are engaged in the Liberation Struggle but do not believe in the institutional church. A conscious effort must be made to demonstrate that the Black church is the emerging all-inclusive Black Nation. Finally, the Black church must call Black people to action in terms of a common philosophy and a common commitment. We must reject the concept of unity for the sake of unity and constantly make clear the basis on which we act as followers of Jesus, the Black Messiah. We urge Black Christians to join with us in this restructuring of the Black church for the Liberation Struggle and for Nation building.

The new Black church, moving in a new direction, is not going to be essentially a preaching church. It will preach and it will teach, but only because they make meaningful action possible. The new church will be an action-oriented institution to which people can come for education and inspiration, in order that they may go back into the Black community and deal with Black people where they are in terms of everyday problems. This is the kind of new Black church which we are building under the banner of Black Christian Nationalism. Shrines of the Black Madonna are being set up in cities across the country. This is the kind of ministry to which we are calling young Black men and women. We have merged the heaven process with the survival process and we are engaged in building a heaven on earth for all Black people everywhere. We are an African people and we walk in the footsteps of a revolutionary Black Messiah, Jesus.

CHAPTER 4

Salvation:
A Group Experience

Today, as Black Christian Nationalists, we seek to rebuild a Black Nation with power. We are engaged in a revolutionary struggle to restructure a society that has excluded us by declaring us inferior. As an oppressed people we bear the mark of slavery and tend to identify with the enemy who oppresses and exploits us. We respond to our oppression not as a people but as individuals, so our efforts are futile and our oppression continues. We need the group experience that Jesus developed as the process for transforming individuals into a people.

Individuals cannot carry on a revolution. Individuals can become angry and strike out in frustration, but this is not revolution. Only a people who struggle together can carry on a revolution. As Black Christian Nationalists, we seek to free ourselves from individualism in order that we may become a people. The most important single aspect of both our faith and our program is the fact that we have rediscovered the process by which the individual can be led to divest himself of individualism and to merge into the mystic, communal oneness of the Black Nation. For us this is an important theological statement, because we have rediscovered how God works in the world. It was not enough for us to say that God does not save individuals one by one and take them to heaven to be with Him for eternity. It was not enough to say that Paul lost the meaning of the life and death of Jesus, the Black Messiah, by making him a pagan atonement symbol. All of this was apparent in the state of man and in the state of the world. But if God does not save individuals one by one—and obviously He does not—then how does God save? If we are not saved by the healing blood of Jesus on Calvary—and obviously we are not—then how does the Black Messiah save? The impotence of the traditional church lies in its inability to understand the process of salvation. The secret lies in the history of the Black Nation Israel, in the teachings of the Black Messiah, Jesus, and in the experience of the disciples at Pentecost. The experience of God can be real for Black people because the mystery of the group experience is an everyday part of the Black man's life.

It is difficult to lose oneself in the group experience in the Western world because all the restrictions and social controls of white society are designed to strengthen the individual's sense of separation from other individuals. The white man feels that venturing out upon the oceanic feeling of togetherness is at best a weakness, and at worst a sensual primitive sin. Everything in the Western world is designed to preserve the icy walls of individualism. The white man struggles to maintain his egocentric psychological isolation so that at the moment of death he can lay at his Saviour's feet a stunted, malformed personality fetus which he dared not permit to live. Many white Christians either "enjoy" sex hurriedly in the dark while overcome with feelings of shame and guilt or use sex as an instrument of oppression and exploitation. For such people the genuine group experience on which Christianity depends is beyond comprehension.

Black people have always recognized the need to help

one another escape from the restrictions of individualism. This is the basis of Black spirituality. The rhythm of the Black experience is determined by the need for regular festivals which submerge the individual in the group. The drum, the dance, the chant, the incantation merged worship, sex, play, and work into one beautiful, unified, Black group experience. Just as it is difficult for the white man to break out of the restrictions of individualism, so it is difficult for a Black man not to break free.

As Black Christian Nationalists, we believe that God touches our lives most fully in our moments of greatest wretchedness. God cannot break through the walls of egocentricity to help an individual who is not willing to face the utter wretchedness of his total Black condition in a white man's world. In desperation we turn away from the white world and to the Black Nation for strength. For us, individualism is the unpardonable sin because it separates a man from his Black brothers and sisters, who constitute his only channel of communication with God. The individualism of the Western world has effectively blocked the power of God in the daily affairs of white people. African communalism is not a socioeconomic system but a theological statement that emerges from the total Black experience. The culture and history of Black people indicate that God works through the Black Nation. Secular socialism and youth communes in the Western world fail to grasp the fact that they have stumbled upon an ancient African spiritual truth. The group can mediate the power of God, but the individual cannot become a part of the group until in desperation he is willing to face the utter wretchedness of his loneliness.

The impotence of the modern church lies in its inability to move people from individualism to communalism. It has no method by which it can effectively change people. It does not even pose the question so that people can turn sadly aside, as did the rich young ruler in the Gospels. Jesus failed, but he knew what he was trying to do, and he had a method in which he believed. The modern church does not know what it is trying to do. Its program is a hodgepodge of unrelated elements indicating total confusion over basic objectives. Jesus called his Disciples and they left everything and followed him. In some way by talking to them he convinced them that being part of a group was important. We don't really know how long it took him to convince them. It might have taken weeks or even months. I believe that he spent time selecting and calling his Disciples. I do not believe that he just said, "Follow me" and they came. It was too important and too complicated an undertaking. He was putting together the basic cadre for the Black Nation. He had to select them well, and then on them he had to test the group experience as a process for welding individuals into a new Black Nation.

The gospel stories which describe the relationship which Jesus had with his Disciples are incomplete, but they tell enough to make clear the discipline he demanded and the process on which he depended. Jesus was always concerned about the thinking of his Disciples. He would stop in the middle of the road to discuss wrong thinking. Even before they said anything he would confront them with dangerous ideas that were just forming in their minds. He would force them to deal with their individualism without warning and without equivocation. He was harsh and uncompromising. "If something is bothering you, say it out," he would demand, and then force the issue to its logical conclusion. He made no pretense of democracy and group decisions. What was to be decided, Jesus decided. When Peter was wrong he denounced him as Satan. The process that Jesus used to create a group involved open confrontation and criticism. His followers could not expect to hide their shortcomings from the group. Jesus used the only process by which the walls of individualism can be broken down and a group can come into being. Individuals cannot be permitted to pretend to have put aside individualism. They must be constantly confronted with the psychological reality of their condition. This entire process was possible with Jesus' followers because the group accepted his leadership without question. Believing that his love and concern were genuine, they could accept his criticism as necessary for the welfare of the group. They could also depend on his protection if they were attacked by members of the group who were selfishly motivated.

A religious community that demands total commitment and the total submergence of individualism in the Liberation Struggle of a people cannot exist without consciously recognized authority. The authority of Jesus depended on the acceptance of his followers. They accepted his interpretation of the struggle in which they were engaged and recognized the fact that all values were derived from that struggle. When the Disciples began to question the basic decisions of Jesus, the existence of the group was finished. Whenever such questioning occurs, it is intended to destroy the group, however idealistic the explanation may be. Jesus was crucified at Bethany in the house of Simon the leper. A woman came and poured an expensive ointment over his head. "But when the disciples saw it they were indignant." Why was the ointment thus wasted? It might have been sold and the money given to the poor. And they reproached her. And Judas Iscariot, who was one of the twelve, went to the chief priest in order to betray Jesus to him. The Disciples reproached the woman, but in fact they were publicly reproaching Jesus. They spoke aloud indignantly. Jesus confronted them because he knew that the life of the group was finished. The Disciples no longer had confidence in Jesus' interpretation of the struggle. It seemed to be a small matter, but his authority had been questioned. It followed naturally that Judas would go to the chief priest and offer to betray him. It followed naturally that Jesus would point out and confront them at the Last Supper with the fact of betrayal already committed. It followed naturally that they would not watch with him one hour at Gethsemane. The Disciples were no longer a group because they no longer had a leader whose authority was accepted without question. Individualism had triumphed over the group.

The group reassembled after the Crucifixion because it was willing to give to a dead leader the loyalty and authority which it had taken from the living Jesus. The synagogue that Peter put together in Jerusalem symbolized the resurrection of the group through the mystical Pentecostal experience. The church that came into being at Pentecost was doomed to impotence from its inception by the weak leadership of Peter and the Disciples who were unable to maintain either political or ideological control of the organization which took the name of Jesus who was called the Christ. The Apostle Paul eventually made it possible to shift church power from Black Jerusalem to white Rome. Peter and the Disciples in Jerusalem did not understand either the emotional Pentecostal experience or the rational process by which Jesus had put together his short-lived group. They had neither a program for liberation nor a process for building a Black Nation.

The Liberation Struggle was lost in the individualistic salvation of Paul, the dream of the Second Coming, and the fall of Jerusalem with its scattering of the Black Nation in A.D. 70. The church which centered in Rome took power without understanding the mysteries of its African beginnings. The concept of nation and African communalism uniting all aspects of life in one basic group experience was lost. The three processes by which the individual is able to submerge his individualism and become part of a group were lost: (1) the process by which the individual is transformed through a rational group experience in which he must face reality as mirrored in group confrontation, criticism, and love; (2) the process by which the individual is transformed through the emotional experience of a rhythmic African religious ceremony deliberately designed to break down the walls of individualism; and (3) the sudden Pentecostal experience which occurs unexpectedly when the walls of individualism have been eroded quietly through sustained, deeply emotional group experiences over an extended period of time.

The Christian church emerged as a powerful political organization, preaching individual salvation through faith releasing the free gift of God's grace, and the sacrificial atonement of Jesus on Calvary as mediated by the sacraments of the church, but with no realization that the individualistic salvation it preached negated the teachings of Jesus and ran counter to the way God works in the world. It had no process for transforming men whose basic sin was individualism, because it did not understand either the teachings of Jesus or the myth of Man's Fall in the Garden of Eden. It could not offer salvation from the very individualism on which its teachings depended. Black Christian Nationalism redefines salvation, calls men to a rejection of individualism, and offers a process of transformation by which the individual may divest himself of individualism and submerge himself in the community life of the group.

An illustration of the process is suggested by the dope addict who turns to Synanon in desperation. He started out with a habit that cost him twenty-five dollars a day. It climbed to fifty and then to one hundred dollars a day. He can't get the stuff, he's in jail half the time, he's aching most of the time. In despair he goes to Synanon. They have receiving stations across the country but their center of operations is in California. Their basic technique is the one which we have been discussing and with dope addicts it seems to work. They break down the barriers of individualism. When an individual turns to Synanon he is desperate. They make him admit it to himself and to the group as the first step in his transformation. He must sit on a bench, on the outside, until they decide to talk to him. He must demonstrate that he is desperate, that he is seriously seeking help, and that he sincerely believes that he can find it in Synanon before the group will accept him. Usually they make him sit outside for at least half a day before they take him in and question him. They work on the assumption that they are dealing with stupidity, and they do not try to find psychological excuses for his weakness. They tell him that he is a dope addict because he has reacted stupidly to the world in which he lives. If he is willing to try to change, they are willing to try to help him. If he decides to stay, he is taken off drugs "cold turkey." They give him a cot in the hall, in the middle of everything, and they watch him day and night. They sit with him when he thinks that he can't make it, talk to him, massage him when his muscles tighten up. In his suffering he is a part of the group. When his pain is gone the community remains with him. He has no secrets. He cannot leave the house. He sleeps in a dormitory. He works with his brothers and they talk together constantly, just as Jesus did with his Disciples. They talk, argue, and criticize. They tear him to pieces, but they deal with him as a person worthy of concern. Gradually he comes to feel a part of the group and he advances step by step in the respect and acceptance of the group. Eventually he may be permitted to work out in the city, returning to the group each night. It is a process that changes people through group participation.

The old-time church was built around the process of changing people called conversion and was psychologically oriented to the way people actually are. The process of being saved was built around the old mourners' bench. Sinners were convicted of their sins by preaching and came forward to be saved. Coming down front indicated only a desire to be saved. The process of being saved was a group experience participated in by everyone present. The congregation would pray, sing, shout, and scream until the walls of individualism crumbled and the sinner confessed and became a part of the group. At that moment he had a conscious experience of God and he was saved. The old mourners' bench represented a process by which an individual submerged himself in a group and escaped from individualism. The mourners' bench worked, but the old-time church had a very limited conception of salvation. Having motivated men to change they could only think in terms of putting an end to petty personal sins. The process was correct, but the conception of the possibilities and power available was simple and childish.

Black Christian Nationalism would adopt the psychological process represented by the mourners' bench to the Black Liberation Struggle. The individual would confess his sin of individualism, saying, "I have been an Uncle Tom and I repent. I have served the interests of my white oppressor all of my life because in ignorance I identified with him and wanted to be like him, to be accepted by him, and to integrate with him. I loved my oppressor more than I loved myself. I have betrayed my Black brothers and sisters to serve the interests of my oppressor. Because of self-hate I did not recognize my enemy. I have been individualistic in everything that I have done. I have done nothing to hasten the liberation of Black people. I have misunderstood the will of God in failing to realize that nothing is more sacred in his sight than the liberation of Black people. I ask forgiveness of God and of my Black brothers and sisters in the Black Nation. With the help and support of the Black Nation I believe that I can change and bury my individualism in the life of the Black Nation. With Jesus, the Black Messiah, as my guide and helper I will try, so help me God. In all honesty and sincerity I can say that I feel that I have been born again." Only an individual who feels the oppression of his people so deeply that he lives in wretchedness and desperation can make such a public confession of guilt and of faith, and only a fellowship of brothers and sisters who have come together in this kind of desperation can honestly work for the liberation of Black people.

The acceptance of group values is the process of re-birth. When the individual confesses that he has accepted new values, he has been saved and we sing because we are happy. But that is not enough. We are not saved once, but many times. Each time we must confess and re-enter the struggle. We must sustain and support each other, just as Synanon does in dealing with dope addicts, because we are all hooked on individualism and cannot be trusted to stay clean alone. We must evaluate and criticize each other constantly but always within the framework of deep love and concern. The individual who does not realize his inner weaknesses and egocentricity is a constant threat to the security of the group. Breaking down the barriers of individualism changes a person's sense of values. This is basic to the Black Revolution. A new Black church must call men from individualism to partici-pation in a Black Liberation Struggle. The process by which we come to commitment is a part of our African heritage, including the method of Jesus and the Pente-costal group experience.

PART 2

We Define the Enemy

CHAPTER 5

The Enemy

As Black people, we have an enemy who is involved in a systematic program of oppression, brutality, and exploitation. If we are to survive we must know who the enemy is and understand how he functions. Brother Malcolm defined our problem very simply when he stated that we are not discriminated against because we are Baptist, Methodist, or Muslim, but because we are Black. We can be discriminated against because our physical characteristics make us recognizable and enable the white group which holds power to keep us separate, powerless, and stigmatized as "inferior." We are oppressed as members of a group, not as individuals. We suffer as individuals and we are humiliated as individuals, but only because we belong to the Black group.

When they discriminate against you, they are discriminating against all of us. They don't care anything about you. If they humiliate you, it is because you are one of us. You can become angry because a white man discriminates against you, and react personally, but it is not you he is discriminating against—it is us. When he refuses to treat you as you think you ought to be treated, it is not because he doesn't like you personally. He doesn't care a thing about you. It is because you are one of us, and you are getting out of our place. We must understand this. We tend to react always as a Black individual confronting a white individual. You go into a place of business and the white man indicates that he does not want your patronage. Your feelings are hurt and you are angry. You wonder, "Why is he acting this way *to me?* I'm clean. I'm dressed all right. I didn't do anything. Why is he acting this way *to me?*" He doesn't care anything about you. He hasn't even seen you. All he saw was something Black come into his store. When you rise up in righteous individualistic anger you are not speaking to the issue. The fact that you have been discriminated against is just an accident of history, because you happened to be the one Black person out of thirty million who walked through the door. Any one of us would have been discriminated against—because the issue of color, not the fact that you are clean or nasty, smell sweet or stink. You can say, "I've been to school. I've tried to learn, I try to be polite." Those are interesting but totally irrelevant observations. We are discriminated against because we are Black. That simple fact is hard for Black people to accept, because we have spent so much time and energy trying to prepare ourselves for integration. If it was just education that the white man wanted, you could get an education. If it was learning how to keep clean, you could learn how to keep clean. If it was dressing in a certain way, you could learn how to dress. But when it begins to sink in that it is not for any of these reasons that you are discriminated against, but because you are Black, you think, My God, I can't do nothing about that! And that's true, you can't do a thing about it because you were born Black, you are going to live Black, and you will die Black. Any attack upon Black people, then, is an attack upon you and your total position with regard to your relationship with white people.

We are discriminated against because we are part of a group that has been declared inferior. We cannot escape this group identity. Our role in a world of white power is determined by the fact of our Blackness and the powerlessness which it connotes. If we are to understand the functioning of society we must think in terms of groups rather than individuals. A group that holds power defines its members as superior to all who are outside the group. White people act differently to any white person than to any Black person because they accept the white person as a part of their group. We look at a white person and wonder how he can accept an ignorant white bum and discriminate against Black people. He is white and therefore a member of one group. Black people are members of another group, and it doesn't make any difference how he looks or how poor he is or how ignorant he is—he is a member of the group with power and Black people are members of a group without power. This is not to say that white people do not also discriminate against poor, ignorant "white trash"; they do in many ways. But this discrimination is within the framework of white superiority and is different from white discrimination against Black people. This pattern is most obvious in the South, where until very recently no white man could be convicted in any court for killing any Black man, and no Black child could attend a white school under any circumstances. This is still true of many jobs that are open to any white person and are closed to every Black person, and of many suburbs where houses are available to any white person with a down payment and not available to any Black person for any amount of money.

We are dealing with group struggle. You may think that it would be easier if you could struggle on an individual basis. Perhaps, but you can't—so why dream about it? The group with power uses it to accomplish group objectives. White people, as a group, do whatever is necessary to secure things white people want. We talk about power as though it were an abstract thing. Power is not abstract. Power is very real. We can see it. We can watch it work. Power is self-determination. Power is the ability to exploit for the benefit of the group. Power is the ability to oppress those who must be held powerless in order that exploitation may take place. The white man oppresses so that he can exploit. Some white people are psychologically sick and enjoy oppression and brutality, but for most white people oppression is for a purpose. We are oppressed so that we can be kept powerless. We are kept powerless so that we can be exploited. We are exploited so that our enemy can become more wealthy and increase his power. It all makes sense. The power of a dominant group is exercised for the benefit of the total group. Individuals act only as agents for the group. The white policeman on the street is just an agent doing what the good white people want him to do. He is only brutal when they want him to be brutal. The white man in the personnel office who will not promote Black people, hires only a limited quota, and puts Black folks in all the worst jobs, is just functioning as a part of the system established by his group. He is working for good white people who do not have to discriminate personally because he is doing it for them. We must realize that it is a system. Exploitation is a very simple thing. White people grow wealthy at our expense. They take part of all we earn. They charge more for everything we buy. We are a basic source of the white man's wealth and power.

A group exercises power through the institutions that it controls, and the institutions function for the benefit of the group. Our enemy does not consist of individuals who in a very limited sense may be either good or bad in terms of personal relationships. If you work in an office, a factory, or a school and most of the people there are white, you begin to define Black-white relationships in terms of how you get along with this little group of white people. If some of them are pleasant and will go out to have a drink with you, or go to lunch, or sit and talk about "the problem," you begin to think white people are not so bad. But you are talking about personal relationships and they have nothing at all to do with the problem of oppression. Personal conversations with individual white people have nothing to do with the problem of institutional white power and racism.

I flew back from New York a few nights ago and a white man had to talk about the race problem. I make a special effort to fly first class so I won't have to hold inane conversations about race. There are just two seats together in the first-class section, and inasmuch as the section is rarely crowded there is little chance that someone will sit down beside you. It was a late flight and there was just one other man in the first class section. But instead of sitting down in his own seat and going to sleep he came over and sat down by me for a friendly chat. He had just attended one of those management sensitivity-training sessions for ten days and it had blown his mind. He was trying to tell me all about what he had learned and asking questions at the same time. "We can talk, can't we? The problem can be solved just like this, can't it?" I tried to suggest that two people talking for forty-five minutes at thirty-two thousand feet between New York and Detroit might not solve the problem immediately. He really was excited about all that he had learned and could hardly wait to get to the office Monday morning with his new understanding. I asked him how many Black people worked in his department. He said he didn't have any but asked if that would help. I said yes, it would help. He said that he had never thought about it, but wouldn't that be tokenism? I said if he put a Black man to work we would accept it. He promised to start looking Monday. He was a pleasant person, but I seriously doubt that he ever found anyone for his department unless the man above him thought that it was a good idea, because otherwise he might mess up his own position in the organization. The Black-white problem cannot be solved upon the basis of personal relationships.

Many white Christians seem to think that the problem is solved in terms of their confession of faith. I don't care what a white man says he believes, he is still white. He can recite any kind of creed, and when he gets through he is still white. He can attend any church, he can preach in any pulpit, and when he gets through he is still white. The Black man's problem is not a matter of what individual white people think or even try to do. White people are in one group and Black people are in another, and the interests of the two groups are in basic conflict. You may be Black and confused and not realize that you are a part of a group, but if you are Black you are in the Black group. Everyone knows it but you. The whole white group— white people who smile at you and those who spit at you —all work together to keep us powerless, and they have no choice. Some may do it in a very suave and sophisticated fashion, but still they must keep us powerless—because only so long as we are powerless can we be exploited, and only so long as we can be exploited are we valuable to white people. We have no value for white people other than the wealth they can extract from us.

The white enemy group strives to maintain its separation. It is a separatist group and it works twenty-four hours a day, 365 days a year to maintain separation. We can say that's evil, but it is not evil. The white group merely finds it necessary to preserve its way of life. Only out of the confusion of our self-hatred have we tried to attach moral value to the white man's desire to be separate. He strives to be separate and to maintain a separate identity for white people because he believes that white people are superior and that Black people are inferior. He is proud of being separate and white. That is his way of life. By maintaining his separate identity he can also maintain our separate identity as an oppressed group to be exploited.

Everything is done for a purpose and at no point is the white group going to give up its separate white identity and let Black people in, because that would involve giving up the wealth which is now derived from the exploitation of Black people. Groups do not voluntarily give up wealth! In the Bible the rich young ruler turned sadly away when asked to give up his wealth.

In struggling to maintain its physical separation from Black people, the white enemy group determines the basic pattern of American social life and population distribution. This is the pattern of Jim Crow segregation and of real-estate conspiracies to restrict Black people to Black communities and to keep Black children out of white schools. Physical separation is supposed to minimize miscegenation, which always threatens the basic pattern of separation. It is reasonable for a white man to ask another white man who suggests easing the barrier of Black-white separation, "Would you want your sister to marry a nigger?" The question reflects the white man's basic separatist position, his fear of miscegenation, and his *declaration of Black inferiority*. Black people recognize the link between white exploitation and the white *declaration of Black inferiority* and have found in it a rationale for the dream of integration, thinking that to end the separation through integration would automatically end the exploitation and the *declaration of Black inferiority*. This naive solution indicates neither a sense of history nor of social dynamics. The white group declared us inferior, enslaved us, deliberately separated itself from us, and has done everything humanly possible to make the *declaration of Black inferiority* a reality through systematic oppression, brutality, and exploitation. What then is the magic program by which the enemy group that has done everything possible to dehumanize and destroy Black people is to be persuaded to integrate with us? Is it to be transformed by Marxian socialism, psychedelic drugs, or religious evangelism?

There is no process by which the white group can be changed except through conflict with an empowered Black group.

The dream of integration is a mechanism of our enslavement. Dreaming of becoming a nonpeople through integration destroys our efforts to build the power, unity, and program necessary to survive in our continuing struggle against a white enemy group. Our separate group existence is a fact. We have been declared inferior. To complete the separation it is necessary for the dominant white group to declare any individual with any "Black blood" to be inferior. This follows logically, even though many Black people seem unable to understand it. I have heard Black people say, "I have so many different kinds of blood in me that I really don't know what I am. I have some Indian, some Spanish, some Portuguese, and some French. I just don't know what I am." Well, let me tell you, if you don't know—you are Black! It doesn't take any special amount of being Black to make you Black. You can mix all of the hues of the rainbow, and if at the end you add a little Black, you are Black. Black is not only beautiful, Black is powerful! The white group knew what was going to happen so they said it clearly. "I don't care how they look, if they are Black at all they are *all* Black." The white man does everything possible to maintain his separate white group identity. This is a very reasonable position for him to take. because he represents a dominant power group and he wishes to limit those who can share the rewards of power with him. We must give the white man credit for reasonableness. We can understand everything he does in terms of his efforts to maintain his separate white identity. Driven by his own logic he was forced to keep Black people separate by separate schools, separate housing, and separate public accommodations. All social intercourse between Black people and white people must be held to a minimum. If legal segregation is outlawed, *de facto* segregation must still be maintained. Separatism remains the cornerstone of the white man's position.

Black people still try to break through the barriers of separation and to integrate. We try to identify with the dominant group. We have been structured out of every power institution in the white world. We are deliberately kept separate for purposes of exploitation. In the middle of all of it, we try to identify with the white man who has built a whole system to keep us separate and inferior. This desire for identification with the dominant group is a psychological sickness. It makes no difference whether you decide to be a part of the Black group or to identify with the white enemy group. You do not have the power to decide. You are already separate and powerless. The white man who controls the system has decided for you. You have been excluded. Efforts to identify with the white enemy group indicates that psychologically you are in the first stages of insanity. You are dominated by a fantasy which you have mistaken for reality. You cannot justify your "persistent non-adjustive behavior." Roy Wilkins of the NAACP bitterly denounces separatism, although he has been Black and separate all his life. For all his sophisticated semantics he thinks of integration in exactly the same simplistic fashion as Booker T. Washington did: "In all things that are purely social we can be as separate as the fingers, yet one as the hand in *all* things essential to mutual progress." * He cannot understand the nature of the separatism which has been forced upon him and all Black people. He cannot understand the white man's *declaration of Black inferiority*, which excludes him today as completely as it excluded his grandfather on the plantation. He thinks that because he verbally repudiates assimilation and amalgamation the white man will share power and status with him. The white man would rather share his bed than his power and his status.

* *Up From Slavery*, New York, 1901.

The argument that Black people only want equal rights in employment, education, housing, government, public accommodations, and a hundred other specific areas of discrimination is a spurious argument because it dodges the basic issue of power. Black people do not only want equal rights granted by a powerful dominant white group. Black people want the power to control their own destiny, to define their own identity and condition. White people understand this even if it seems beyond the comprehension of Roy Wilkins, the NAACP, the Urban League, and the Southern Christian Leadership Conference. Roy Wilkins screams like a stuck hog when Black people put together a Black power institution they can control, as Black preachers did in Boston. He did everything but crawl from New York to Boston in an effort to block a white grant of one million dollars to a Black ecumenical project. He opposed it because it was "separatist." It was "separatist" in contrast to the NAACP, which is "integrationist." Obviously, then, "integrationist" means controlled by white people and "separatist" means controlled by Black people. Roy Wilkins has no conception of the dynamics of conflict nor of the institutional basis of racial oppression. His position would be too insignificant to mention, but for the fact that some elderly Black people are still confused by it.

There are groups of Black people across the country who try to maintain the fiction that they have nothing to do with the Black problem. The first church I pastored in Lexington, Kentucky, had a little group of light-Black folks in the congregation. They didn't buy in Lexington. They didn't go downtown in Lexington. They drove forty miles to buy in another town where they would be accepted as white people. They never shopped in downtown Lexington because people there knew that they were Black. They tried to pretend that by having their own little social life and driving forty miles every time they wanted to buy a pair of shoes they had somehow escaped the Black problem. Everyone in town, including the white folks knew what they were doing, and they still had all the everyday problems of Black people. It was harmless fantasy they enjoyed. They were very pleasantly and graciously insane. Sometimes we forget the numbers of Black people who are insane, and the varieties of Black insanity. We could do a study on varieties of Black insanity, describing how Black people try to pretend that it is possible to escape the stigma of Blackness in these United States through identification with white people. (But E. Franklin Frazier has already described it and it needs little amplification.)

To be the first negro on the job, the first negro on the street, the first negro in a community, the first negro anywhere gives the individual a sense of being somehow separate and apart from other Black people. And he will announce proudly that he was the *first* negro. Forty years later he will still tell you all about how he was the first negro in some place or other. He was permitted to remain because he was no threat as the first negro, or the only negro. They will let him go wherever it was that he went, which was totally meaningless, and let him stay because he was no threat. He lived a little weird life as the first negro. His life was a pattern of total insanity because he thought that being in this "first" position separated him from other Black people. He did not bother white people at all because he was the first, and he thought that being first on a street or a job meant that he was the first one in paradise and that he had been accepted. Every white person who saw him knew that he was still Black and he could feel, if he wanted to be honest, the restrictions which hemmed him in on every side of his "first" position. The "successful negro" often feels that somehow he has been accepted because he has risen above most Black people economically. He will boast, "I did it the hard way, by ability. I got to my position by hard work, the rest of them niggers can do the same thing. I don't have any responsibility to them. I made it by myself." He is a "successful negro." He has escaped Black people by virtue of his success, and he will tell you in a minute that he cannot really understand the Black problem. He has not escaped a thing. If he lives outside the ghetto, white people still know that he is Black and they treat him as an inferior unless they are using him for some purpose. The white man will not hesitate to confuse you if he can use you. He will let you think that you are white as long as you serve his purpose. But the first time you get out of line and think that you have a purpose of your own, that's when he reminds you, "Black boy, you are just here on sufferance and don't you forget it." There is no such thing as a successful negro who is accepted by white people. The dominant enemy group maintains its identity and its separateness.

In a homogeneous white society there is a totally different pattern of behavior. For many people Marxism offers a rational view of society. Patterns of thought and behavior are but reflections of the economic system determined by control of the means of production. If you can change the economic system you can change the way people think, because you change class interests. Karl Marx worked out that theory in a country where there were no Black people. He spoke of the dictatorship of the proletariat, of the masses. Marx recognized the fact that people must struggle, even in societies in which there is no race issue. You have two groups: a wealthy group in control of the means of production and a poor group. The poor group is only identifiable by its poverty. The wealthy group can be identified by its wealth and its power. The groups are in conflict but neither group is distinguishable by physical characteristics, so to change control of the means of production will actually change the relationship between members of the two groups. Change control of the means of production, and you no longer have a wealthy group and a poor group. Behavior patterns will change. A shift in control of the means of production will take power away from the rich and give it to the poor. The cause of class differences will be removed, so the groups will disappear. There will be no physical differences to distinguish one from the other. Separation and conflict can give way to the perfect society in which all people live together as brothers. Marxian philosophy and economics do not apply to America for the very simple reason that we have a physically distinguishable group which is oppressed. Whatever you do to the economic system (I am not defending capitalism) is not going to change Black-white relations. White people in America would oppress Black people under communism or socialism just as they do under capitalism. As Brother Malcolm said, they don't hate us for any reason other than the fact that we are Black. Unless socialism has some way of changing our color, it cannot change our condition. We must recognize the basic difference between America, which is a racist society, and a homogeneous society in which the basic difference separating people is economics. Marxism offers no solution to the Black man's problem. For Black people in America to try to be Marxists by identifying with a small radical wing of white people is a total waste of energy and in this particular time only serves to confuse Black young people. There is no solution to the Black problem in Marxism. It is valid in other countries but not in America.

The Black politician who says on the night he is elected that he wants to represent all the people has no sense of reality. There is no way he can represent all the people because all the people do not want to be represented by him. He is saying that he would like to be able to represent all the people. He is not a part of the white group, he is a part of the Black group. There is no way he can represent white people. He can be used by white people. (White people sometimes put a Black man in an office because they can use him better than they could a white person in the same office.) Black teachers and school administrators do not think of themselves as having infiltrated an oppressive white structure in order to use it for the benefit of Black people (insofar as an oppressive white institution can be used for the benefit of Black people). Black teachers and administrators should realize that they have infiltrated an enemy institution and cannot always follow the enemy's rules and serve the best interests of Black children.

Black preachers are also in an enemy institution. Even if everyone they see on Sunday morning is Black, the institution itself is an enemy institution which we have not yet liberated. A Black preacher who does not realize that he is utilizing an enemy institution in the interest of Black people who are fighting against oppression does not have the realism necessary to function in the pulpit of a Black church. Black preachers are not using the Black church as a revolutionary institution in opposition to the white church which serves the enemy white group. The Black church is an extension of the white enemy institution. There is no difference in the roles they play. In Milwaukee I attended a demonstration sponsored by the National Welfare Rights Organization seeking clothing for ADC (Aid to Dependent Children) mothers. Father James G. Groppi was there. He had been arrested seven or eight times and had at least a dozen charges still pending against him. He could not participate because the police were going to arrest the marchers, but he was in the church. A Black brother who was working with the movement asked if there wasn't something I could do to involve local Black preachers in the struggle. I answered honestly that there was nothing I could do. He said that not one Black preacher would support anything that the Black community tried to do. Even if he exaggerated, obviously most Black preachers in every city do not understand that the Black church is a revolutionary institution. In almost every city young Black people cry out that they cannot find a

Black church willing to support the Black Liberation Struggle.

Black lawyers and Black judges are much the same. They are part of an institution designed to oppress Black people but they do not understand it. They do not realize that they are attempting to serve the needs of Black people within an enemy institution. Detroit's Judge George William Crockett, Jr., demonstrated on at least one occasion an awareness of the unique role of a Black judge in American society. In the New Bethel Baptist Church-RNA (Republic of New Africa) incident, he released hundreds of innocent Black men and women being held on suspicion without formal charge. In a sense Judge Crockett liberated the court to serve Black people.

Social workers must do the same thing. A social worker thinks that what she learned in college can help empower Black people. She does not realize that college was not designed to teach her how to liberate Black people, but how to corrupt Black people, to destroy Black people, and to enslave Black people. A social worker must use the white man's own institutions to fight him. Too many Black people are hung up on little individualistic fantasies. We keep trying to play by the enemy's rules to get ahead, without realizing that the institution itself is designed to destroy us and all other Black people.

Insofar as possible, enemy institutions must be used in the interests of Black people. We are functioning within white institutions which were set up to perpetuate white supremacy. We live in a very critical time, and it is important that we carefully define our enemy. Our oppression is a very complicated thing. We must understand it if we are to struggle intelligently for our liberation. An oppressed people must analyze every situation carefully and use it for the benefit of Black people. We are struggling against an enemy who has the power to destroy us. We are fighting for our very survival.

CHAPTER 6

The Yakub Myth

Today if you advance the thesis that all people are the same, Black people will reject it, saying that we could not do the bestial things that white people do. We possess human qualities commonly called soul which white people cannot even understand. We are creative because we can feel deeply and we can respond to the feelings of others. White people cannot grasp the meaning of love, music, or religion because they exist on a lower, bestial level of violence, materialism, and individualism.

As Black people we are reacting emotionally to the totality of the white man's oppression, brutality, and exploitation, but we are able to marshal an impressive array of facts to support our argument. I have heard Black elementary-school children use the same arguments echoed in high-school Black-student-association discussions, on college campuses, on street corners, at block-club meetings, and in church discussion groups. As Black people seriously begin to put together a new Black identity, this almost universal denial of the white man's humanity is becoming a cornerstone. Many Black people who still consider themselves integrationists will earnestly deny the white man's humanity without realizing that they have taken the first giant step toward separatism. No individual can long seek integration with a "beast," no matter what his color nor the extent of his power. White people have found it impossible to accept integration with Black people because we have been declared inferior. Black people will find it equally difficult to accept integration with a white beast.

We have spent a lot of time watching the beast, observing how he acts, and analyzing him in a way we never did before. We used to take it for granted that whatever a white person did was right and good. All of his worst characteristics we tried to copy. But on the basis of observation we now resent being told that there is no basic difference between white people and Black people. The white man's culture is vicious and brutal. Everywhere in the world he is essentially the same. His history is a story of human oppression and exploitation. From the moment he first climbed down out of the tree he has used power to enslave other peoples. He has tortured, exploited, and used people for his selfish benefit. He corrupts and cheapens everything he touches. Everything the white man has done in relationship both to his environment and to other people has been vicious and brutal. We can say that he is capable only of violence and oppression because we have never seen him act in any other way. The white man is the only animal on the face of the earth who deliberately fouls the very air he must breathe, the water he must drink, and the earth upon which he must live. The air we breathe grows more foul day by day, and the white man continues his nasty contamination. He does it simply because it is cheaper to contaminate. He makes a bigger profit. He fouls the water he must drink because it is cheaper to throw trash and contamination into the water. He makes a bigger profit. He must be a beast. Everything he does is designed to destroy mankind and the earth. Atomic fallout has contaminated most of the earth from which his food must come. Parts of the earth will be contaminated for hundreds if not thousands of years. Even though he knows this to be true, he continues.

There is ample justification for saying that the white man is a beast. How else can we explain his treatment of the American Indian, who met him at the shore and taught him how to live in this strange land and kept him alive? How else can we explain his treatment of the Africans, whom he enslaved? He went across the world to rape a continent and enslave a people. Every civilization he has touched he has destroyed. To live in Latin America is to be exploited by the white man. There are double standards for everything that exists because the white man controls everything. Recently some of the white man's inhumanity was exposed following Rockefeller's trip to South America. The white man has only one pattern of behavior in his relationships with other people. For every nonwhite people the "final solution" is genocide. How else can we explain genocide in Vietnam with napalm and saturation bombing? This war has no parallel in human history. Certainly the white man is bestial in the things he does. It is no wonder that Black people recoil if you say that there is no basic difference in the nature of a Black man and a white man.

The things that the white man has done and is doing will continue as long as the white man has power, but they do not prove conclusively that he is subhuman or nonhuman. They do not prove conclusively that he is either a devil or a beast, or therefore inherently inferior and different in nature. They prove that he is bestial in everything he does. If we conclude that the white man and the Black man are different in nature, then we must demonstrate that the Black man is essentially kindly, good, loving, considerate, nonviolent, and nonbestial by nature. There are many who are willing to go that far and are prepared to assert that the white man is nonhuman and the Black man is human. Many Black people are ready to take the argument to its logical conclusion and to contend that Black people could never act as the white beast has acted, because the Black man is the essence of humanity. And here again evidence can be assembled. There is a certain reasonableness about the position Black people are in the process of developing. We can say that in Africa Black people developed a happy communal pattern of living in which Black people loved and took care of one other. In some parts of Africa at certain times this kind of Black culture existed. The hunter's kill was shared with the village. Individualism did not exist. The children belonged to the village, and everyone was concerned about them. The people moved their villages systematically. They did not destroy and deplete the land on which they lived or the resources or the air on which they depended for life. We can say that Black people did not oppress, exploit, or brutalize one another. Their human relationships were kind and tempered with love and compassion. We are looking back to the days before the white man contaminated us with his materialistic individualism. The Black man had a culture which was human as opposed to the bestial white culture. This is a position. We must conclude, then, that basic cultural differences between white people and Black people stem from basic differences in their natures. Black people are human and white people are nonhuman or beasts. I am not manufacturing a hypothetical position. You can go anywhere in America today and talk to Black people and you will find this position increasingly dominant.

This is the new Black cultural mythology and you can find it everywhere. Young Black high-school students writing poetry and plays are writing out of this kind of conviction. It is given wide credence and acceptability by creative Black artists. As attractive as it is for Black people who are sick and tired of everything white, it is essentially bad psychology. It is bad sociology; it's not true in terms of basic sociological principles, studies, or findings. It is bad anthropology, and it is bad history. But that does not dismiss it. It is still an important reality in the thinking of Black people. In the teachings of the Honorable Elijah Muhammad it finds direct expression. Black people up and down the street believe it without knowing where it originated. They have picked up pieces of information here and there which lead them to believe that white people are beasts. But only in the teachings of Elijah Muhammad, who has exerted a phenomenal influence upon the thinking of Black people during the past fifty years, does this position find full expression in the Yakub myth.

This myth is basic to the teachings of the nation of Islam. The myth of Yakub tells the story of the mad Black scientist who created the white beast, who was permitted by Allah to reign for six thousand years. His time ran out in 1914. This story is not different in kind from the Christian story of Creation; they are both myths. We do not throw one out because it is a myth and keep the other because it is true. They are both myths, and both are capable of being true. To say that something is a myth does not say it cannot contain the elements of truth. Those who believe in the myth of Yakub are waiting for the end of the white man's rule. The six thousand years are over, and the seventy years of grace are nearing their end. Many Black people do not have any religious basis for their belief. Without a religious myth, they affirm that the white man is a beast. Some reject all religions but give a passing nod to the Honorable Elijah Muhammad and the myth of Yakub. The Yakub myth actually underlies much Black poetry that is being written today. Black drama also reflects this position, as does Black creative dance. The researching of the African religions Youba and Voodoo in the twentieth century ghetto is another expression of the cultural influence of the Yakub myth.

The Honorable Elijah Muhammad has exerted a most profound cultural influence upon Black people in the second half of the twentieth century. Two outstanding Black writers in this generation, Maulana Ron Karenga in Los Angeles and Imamu Amiri Baraka (LeRoi Jones) in Newark, have been able to build creatively upon the Yakub myth. Don Lee, the young Black poet, can't decide whether he accepts the Yakub myth or rejects it, but certainly it has influenced his writing as it has the poetry of Sonia Sanchez and Nikki Giovanni. This new Black cultural mythology is important to Black people at this time in history when we are trying to break our identification with white people. We are not conscious of it every day as we go about our daily activities, but we are all engaged in an important task; we are trying to break our identification with white people. It is not easy. We break it bit by bit because we are living in a white man's world. Everything is prepared to brainwash us. The white man taught us from the time we could breathe; he has indoctrinated us and programmed us. Trying to break free of our identification is a difficult and complicated thing. Black cultural mythology is important because it is a part of our trying. We cannot do anything until we break free of our identification with white people. Any Black man who accepts his identification and does not fight against it is hopelessly lost. A Black man who says, "I'm struggling to break my identification, and I believe that the white man is a beast," has made a big step. At least he has found a basis for breaking free.

Our whole Black cultural mythology stems from a broken love affair. We don't like to admit it, but that is what it is. If we hadn't loved the white man so much, we wouldn't need the Yakub myth. We would not have been forced to declare him a nonhuman beast. When you love someone madly and you live and breathe for him, and you are convinced that you could not exist without him, and suddenly something happens to your affair, you cannot accept it as an affair that has come to an end. You must somehow destroy the image which still remains in

your mind. No matter what happened, the image of perfection remains in your mind. Somehow you must oblit-
erate it. Facts are of little help. If you are a man you must
convince yourself that certain things are true, whether or
not they really are. Before you can be free you must
destroy the image of the one you loved. Somehow you
must make your love object unfit for love. You must move
beyond the thing that destroyed your love affair, the
thing you saw, or the thing someone told you, the thing
you know is true—you must move beyond that. If you
have loved a woman, you must convince yourself that
she wasn't any good to begin with. "There never was any
good in her! I don't know why I didn't see it all the time.
She wasn't a woman." You must declare her a devil and
destroy her. Then you can live. Then you have a reason
to put her aside and to hate her.

When we are willing to admit that our Black cultural
mythology represents a broken love affair, we shall be able
to understand the psychological problem that confronts us.
Our identification with the white man lasted from the
slave ship right through Dr. King's mass demonstrations
and was given its final anguished utterance in his "I Have
a Dream" speech. The love affair would not end because
the white man revealed himself and we suddenly realized
that he hated us. How could we have lived on the plantation with him and watched him rape our wives and daughters and not have known that he was a beast? How could
we have been exploited by him every day and not have
known that he was a beast? We did know—but beast
and all, we still wanted to be like him and to be accepted
by him. Now we are ashamed of the memory of our
broken love affair. We are going to break away. We are
no longer going to seek acceptance by him. We are going
to be ourselves. We are not going to seek acceptance by
him. We are going to be ourselves. We are going to love
ourselves and look at the world through our own eyes.
Our historic identification with the white man was more

than a matter of expediency, of trying to accommodate to power, or we would not be experiencing these emotional overtones in our efforts to break away. It was an affair of the heart of which we are now ashamed.

In reality we are dealing with a man with a human nature just like our own, but with power. We ought to realize that this is what power does to human nature. This is reality. The white man is not a beast. He's not a devil. He's just a human being with power. A human being will do anything to get power and to keep power. There are no limitations to what a man will do for power. He'll kill his own mother and find good reasons to explain why it had to be done. We must look honestly at the white man and realize that he demonstrates the effects of power upon any individual who is not protected against it by adequate group controls. As Black men get little bits of power they become a little bestial. Even as Black men scramble after individual power they become bestial. This "beast" idea is only a question of power. Those of us who cannot face reality have to have a Yakub myth. It serves to bridge and justify our transition from love to independence. It makes acceptable our struggle from powerlessness to power. It is the bridge from where we were to where we are going. Some Black people are already across and no longer need a bridge. We must all get to the place where we no longer need it, because it is a weakness. At the moment it is necessary, but eventually Black people must face reality. We thank God that the Yakub myth exists for those who need it as they break their identification with white people.

Black Christian Nationalists do not need the Yakub myth. The white man for us is neither a devil nor a beast but a power-crazy individualist who can be dealt with and defeated in struggle. We seek to shift the creative dynamics of the Black Liberation Struggle from cultural mythology to pragmatic realism. The white man is not a beast. The Yakub myth is a lie, but it contains the elements of truth. Certainly it is not true in a scientific sense and actually it is not true in a mythological sense, because it does not serve to reveal the truth but to obscure it. But it is an important stepping-stone to truth. Black people and white people are not different in nature, and cultural differences can be explained in terms of differences in experience and environment. The white man—even though he acts as a beast, and certainly he does—is not subhuman or nonhuman, and the Black man, though he accepts all of the indignities heaped upon him by the white man, is not an angel. The Black man is not a uniquely perfect human being. The Black man and the white man must be understood in terms of a universal will to power. All men seek power to dominate, to rule, to govern, and to control. As Black Christian Nationalists we accept this Biblical definition of human nature. We interpret human behavior in terms of the will to power, because the cultural manifestations of power are no more significant than the cultural manifestations of powerlessness. We all want power. We act in one way if we have power and we act in another way if we are powerless. White people have been ruthless in their use of power. Under the same circumstances the Black man *will* act in the same way. Someday the circumstances will be the same unless we create a community in which Black people can establish a different value system.

The Black Nation is important because we do not want to become the "beast" that the white man has become. We want to secure power within a communal framework that will enable us to preserve our humanity. As Black Christian Nationalists we know how this is to be accomplished. Each individual must submerge himself in the Black Nation. All values must derive from the Black Liberation Struggle and the welfare of Black people. All of the systems necessary for a people to live together must be developed from a communal philosophy of life. This does not mean that we disdain power. Acceptable power for us is the power of the Black community. The white man's power is the power of the individual, and this is the basis of his bestiality. They come together temporarily in mergers of convenience, but essentially each white man seeks only individual power, and he will destroy not only Black people but anyone who blocks his quest for power. Black Christian Nationalism seeks to lead Black people away from the pitfalls of an individualistic concept of power. Our concept of power includes all Black people everywhere. No concept of power short of a worldwide Pan-Africanism can protect Black people from the dehumanizing effects of white individualism. We must realize that individual power can stand between us and the accomplishment of power for Black people. We are not different from the white man by nature, but we have been able to watch the way he lives, the way he acts, and the mistakes he has made. We have begun to put together a structure that can protect us against the white man's bestiality if we are willing to put aside individualism and become a people.

The ability to face reality is important. We must understand that by nature all men are the same. We are capable of violence, brutality, and bestiality. Only in the light of this realization can we come together with a sense of urgency and say that, in the name of God, we must protect ourselves from the forces that have destroyed the white man, his world, and his civilization. If we assume that we are different and that automatically we are protected because we were created different, then we are not going to do the things that are essential for our protection. We have two beasts to fight: the beast within and the beast without. To neglect one is as dangerous as to neglect the other, and to misunderstand one is as dangerous as to misunderstand the other. We reject the Yakub myth because it obscures an understanding of our own inner nature, and makes it difficult to comprehend the motivation and strategy of our enemy.

CHAPTER 7

The Philosophy of
Brother Malcolm*

There is a tendency for Black people who loved Malcolm to try to freeze his ideas at the moment which seems best to them. They say, "This was Malcolm." Or they take a favorite idea out of the context of his total philosophy, as many young people do with the concept of revolution, saying, "Revolution is for land, and there must be bloodshed." At Ohio State University, I spent an entire afternoon with a group of students who were convinced that revolution must involve the struggle for land over which a flag could fly. Beyond this they had no comprehension of the nature of struggle and conflict. Brother Malcolm understood the Black Liberation Struggle because he was chained to no fixed ideological position. He was able to adjust his analysis to fit new realities. He was not afraid to accept the implications of truth as they were revealed to him by the Struggle itself.

Of all our Black national leaders, Brother Malcolm was the only one who could understand the pragmatic realism

* Author's Note: "In this chapter, I quote and paraphrase Brother Malcolm from memory, quoting conversations I had with him, and speeches I heard him deliver."

of Black Christian Nationalism as it was developed at the Shrine of the Black Madonna in Detroit. Other leaders such as Dr. Martin Luther King came to Detroit, but they only made speeches, the same speeches they had delivered a hundred times to Black people in a hundred different cities. I knew Dr. King, spoke on the platform with him, attended small informal receptions in his honor, and I am sure that he scarcely knew what city he was in, who the people groveling around him were, and could not have cared less. He made no effort to relate what he had to say to the Black brothers and sisters who came out to hear him. I heard him deliver his "I Have a Dream" speech in three distinctly different situations. It was slightly different each time only because he was in the process of smoothing out the rough spots. He responded to his audience as an actor in a play responds. He could not change the lines but he needed the emotional stimulation of their approval. This was most obvious when he spoke at the Detroit Freedom March in 1963.

More than two hundred thousand Black people "walked to freedom with Dr. Martin Luther King." This was the first Freedom March and was considerably larger than the Washington March, which was national in scope. The rally following the march was held at Cobo Hall. The Arena and every convention auditorium was jammed to capacity, and an overflow of more than one hundred and fifty thousand Black people filled the streets and the area adjacent to the Convention Center. It was undoubtedly the largest crowd that Dr. King had ever seen. I spoke just before him on the program. The mayor, Walter Reuther, and a representative of Governor Romney had spoken, even though the committee at my insistence had unanimously voted to keep all white people off the platform and to make the meeting a protest meeting. Black people did not "walk to freedom with Dr. Martin Luther King" to listen to white liberals give the same old condescending words of encouragement. The crowd began to boo and scream for white folks to sit down and shut up. The meeting was out of hand. I got up to speak in the midst of bedlam because the committee could think of no other way to secure enough order to have an offering and let Dr. King speak. I articulated the feelings of protest that had brought Black people together, and the response threatened to bring down the building. I spoke not longer than fifteen minutes. Then I called upon Black people to boycott a national food-store chain which at that time refused to hire Black people and asked Black people to contribute financially to continue the fight in Birmingham where Black children had been bombed while attending Sunday school. I have never heard such a soul-stirring response. I have never seen so many five- and ten-dollar bills waving in the air. It was a beautiful moment. But Dr. King made no change in his presentation. It was as though he had not been present. When he found a box to stand on so he could reach the microphone, he delivered his "Dream." It was a moving speech, but it did not speak to the Black man's condition in Detroit. For once in his life Dr. King had been upstaged by reality. The response to my protest was far greater than the response to his dream. I don't think he either noticed or cared.

Dr. King's entire approach was a mystical kind of idealism which had no roots in objective reality. The same is true of other Black leaders who wandered into Detroit from time to time. Adam Clayton Powell had no real comprehension of reality. In his finest hour he had no sense of program. He did not understand how society functioned. This is true of most Black leaders if we look at them one by one, with the possible exceptions of Imamu Amiri Baraka (LeRoi Jones), Roy Innis, Floyd McKissick, and Stokely Carmichael, for all of whom I have deep respect and affection.

If Brother Malcolm had lived we would have seen a gradual development of his ideas, because he was able to understand the dynamics of society. This put him in a different category from most Black people who step onto the stage and are hailed as leaders at a particular moment in time. I shared the platform with Brother Malcolm for the first time at the Grass Roots Conference in Detroit.* I had seen him briefly on television, but this was the first time I had had an opportunity to talk with him, to listen to him, and to understand the kind of person he was. You really can't tell much about a Black man's position by the fragments the white man puts on television. At the Grass Roots Conference I heard his best speech, and it was an amazing experience. I spoke just before Brother Malcolm and I was surprised to see that we spoke from the same basic position and projected the same basic conclusions, even though we had not talked together before and had developed our positions independently. It was startling to me because so few Black people could understand anything that I was saying at the time. He was able to grasp my position and to understand that it was essentially the same as his own. His "Message to the Grass Roots," which was recorded, referred again and again to the things that I had projected before he spoke.

Brother Malcolm was a totally different kind of person from Dr. King. For him speeches were not cut-and-dried

* Editor's Note: "In late 1963, the Detroit Council for Human Rights announced a Northern Negro Leadership Conference to be held in Detroit on November 9 and 10. When the council's Chairman, Rev. C. L. Franklin, sought to exclude black nationalists and Freedom Now Party advocates from the conference, Rev. Albert B. Cleage, Jr., resigned from the council and, in collaboration with the Group On Advanced Leadership (GOAL), arranged for a Northern Negro Grass Roots Leadership Conference. This was held in Detroit at the same time as the more conservative gathering, which was addressed by Congressman Adam Clayton Powell among others. The two-day Grass Roots conference was climaxed by a large public rally at the King Solomon Baptist Church, with Rev. Cleage, journalist William Worthy and Malcolm X as the chief speakers." (Quoted from *Malcolm X Speaks*, edited by George Brietnam, Grove Press, New York, Page 3, Introduction to Message to the Grass Roots.)

performances repeated endlessly for faceless audiences who did not really matter. Although he used much of the same material many times, each speech was different because it was directed to a particular audience with particular problems. Brother Malcolm talked to an audience as though each individual was important and must somehow be made to understand the urgency of the problem. Dr. King spoke to inspire. Brother Malcolm spoke to teach. Dr. King sought no response beyond appreciation. Brother Malcolm sought total commitment to the Black Liberation Struggle. Dr. King was preoccupied by a speech, thinking about what he was going to say in a way that was totally unrelated to the actual situation. Brother Malcolm was never really sure of what he was going to say until he stood up, looked at his audience, and started to speak. I have been backstage with him talking just before a meeting started. He would have his pad and paper containing his rough outline in his hand. Suddenly he would stop and tear off the old outline and make a completely new one. Once when we were at the King Solomon Baptist Church, after he had broken with the Honorable Elijah Muhammad, he just added a few lines to his outline and explained, "I am going to tell the brothers and sisters who live in Detroit to join the Shrine of the Black Madonna." (And he did, as Sister Betty did years later when she spoke for our Women's Day Service.)

In an essay entitled "Myths about Malcolm X," which is included in a collection edited by John Henrik Clarke, *Malcolm X, The Man and His Times,* I state that I do not feel that I need to read critical evaluations to understand what Brother Malcolm was saying and what he meant. It is my considered opinion that most of the books and pamphlets being published about Brother Malcolm are distortions of his ideas and of his philosophy. I understood his position because it was my position, arrived at independently before I ever saw or heard him. I understood the changes in his position because I understood the logic which forced those same changes in my own thinking. Brother Malcolm was concerned about social dynamics. He was trying to understand how society functions and why. Why do people do what they do? Why are Black people oppressed, discriminated against, and brutalized? Why does the white man act as he does in his relationship with Black people? Why do Black people act as they do in their relationship with white people? He began with the moral, ethical, and religious position of a Muslim minister. This was the basis on which he stood. I began from the same kind of basic position—the moral, ethical, and religious position of a Christian minister. We both had to come a long way to be able to look at the world realistically. I understood the road he had to travel to reach truth because we took the same journey, though from different starting points. Perhaps he had the easier task, because I was a sociologist and a psychologist before I became a religionist, so I had more to unlearn! I went into the church because I could not see anything that you could do for Black people with white-oriented sociology and psychology, but it still had to be unlearned. Brother Malcolm had to build all by himself, step by step, beginning with the teachings of the Honorable Elijah Muhammad. At the time he was murdered he was just beginning to find new answers to old questions. It was unfortunate that he was killed when he was, in terms of the development of his philosophy. But in another sense he knew when to die because dead he has more followers than he could ever have had alive.

At the Shrine of the Black Madonna, with the philosophy which we call Black Christian Nationalism, we have moved from Brother Malcolm's final position as he would have moved if he had lived. This development is tremendously important because in no other place can Black people see the evolution of his basic philosophy and program. If he had lived, his position today would be the same as ours. This is not to say that he would have been

Christian, because he was a Muslim; but his analysis of the
nature of the Black Liberation Struggle in terms of struggle, power, conflict, and the institutional basis of white
racism would have been the same as ours. I understood
what he said, where he was going, and where he would
have ended. I understood what he said while he lived, even
during the confusing last year before his assassination, and
if he were still alive and could stand up and speak when
I have finished, as he did in his "Message to the Grass
Roots," he would echo the same message now as he did
then. This is important to us as Black Christian Nationalists
and to Black people everywhere. We shall outline briefly:
(1) the basic message of Brother Malcolm; (2) develop-
mental changes in his philosophy; and (3) a summary of
what Brother Malcolm would be teaching if he were alive
today.

Brother Malcolm grew enormously in his ability to
analyze the social dynamics of the Black Struggle. From
the very beginning he understood that Black people are
engaged in a power struggle against white people. Very
few Black leaders understood this. They thought that
Black people were only trying to get into something that
white people had. There is a basic difference. If you are
struggling against someone, you are on a level of equality;
but if you are just trying to be accepted by them, you
admit the superiority of the people by whom you are
trying to be accepted. You are crawling, you are begging,
you are pleading. You are trying to make them feel sorry
for you so that they will accept you. Because you have
no pride and no understanding of your worth and value,
you are trying just to beg your way in, plead your way
in, or talk your way in. Most Black leaders have no comprehension of a struggle. They view the Black man's
problem in static terms. They are constantly seeking specific solutions to specific problems. We have a housing
problem. We have an educational problem. We have an
employment problem. We have all kinds of little problems

to be worked on. The NAACP, the Urban League, and SCLC are all working on these little problems. They have no sense of struggle, of a people coming together as a people and struggling against a common enemy. So all cries for Black unity have been utterly and completely meaningless because there was no basis on which Black unity could be brought into being. How could Black people unite when they were not engaged in a common struggle, and each individual was trying to get ahead of his Black brothers and sisters so that he could sneak into the white thing all by himself? Black sociologists didn't understand it. Dr. E. Franklin Frazier had little comprehension of struggle. In *Black Bourgeoisie*, he described the way Black people behave as though describing a funny act seen at the circus. No Black university dared provide as comprehensive a definition of the Black Struggle as did Brother Malcolm. In every speech he was ahead of Black sociologists, psychologists, and historians in being able to interpret the Black Struggle, because he knew that we have a common enemy, the white man, who oppresses, brutalizes, and exploits us. A Black man is totally incapable of comprehending reality until he can accept this simple basic fact with all of its implications. Brother Malcolm said, "We are oppressed because we are Black and upon the basis of our common Blackness we must come together in a unity which is born out of our common struggle against a common white enemy."

Brother Malcolm built upon the Honorable Elijah Muhammad's religious mythology, which has a beautiful, simple power. It can be taken into a penitentiary and presented to Black men who dropped out of grammar school. They can understand it and accept it. "The white man is our enemy. God has permitted him to have power for six thousand years, but now his days are numbered. The reign of the beast will soon be ended and God will re-establish his original Black Nation in power." This simple picturesque mythology offered little room for the kind of comprehensive analysis of struggle, conflict, and power of which Malcolm himself was capable. Near the end of his life he said, "I feel like a man who has been asleep somewhere and under someone else's control. I feel that I am thinking and seeing now and for myself. Before it was for and by the guidance of Elijah Muhammad. Now I think with my own mind." This was important because it indicated that Malcolm had consciously begun to reject some of the basic concepts of Mr. Muhammad. He had at least begun to reject the Yakub myth, with its focus on the evil nature of the individual white "beast" as a rational explanation of the oppression of Black people.

In his early speeches Malcolm did not yet understand the basic limitations of the Yakub myth, which avers that the white man is a beast and this is sufficient explanation of his actions (when he is wet he even smells like a wet dog). After his break with Mr. Muhammad, Malcolm gradually came to see that the individual white man is not important unless it is clearly understood that he is manipulated and controlled by a power system that serves his interests and of which he is a part. To declare him a beast only serves to obscure the social dynamics of the white-racist American situation. We are not oppressed by white beasts. We are not oppressed by white individuals. We are oppressed by a white institutionalized power establishment from which we are excluded. We are dealing with white power exercised by a white group that is engaged systematically in the oppression and exploitation of Black people. Malcolm came to realize that it was an oversimplification merely to call the white man a beast, and he was moving toward an understanding of institutionalized power as outlined by Reinhold Niebuhr in *Moral Man and Immoral Society*. Niebuhr recognized the fact that a man may try to function morally as an individual but cannot escape the fact that he is part of an immoral society which dominates and controls him. Even when he would do right he does wrong!

Malcolm was trying to develop the implications of this position for the Black Liberation Struggle during his last hectic year. He had moved beyond the Yakub myth, and the complexity of his emerging new analysis was generally misunderstood and interpreted as a repudiation of his basic premise that the white man was the Black man's enemy. To admit that white people are human beings and that individual white people do not constitute an oppressive white power system in and of themselves is not to deny that white people functioning together as a white power establishment are the Black man's enemy. It is perhaps unfortunate that Brother Malcolm did not have an opportunity to edit the final portion of his autobiography and to correct an unintentional overemphasis on the change which took place in his thinking in Mecca, without any real interpretation of its meaning. Malcolm is interpreted as believing that an individual white man (particularly outside the United States) might somehow escape involvement in the white institutional oppression of Black people. I am certain that Alex Haley succumbed to the drama inherent in presenting two contrasting positions rather than showing the normal development of Malcolm's thought after he had discarded the simplistic Yakub myth. No white individual can escape involvement in white racist society, not in Mecca or anywhere else. But the white individual is not the entity with which we must deal.

American white racism permeates the earth. Moral white individuals cannot long resist the power of the white racist institutions! We have wasted far too much time trying to convince individual white people to do things which they cannot do. We cannot talk a mayor or a city council into acting in opposition to the white-supremacy interests of their constituency. We cannot persuade the heads of industry to empower the very Black people they must exploit in order to maintain their position. We cannot deal with white people as individuals, but only through the power establishment they have created. Malcolm was coming to recognize this in his last year. He began to see that all his talk about individual white people was not relevant to the Black man's problem. He did not say that he had changed his mind about white people. In fact, he denied it explicitly in one of his last interviews. He said, "I have never changed." The white man in this country is the Black man's enemy and will do anything possible to destroy him. Only the unity of Black people engaged in a serious revolutionary struggle will enable us to survive. Malcolm also was coming to understand the devastating influence of the white man's *declaration of Black inferiority*. In an interview he stated that you cannot organize a sleeping people around specific goals. You must wake the people up first. And the white man asked, "Do you mean to their exploitation?" Malcolm replied, "No, to their humanity, to their own worth."

Malcolm realized that we cannot begin to struggle for freedom until we decide that we are equal and reject Black inferiority as a myth created by the white man to destroy us. Malcolm was moving rapidly as he neared the end. His trip to Mecca and to the independent countries of Africa was very important. He was beginning to develop a philosophy which went far beyond the simple mythology of the Honorable Elijah Muhammad. He was beginning to understand the social dynamics of the white man's society. This white people could not understand then, and they cannot understand now. Very few white people understand the social dynamics of their own society. Very few white people realize how completely they are controlled by the institutions of their society. A white person will tell you in all sincerity that he is not like other white people, and perhaps in a superficial sense he is not; but in a profound sense he is. He is controlled by the institutions of which he is a part. He is not free. He is controlled by the institutions and the institutions are controlled by the self-interest of white people who fight to maintain white supremacy.

You may ask, Why do white people want a superior position? For two very simple reasons. One is a drive for status. Everyone fights for status and a white man secures status by keeping Black people worse off than he is. This is white supremacy. The ugliest, nastiest, poorest, and most ignorant white man in the world takes pride in the fact that his skin is white. He must give that whiteness value and maintain it at any cost. No matter how bad off he is, or how far down he falls, he still feels that he is on top because someone is below him. He is superior because the Black man has been declared inferior. This is important to most white people. They have their own white community, their own white clubs, and their own white schools. In the South parents are taking white children out of public schools and putting them in inferior white private schools. It gives them a sense of status not to let their children go to school with "niggers." That is one of the reasons. The second reason is that the exploitation of Black people puts wealth in the pockets of white people. This includes everyone. There is a ceiling on Black employment so white people have a higher income. The white man pays less for his house because Black people pay more. Black children get less education so white children get more. Status and wealth are important to all white people, and white supremacy is the basis on which both white status and white wealth depend.

Malcolm was moving toward a concept of institutional power during his last year. He spoke of "internationalizing" the Black struggle in America. He still underestimated the power of the American white man's institutional racism, which controls the United Nations even as it controls Congress. But Malcolm recognized the basic need to indict American society with the charge of genocide before the United Nations. This was a far cry from the simple declaration that the white man is a beast. In his efforts to internationalize the Black man's struggle in America Malcolm was not original. The Civil Rights Congress presented a petition to the United Nations in 1951 charging genocide and offering as evidence "various acts of genocide against the Negro people of the United States from January 1, 1945, to June, 1951, chronologically arranged under those articles and provisions of the Genocide Convention which they violate." He was not original in thinking of going before the United Nations, but certainly he was unique in the kind of international support he might have mobilized for such a move. He was not original in his growing Pan-African emphasis, but like Marcus Garvey before him, he brought a new sense of urgency to the growing recognition that Black people everywhere constitute one people, an African people struggling for survival against a common white enemy. Malcolm said, "We will indict the white man's power system before the world. Even if he controls the world, the world will know what he is doing and how he is destroying us. The Black man's revolution must become worldwide." So Malcolm moved from provincialism toward Pan-Africanism. He said that we are not by ourselves. We are a minority being oppressed by a white majority, but we are a minority only in the United States. We are part of a Black majority which is worldwide, and it is to these Black brothers and sisters that we must speak!

We are handicapped by the fact that as Black people we are a very moralistic people. We believe in right and wrong, and we do not want to do wrong because we are convinced that ultimately right will prevail. This was the basic weakness in the philosophy of Brother Malcolm when he broke free of the Muslim mythology—which escaped the confusion of human morality by attributing the immorality of vengeance and punishment to God. Obviously God does not prevail automatically. Apparently

God does not choose to intervene on the side of right or He would have done so long ago. In a world in which God does not choose to intervene, power must prevail. The Black man's effort to change the course of events by touching the white man's conscience has been as futile as it was foolish. The white man's conscience has nothing to do with his institutional power struggle. Touching his conscience is a waste of time. Malcolm never completely escaped from Black morality. In all his speeches he was judging in terms of right and wrong. If he had lived, he would have discovered by now that right and wrong do not have a thing to do with what is going to happen. Right prevails when right is supported by power. Black people do not have any power, so we can expect that right is not going to prevail until we can figure out how to get some. Anyone who won a war was right. This is crystal clear in the history books. Whoever won was right. Whoever lost was wrong. The Indians were definitely wrong or they would have won their struggle against the white man. If they had won they would have written the books, and if they had written the books they would certainly have been right. Obviously Black people were wrong in Africa, and the white man was right. The moral justification for slavery is the simple fact that we were enslaved. The slave trade and slavery were moral institutions because the white man had power. The whole concept of morality must be re-evaluated in terms of power and victory.

Religion holds that there is a God up there who has power, and the unsophisticated say that God can do anything but fail. But if we look at the world around us, we must confess that God cannot do anything but fail. If God is trying to do anything on earth He has failed! During the last four hundred years, everything that has been done on earth has been wrong. If God has the power and the will to intervene, then obviously He is on the side of evil and Black people need to find another God. I prefer to believe that God is not on the side of evil, but is waiting for Black people to get enough common sense to do what has to be done for themselves. In the Old Testament God helped the Black Nation Israel fight for dignity, manhood, and nationhood. But God can't help a people who aren't doing anything to help themselves. God does not "prevail" in the way Black people have been waiting for Him to "prevail." God didn't intervene when more than one hundred million Black people were killed in the slave trade. God didn't do a thing, not a thing! Millions were killed on the plantations and God didn't do a thing! Black people moved into the slums and ghettos of the North and millions died from starvation, hunger, cold, and everything else that happens to Black people in the slums—and God didn't do a thing! If you have ever been on a dark street at night with a policeman whipping your head, you know that you could pray until the sun came up and God won't do a thing because that is not the way God works.

Malcolm never entirely escaped the Black man's naive faith that God would somehow intervene on the side of right. Up until the very end Malcolm was a moralist, thinking in terms of people being good and bad. Malcolm also had some (peculiar) ideas about the nature of revolution. At the Grass Roots Conference he talked about revolution. Revolutions are for land and blood must be spilled. He mentioned the American Revolution as an illustration. The American Revolution involved colonists fighting to control the land on which they lived. He was right, they were fighting for land. In the French Revolution, the majority of the French people were fighting to control their own land. In the Russian Revolution, the Russian peasants, the majority of the Russian people, were fighting to control their own land. In the Chinese Revolution, the majority of the Chinese people were fighting to control their own land. In Africa every liberation struggle involved a racial majority fighting against a racial minority to control its own land. But in America conditions are different. We are a minority. The concept of revolution in terms of land must be re-evaluated. It is foolish to talk about the struggle for land as the basis for revolution without an analysis of our unique condition. We are a minority and we are struggling against a majority. Past revolutions do not furnish guidelines for our struggle. The concept of revolution must be developed by a people out of their particular situation. Malcolm's concept of revolution was a changing one. At one point he stated that perhaps we could have bloodless revolution in America. But then he added, "But I don't think it is possible because the American white man is not morally equipped to do so." So he dragged morals back into the picture. It isn't the fact that the white man is not morally equipped to accept a bloodless revolution, but the fact that the white man is controlled by power institutions which will not permit him to do so. Malcolm was moving in the direction of Nation within a nation and a dynamic concept of society. So do not leave him where he was at the Grass Roots Conference. His was a growing philosophy and what that philosophy would have become can be seen only in the theology, philosophy, and program of Black Christian Nationalism. We have developed from the point where Malcolm stopped. We serve the cause he served best by developing his position to its logical conclusion, remembering that nothing is more sacred than the liberation of Black people. Malcolm said that you cannot organize a sleeping people around specific goals. You must wake the people up first. And the white man asked, "Do you mean to their exploitation?" "No," he replied, "to their humanity, to their own worth." This is the program of Black Christian Nationalism.

PART 3

We Define Our Struggle

CHAPTER 8

The Institutional Basis
of Power

Jesus turned his face steadfastly toward Jerusalem seeking with the white gentile enemy the final confrontation —which he would lose, because he lacked the power to defeat the institutionalized forces which were arrayed against him. Black people did not understand institutionalized power. Jesus spoke to the needs of an oppressed Black people and when he talked they felt good. They were persuaded that the things he was saying were true and that the institutions that he was attacking were evil. But they did not understand that in many ways they were a part of the mechanism of their own enslavement.

The Zealots advised Israel to withhold taxes from Caesar, but Black Jews grew fat as tax gatherers, exploiting their own people for the benefit of Rome. The institution of government was evil because its power was used to oppress the people. When Jesus explained it there was no question in their minds. Jesus was right and the Roman government was wrong. Jesus told them that the religious institution was exploitative. The priests, the scribes, and the Pharisees had turned the House of God into a den of thieves. The institutionalized church was one of the forces oppressing the people. When he explained it to them they understood. They said Jesus was right and the church was wrong. Jesus explained that they were being oppressed by the economic institution. He said, "It is not right to use money to exploit people. Divide your material possessions with the poor and follow me." They said, "That's the way it ought to be." When the rich young ruler said, "I have obeyed the Commandments since the days of my youth. What now shall I do to inherit eternal life?" Jesus said, "Give your riches to the poor and follow me." The rich young ruler turned sadly away. He was not prepared to sacrifice his power. He wanted to be "good" without attacking the institutional basis of evil. He did not recognize his involvement in the oppression which was all about him. The people said, "Jesus is right and the rich young man is wrong. An economic system which is exploitative is evil." Ordinary Black people were convinced. This could be the only reason that multitudes came out to hear Jesus. They knew that what he said was true and that institutions were the instruments of their oppression. People followed him out into the countryside. When they listened to Jesus they would say, "That's right," the way people would when Brother Malcolm was talking. Basically Jesus was saying the same thing. The institutions of the enemy are the basis of your oppression and exploitation. The government belongs to the enemy. The church is controlled by the enemy. The economy serves the enemy. The oppressed would say, "That's right. That's right." But having no institutions of their own, they had no power. That's the way it was with Brother Malcolm, and that's the way it was with Jesus. They could not comprehend a basic attack upon the institutions which oppressed them. They were content to declare them evil.

The Disciples did not understand the power of the institutions and we do not understand it today. Most of the things we do as Black people fail to take into account the institutional basis of our oppression. Explain what's wrong with a particular institution and everyone says, "That's right," but no one is moved to action. So long as institutions are permitted to exercise unchallenged power in serving the interests of the enemy, the oppressed are helpless. Institutions are the basis of the white oppressor's power. They were created to serve his interests. As oppressed Black people, we have a different relationship with American institutions from that of the white oppressor. That which serves his interests cannot possibly serve ours. Members of the white enemy group who criticize white institutions realize that they cannot afford to make basic changes without risking their power position. Enemy factions jockey for power within the enemy system without ever seriously questioning the necessity for its preservation. The enemy is as controlled by his institutions as we are, with one significant difference. White institutions serve him, but they enslave us. This can be easily seen in the field of politics. We voted for LBJ to end the war in Vietnam, and the things he actually did were the things we defeated Goldwater to prevent. Again, we voted for Nixon because Hubert Humphrey would continue the LBJ policies and prolong the war in Vietnam. Nixon in office is carrying out the same policies enunciated by LBJ. Obviously the President does not make policy. Institutions determine what happens. The program is not dictated from the White House but from the power institutions which control America just as they control every society.

People set up institutions as a necessary step in the struggle for power, because, as Chairman Mao has correctly observed, the social tendency is not for people to come together, but for people to fly apart. People find it difficult to unite in groups, and when they do, they find it difficult to stay together. We have deep individualistic tendencies and we do not like external controls of any kind. But out of basic human experience individuals learn that only groups are capable of developing the power necessary for survival. And only individuals who can recognize the necessity for delegating power and authority are capable of merging themselves into a group, a tribe, or a nation. The group is born out of individual desperation. Only individuals who realize that they cannot make it by themselves are willing to sacrifice enough to bring a group into being. To reduce the process to diagrammatic simplicity, it is as though an individual hiding in a cave suddenly realized the benefits to be derived from making some kind of defense pact with other isolated individuals hiding in caves. So instead of killing his next victim he lets him live and makes a bargain. Then the two of them overpower other individuals and bring them into the group. The group grows in numbers and in power. Individuals are helpless against it. The group exists because of a purely selfish, power-hungry agreement. The members of the group say, "We are going to work together for our mutual protection, and together we will secure power and status for our group and its members. As a group we must do certain things. We must select leadership and we must delegate authority. The strongest member of the group cannot take leadership and depend on the authority of his strength, because no individual in the group has strength enough to challenge the groups. Leaders must be selected by the group and exercise delegated authority. Those who refuse to accept authority will be tracked down like animals and destroyed for the good of the group."

This little group has contrived a crude social compact. It selects a leader and begins to create institutions. The church is a basic social institution because it gives divine sanction. Not only does a group need a leader, but it wants to know that God is on its side. So the group will seek a divine revelation and will hear the voice of God in the commonplace events of its daily life. Then the members of the group will say, "We are surely on the right side because God is with us." So the little group which came together upon the basis of a purely selfish, power-hungry agreement now begins to build a religious institution upon the basis of its unique revelation of God. It will develop a religion which belongs to it alone. Other people may be converted, but they must understand that the group controls the revelation, the institution, and the rituals, and can mediate the power of God to whomever it will. Other people must accept the group's interpretation of the revelation, and the fact that the group constitutes God's Chosen People. Why else would God have elected to speak through the group and its history? So the group undertakes to convert outsiders to the worship of the one true God. The group realizes that in sharing its divine blessing it is also establishing an institutional control over those who are converted. It is easier to convert than to conquer in battle, and even after a battle it is useful in dealing with those conquered and serves to underscore their acceptance of inferiority. Who can question the superiority of those Chosen by God as His very own People?

The group institutionalizes its government with the acceptance of a compact of association and the selection of a leader with delegated power. From the institutionalization of the church the group naturally turns to education. It must interpret history with itself at the center. All history begins with the moment the group formalizes its existence with a social compact. Everything that happened before was but a pagan prelude to history. Psychology and sociology are written to reflect the self-interest of the group. The group describes its behavior patterns and projects them as human norms. Anything else is deviant behavior reflecting primitive patterns or the behavior of inferior peoples. The group sociologist and psychologist have but to determine how the group functions to know how all human society is supposed to function. With this rather simple process, a huge educational institution with libraries, research centers, and academic degrees is brought into being. Everything the group puts together is taken out to the world and proclaimed with authority. Other people accept it and are automatically declared inferior. Without any authoritative revelation of God (the group declares all other revelations questionable or primitive) and no knowledge or books of consequence, other people are disadvantaged in the struggle for power. The institutions belonging to the group dominate the world. Other people do not understand the mechanism of their enslavement. The group hands the control of its institutions down to its children. They accept their dominant position as just and right and fight to expand their worldwide control.

Gradually, however, institutions appear to take on a life of their own. They no longer seem to be undergirding the power establishment, largely because the power establishment no longer seems to need undergirding. Individuals inside the church think that they can reinterpret the original revelation that came to the group. Some even try to reinterpret it in such a way that it can ease the oppression of those who have been structured out of the group. This is not what the revelation was intended for and not what the religious institution was created to accomplish. Some even begin to say that the revelation was intended for all people, and the purpose of religion is to make all "one in God." This is not true. The revelation came out of the experience of the group and was intended to strengthen the group in its struggle against outsiders. The outsiders rejoice at the sound of a "liberal" voice within the institution. The oppressed began to feel that the church is changing. It is beginning to speak for those who are discriminated against. They have forgotten that it is an institution! An individual making "liberal" pronouncements does not speak for the church but against the church. Soon "liberal" voices can be heard in other institutions. The group seems to be falling apart. The thing which brought them together in the first place was the simple fact that they needed each other to secure power and to maintain power. What can hold them together now that they control the world?

Individuals within the institutional framework begin to exploit others within the group. Young people refuse to defend the group, rejecting the idea that war is necessary to maintain the group's control of the world, announcing that they reject control of the world as a justifiable goal. Everywhere people are trying to get rich at the expense of the group and the economic institution is falling apart. Individual greed begins to make social life impossible. The cities begin to die of decay and pollution fouls the earth, the air, and the seas. Finally the group approaches the death stage. But something strange begins to happen. The people become frightened and the same selfish power hunger which brought them together serves to protect them. They feel the need for the group to protect them against attacks by outsiders. The institutions evidence an inner strength of their own when the oppressed on the outside begin to attack. The group does not react to criticism that does not constitute an attack upon its power institutions, but any hostile act by outsiders triggers an instantaneous response. Without an attack by outsiders the group might not be able to halt its disintegration before reaching the point of no return. The group is saved by the automatic reaction of its basic institutional structures. An automatic defense mechanism comes into play and the institutions which have appeared to be fragmented beyond repair come back together. This is a diagrammatic outline of the institutional basis of group power.

Today we see this process at work as American society in the midst of social disorganization and fragmentation interprets the Black Revolution as an attack upon its basic power institutions. At conference after conference white ministers will admit that they are in a very bad position because of their "liberal" views. They make heroic statements promising to continue to stand up for what they believe. They can stand up if they want to, but they are not going to stand long because the white religious institution is going to defend the white power establishment. The church, the government, the schools, the economic institution, and everything else in America is going to be taken over by white-supremacy advocates. The silent majority have always believed in white superiority and have struggled in their own way to keep oppressed and exploited Black people outside the white power establishment by maintaining the white *declaration of Black inferiority*. They do not intend to let the white group be driven out of power. Ignorant and inarticulate as they have been and still are, they have taken control of government and are moving to take back control of the white church. Gradually the national white church will begin to sound more and more like the old southern white preacher praying that God would give the Klan strength to kill a "nigger" today. The white church cannot escape that frame of mind when it considers itself God's instrument for the protection of a dominant white racist majority. The same thing is happening in the economic field. Black people have made no progress economically. We still do not own anything. In fact we own less and less. The white economic institution is reacting, as evidenced by growing Black unemployment.

In the final analysis the white group feels that its dominant position depends on its use of police power. It is willing to establish a police state if a police state is necessary to re-establish its power establishment. The national police conspiracy to kill Black Panthers is just a part of the process of re-establishing a white position of authority and power. Anyone engaged in any kind of dissent is going to get clobbered as quickly as possible because the white group has decided that it can no longer tolerate dissent by individuals who oppose the white power position. Now we are dealing with the same reality that existed before the 1954 Supreme Court decision. We are now dealing with white institutions controlled by individuals who will stop at nothing to maintain white supremacy. Poor oppressed Black people did not realize that institutions had anything to do with the Black Revolution and its demands. We thought that we were dealing with "good white people" and "bad white people," and now we are totally confused. Good white people are not talking so good anymore and they are doing very few good things, and bad white people are multiplying like rabbits. There never were good white people and bad white people. There were just white people controlled by the institutional structure created to serve their interests. They couldn't possibly be good to the oppressed people who were structured out of their power establishment. White people now have the boldness of desperation. The Federal government is acting to nullify in one way or another most of the legislation and court decisions that had given Black people the feeling that they were at last becoming a part of America. Time is to be rolled back to some point before the 1954 Supreme Court decision outlawing segregation in public education. The attack upon the Supreme Court is now a real attack. The IMPEACH EARL WARREN signs didn't mean much. White folks were just playing then. Now they are not playing. Judges are being selected so that decisions will be designed to re-establish the power of white institutions. This is not strange. The Supreme Court is supposed to serve the dominant group; that's what it was created for. Because their power was absolute white people forgot for a moment. But with the white group under attack, the Supreme Court will again take its rightful position.

All the white man's institutions are rising to defend white supremacy. The communications media are beautiful to watch. One of their effective techniques is "no news." No news is good news. Things are happening to Black people all over America but they are never reported. You wonder what happened to the Black Revolution. White people just took it out of the paper and off TV. Many things happening on Black college campuses are never reported. There was a boycott down at Fisk University which lasted until the entire student body was sent home. It never got into the newspapers. Black protest is being deliberately ignored by the media. The communications media have come together to defend white supremacy and white power. This is natural because the communications media are an institution and as an institution they do what has to be done to fulfill their function. They serve the interest of their own group. Individuals are unimportant. If one won't do what he is supposed to do, others will. Integrity has nothing to do with it. The institution really couldn't care less about who reads the news or who writes the news. Any commentator can be built into a "personality" within a matter of months and any big-headed personality who feels bigger than the institution can be forgotten within weeks. The media project "liberals" when the group is secure and "liberal," and they project conservatives and reactionaries when the power institutions of the group are under attack. No directive or conscious conspiracy is necessary. Institutions merely react to the realities of the situation. So we now have "no news" or "controlled news." Spiro Agnew has issued a warning to the communications media. (The only question is whether or not anyone so crude can really speak for the white power establishment.)

More typical is the finesse of the communications industry in exploiting Detroit's Mother Waddles, who was sent to Nixon's inauguration. Mother Waddles is a beautiful Black woman who is perfectly described by her name. She operates a soup kitchen and "perpetual mission" for the down and out. She understands perfectly the art of handling white folks and has a knack for public relations. She is constantly on the front page of Detroit newspapers. But however sweet she may be, she does not merit all the attention white folks give her in Detroit. Obviously she is being used to prove that white people are really friendly to nice Black people. In Grosse Pointe the high-school kids got together and raised a thousand dollars for Mother Waddles. Black people can't live in Grosse Pointe but a thousand dollars was raised there for Mother Waddles. So Black people must admit that white people are not all bad after all. And Channel Two, not especially noted for a friendly attitude toward Black people, devotes its daily editorial to Mother Waddles and offers to double any money mailed in for Mother Waddles. She is given a daily radio program and a TV program, and City Hall refers applications for assistance to her without offering any financial aid. Why is Mother Waddles the darling of Detroit's communications media? She doesn't threaten anything, that's the first thing we must understand. If you do not threaten anything you can be supported. James Forman didn't get that kind of response, even though his program was much more realistic than the program of Mother Waddles. The Black Manifesto demanded five hundred million dollars for Black self-determination. He suggested a southern land bank, a Black university, publishing houses, and a communications network. The Black Manifesto was hardly mentioned in the Detroit newspapers. No TV channel offered to double all money raised. The churches were afraid, the communications media were afraid. Everyone was afraid. Mother Waddles is talking about love. Forman is talking about power. As long as Black people are talking about love no one is worried, but when we start talking about power everyone is worried, because we are attacking the basic white power structure.

All white institutions come together to fight against any kind of an attack on the white establishment, and we are still dealing with an unstructured Black Revolution. No Black people in America are really trying to structure a Black Revolution except Black Christian Nationalists.

Everyone is still talking about how bad things are, and some Black folks are saying that the worse it gets the better it is because then we will react. React to what? With what? React to a policeman shooting a Black man down in the street? That's not reacting to institutional power. A policeman works for twenty-five dollars a day. He is no power instrument. How can we attack the institution that keeps him out there with his stoner rifle, Mace, and shotguns? To structure a revolution we must begin to build institutions of our own. We have no institutional power as Black people. White institutions cannot be expected to serve Black interests. The Black church is not an institution; it is only the shadow of the white church. But it can become an institution. Black Christian Nationalism points the way to a relevant Black church, capable of structuring Black institutions and spearheading a Black Revolution.

CHAPTER 9

The White Power
Establishment

Jesus lived in a world of tension, conflict, and hostility.
Only a few people were able to free their minds and
seriously try to follow him. He realized this when he told
his Disciples, "The world hates me because I testify that
its works are evil." It is important to remember this when
we approach a critical evaluation of Black Christian Nationalism. BCN challenges the very foundations of Western civilization, which has enslaved Black people and
forced upon them a culture inferior to their own as well
as the absurd, otherworldly Christian theology of a Black
slave church, incapacitating generations of Black people
for intelligent revolutionary struggle against oppression
and powerlessness. Like Jesus, BCN criticizes society and
its existing institutions, and calls Black men to a revolutionary struggle to change the world.

It is uncomfortable for us when anyone challenges the
things in which we believe. Most of our basic beliefs were
absorbed uncritically and are taken for granted. When
these things are challenged we feel that we are under personal attack. We learned much of our religious faith at
our mother's knee and accepted it without critical evalua-

tion. Certainly we learned the white man's *declaration of Black inferiority* uncritically. These things have become emotion-filled parts of our thought patterns. Any attack on white supremacy threatens even Black people, whose minds have been twisted by self-hate and a deep desire to identify with their white oppressors. Jesus understood why he alienated people and created hostility. He attempted to avoid it by trying to build the new upon the old, "fulfilling the Law rather than destroying it." But even so, people were disturbed by the inescapable implication that many of the things they believed were not true.

Many people feel uncomfortable when they come to the Shrine of the Black Madonna to worship. We are relevant, we are friendly, and our Black theology makes sense, but there is a tension about the entire experience. It is not by accident that we have modified the rituals and outer forms of worship more slowly than we have our basic theology. Some visitors who have come to the Shrine on a kind of sight-seeing trip are surprised. The large chancel mural of the Black Madonna and Child is striking and not easily forgotten. It is not the soft, childishly pretty Madonna of the Roman Church, but a woman, beautiful because she is Black and of the earth and has borne a man-child for the Liberation Struggle of his people. She is all of the Black women of the ages who have made it possible for the Black Nation to survive in the midst of oppression, exploitation, and brutality. She resembles the Madonnas of the Orthodox churches that have retained a closer kinship to their African beginnings. But our order of service is traditional, as is our use of Black gospel music. We have been willing to surround the new Black theology with familiar outer forms to soften the initial impact. Like Jesus, we seek not to destroy but to fulfill. We explain that the old theology is the theology of Paul and not of Jesus, and that Jesus was a revolutionary leader seeking to build a heaven in the here and now on earth, but we do not hesitate to sing "O Happy Day, When Jesus Washed My Sins Away." More and more, however, we are being forced to restructure BCN ritual, music, and program to conform to the new Black theology. Like Jesus, we have discovered that you cannot put new wine into old wineskins. Increasingly, therefore, we are challenging people either to accept or reject the new Black theology with the ritual, music, and program that it demands. Either you are waiting for God to take you up to heaven, or you are seeking God's guidance in building heaven here on earth. You have been taught that heaven is up in the sky, and when we challenge this absurdity you feel uncomfortable. Many people dare not visit because they fear that we will shake their faith.

We have a Black teacher's caucus which meets twice a week and, in co-operation with our ministerial training group, sponsors a school of Black studies for elementary and junior-high children. Many militant Black teachers are afraid to attend until they are attacked by the system and need support. They hesitate to accept our basic position—that Black people are engaged in a never-ending power struggle against a white enemy who oppresses and exploits us and from whom we must break our identification. For no people in the world is the acceptance of this basic premise more important than it is for Black teachers. They hesitate because it brings into question their acceptance of the white *declaration of Black inferiority* and of the old theology, both pillars of the Black man's dream of integration. They ask, "Can't we just attack educational problems and teacher problems without accepting a totally new philosophy of life?" The answer is an unequivocal No. The basic problem confronting Black teachers, lawyers, doctors, social workers, and all other Black people is the simple fact that they are trying to function as intelligent beings without a rational philosophy of life. Many Black teachers are afraid of the Shrine of the Black Madonna Black teacher's caucus because it challenges their

basic beliefs. Sooner or later they must come to our position, but they equivocate because our challenge to their
irrational beliefs makes them feel uncomfortable. People
react to Black Christian Nationalism just as they reacted
to Jesus. We take pride in the fact that the truth we
proclaim stirs up the people, even if for the moment many
turn aside. People telling the same old lies back and forth
is a luxury that Black people can no longer afford.

We are engaged in a Black Liberation Struggle. At the
Shrine of the Black Madonna, we teach that nothing is
more sacred than the liberation of Black people and that
active participation and leadership in the Struggle are the
basic function of the Black church. We accept the in-
evitability of confrontation and conflict in a power struggle. Many people who talk about power are uncomfortable
and guilty about it. We seek power unashamedly, because
it is basic to the liberation of Black people. All Black
people must become involved in the Black man's struggle
for liberation, because it is also his struggle for survival.
We struggle to escape the framework of existence within
which the white man has confined us by his *declaration
of Black inferiority*. Our fight for liberation is a very
definite and specific thing. We do not merely urge Black
people to unite. When we fight for Black liberation, we
fight to destroy white supremacy. We have no other
choice. We must either destroy it, or accept Black
inferiority.

Our struggle for survival is the foundation on which we
must build a total interpretation of life. Quite simply,
that means that a Black person who does not realize that
he is engaged in a Liberation Struggle against a white
enemy cannot think correctly about anything. If he does
not realize that he is engaged in a struggle for survival
against an enemy, he cannot possibly understand anything
about the world in which he lives. If he thinks that he is
living in a world in which right will prevail because God
is going to see to it that right does prevail, then obviously

his every interpretation of life and events is going to be wrong because God does not work that way. We have no assurance that things are going to work out all right unless we have the skill and the power to work them out together for ourselves. When we talk about a struggle for survival we are talking about a real struggle which we can either win or lose. Let us challenge the empty platitudes. Things are not going to work out all right. Give the world the best that you have, and the best will not necessarily come back to you. Try to love everybody and you will probably be beaten to death before the week is over. We must cleanse our minds of this old slave theology. If we are engaged in a struggle for survival we must recognize the nature of that struggle. We must not say a word without realizing that struggle means confrontation and conflict. It means that we pit ourselves against others. We must be willing to risk everything, or we are not seriously engaged in a struggle for survival.

Another fallacy which troubles us is the feeling that the Struggle in which we are engaged will last only for a limited period of time. We hope that if we work hard it may be over by next year. But it is not going to be over in ten years, or a hundred years, or a hundred thousand years. We will always be engaged in struggle. There is nothing immoral about struggle and conflict. Black people are not good because they are poor and powerless. We want power and everything everyone else wants, but we have been taught that we ought not to want them, so we feel guilty and try to make a virtue out of weakness. We try to believe that God has blessed us with second-class citizenship because He did not want to contaminate us with power. We must eventually realize that we are powerless because we have been fools for hundreds of years. We want power because a people cannot survive without power, and because we want the status which comes with power. We want everything that comes with power. We want to run the factories, control the cities, control the nation, and control the world. We want all of it, and our new Black theology teaches us that there is nothing immoral about our quest for power. Immorality lies in weakness and in the fear of power. Immorality lies in the acceptance of powerlessness and the indignities which powerlessness forces upon a people who are created in the image of God and are expected to maintain dignity.

When we secure power, white people will have the same protection open to them which is now open to us. They can struggle to secure sufficient power to establish a balance that can protect them against our oppression, confident that power corrupts and fragments a people whenever the people whom they oppress sink to total powerlessness and are for the moment unable to fight their way back to a reasonable balance. If human beings were rational, a group in power, for purely selfish reasons, would never permit those whom they oppress to fall below a certain level of power because the total powerlessness of the oppressed offers the only real threat to the essential cohesion of the dominant group. A group in power fragments into competitive individualism when it has no attacking enemy to make its unity essential for survival.

Humans have been condemned to live by the sweat of their brows. This is the truth of the Fall, the driving of Adam and Eve out of the Garden of Eden by God. Struggle is an inescapable part of human existence, as the desire for status is an inescapable aspect of human nature. Cain slew Abel because Cain wanted status in the eyes of God. In all generations men have struggled for status and power. Those who do not enjoy the struggle have been emasculated by powerlessness and oppression. The struggle is without joy when you struggle for survival from a position of total powerlessness. You are disadvantaged. No one likes to fight an opponent who is standing up when he is on his back. Many Black people do not like to struggle, because the old slave theology teaches that struggle and conflict are wrong. They think that God expects them to be meek and humble and accept whatever happens. You feel guilty when you are on your knees and' the white man is kicking your brains out and you try to hold his feet. The old theology teaches you that your suffering is redemptive. You feel guilty when you fight back, when you try to get up, or when you try to hit back. You feel that there is something wrong with you, fighting when you ought to be praying. You are bound hand and foot by your slave theology. The old theology is an integrationist theology which leads Black men to follow the dream of integration wherever it may lead. Suffering is redemptive —if the Black man can suffer enough, the white man may be persuaded to love him. The new theology says that this is total absurdity. The Black man's acceptance of indignity leads the white man to despise and hate him the more. The only possibility of redemption for either the powerful or the powerless lies in confrontation and conflict.

Individuals are relatively powerless when confronted by a group. Any group has the power to enslave individuals. If we are a thousand individuals, a group of twenty organized men can enslave us. They would have organization and a plan of action. Each of us would be trying to make individual plans, and we would end up aiding the enemy and trampling each other in our efforts to escape as individuals. A collection of individuals must pass through definite stages of development in the process of becoming a group. Groups do not just happen. As powerless *individuals*, we denounce the members of a *group* as vicious men. We denounce the system by which they operate. We are talking from weakness while they are acting from strength. Each individual who has gone into the group has made sacrifices in order to make it possible for the group to come into being. Each one has given up something of his individualism to create the collective power of the group. Each has agreed to accept the authority of leadership and the structured behavior of institutions. Without leadership and without institutional strength, individuals can constitute only a mob.

Institutions are created by a group out of specific needs, and they exist only to serve the needs of the group that created them. A group creates institutions as instruments of power, preservers of power, and transmitters of power. Government is an institution. It doesn't just come into being; people struggle to create it. The military establishment is an institution, a part of the institution of government, but an institution in and of itself. A complex of institutions undergirds the white man's power in the Western world. When we discuss the behavior of white individuals, we must recognize and understand the institutional structures that control them and constitute the foundation of their power. Institutions must have leadership, but the basis of group power is the institutional structure. The members of the group recognize this and fight to preserve their institutions at any cost. How the individual fights to preserve his institutions is not always apparent. A white man feels personally threatened when any one of his institutions is attacked. He does not have to think about it or wait for instructions. He reacts. A suburban white preacher who talks too much about the oppression of Black people will lose his church. His congregation will feel threatened, because they know that the thing he is talking about will undermine the white supremacy which is the basis of their power. In spite of liberal Judeo-Christion traditions, they will react to this reality. If a liberal white politician decides to respond to the demands of Black people when Black people do not have the power to keep him in office, white people are going to take him out of office, because they will feel threatened when he makes the slightest concession to Black demands. They will interpret his act as a betrayal of white supremacy. Anytime an attack is made on any white institution, all nonalienated white people will move to its defense.

Today Black people are attacking all white institutions. It makes little difference how the attack is launched, the response is the same. White institutions have protective mechanisms set up to ward off attack. If you strike at the white institutions, a protective mechanism meets you before you can touch the institution. I attended a meeting recently. It was a conference on repression called by Detroit's liberal white establishment. A few Black "leaders" were invited to lend it legitimacy. There were the New Democratic Coalition, the Urban Coalition, organized labor (the Teamsters Union and the UAW), Jewish community groups, Protestant community groups, and Catholic community groups. Basically it was the white liberal establishment. Usually when we say liberal establishment no one knows exactly what we mean. The liberal establishment is the automatic defense mechanism of the white power establishment, which must fend off institutional attacks when they occur. Oftentimes we think that we are dealing with the power establishment when we are engaged in dialogue with this deliberately created buffer.

No one at the meeting had power. No one was a decision-maker. They were the discussers. They had come to the meeting to discuss a serious problem. They were genuinely concerned about repression and wanted it stopped. The harassment and murder of Black Panthers across the country really worried them. They could see the danger to every American's civil rights. If the police were permitted to attack the Black Panthers and shoot them down in the street today, tomorrow they would be killing the Jews in the street. The next day they would be shooting Catholics, and the following day they would be shooting down working people in the street. It must be stopped now. Many suggestions were made. The committee would issue a statement. The committee would send representatives to talk to the police commissioner. The committee would hold a press conference and have distinguished representatives speak on television. These were the methods they knew and understood. They did not seem to understand that their own constituencies were demanding and supporting the very repression they were denouncing. They were the protective mechanism of the white power establishment, moving to soften the blow of increasing repression and to confuse and fragment the natural response of the Black community. They were for the most part the human-relations representatives of their various organizations, without power to act, but only to discuss. We had the human-relations departments of the Catholic Church, the Jewish community, the Protestant denominations, and the liberal coalitions.

Why do these organizations all need human-relations committees? These departments, councils, and committees have all been set up to deal with us and our Black problems. They will meet and discuss anything with us at any time, but they have no power to commit their organizations to any real programmatic action. To get through them to the centers of power is like fighting through quicksand. They will talk for days, months, weeks, years —because that is their whole function. They are designed to absorb the impact of hostility. They cannot be insulted. Every discussion ends with "Come in again. It was so nice to talk to you, because we really want to understand how you people feel. Next time bring some of your friends, anyone you know who feels the way you do. We just want you to 'tell it like it is.'" So you become involved in a whole series of meetings with human-relations people. The organizations go right on doing whatever they have been doing. They tell you, "Our Human Relations Department will make recommendations to us." That is true, they will. Sometimes they get even well-meaning, intelligent white people on these things who really understand the process and are willing to take terrible psychological beatings daily for the little good they can sneak in once every five years or so. You can talk to them like dogs. They will get red and go right on talking because that is their job; to keep you there as long as possible, because as long as you are sitting there talking to the human-relations committee you are not doing any of the other things you might be doing, like organizing, confronting, and resisting.

So we all sat there and agreed that repression was a bad thing, a very bad thing, and a statement must be issued immediately. We do not like the way the Black Panthers are being killed everywhere. We do not like the way Angela Davis was taken back to California. We do not like! We do not like! Human-relations committees can sign any kind of statement without committing the organization itself. Institutions do not get involved with their human-relations departments. What white folks really don't like is Black people stepping over the human-relations department to start fighting decision-making white folks. That is what they did not like at the National Council of Churches meeting in Detroit.

The National Committee of Black Churchmen stepped over the human-relations committee and struck at the people who control the denominations. They did not like that. At the United Church of Christ synod in Boston, the Black caucus stepped over the human-relations people and brought the fight to the floor of the synod, the center of power. The individuals who control the basic instrumentalities of the church were forced to fight back openly. This is the new pattern for Black action. Attack the center of power. Do not discuss your problems with the office boy. Even if you convince him, he is as powerless as you are. James Forman understood this clearly when he moved into 475 Riverside Drive, New York City. He was attacking the center of denominational power in America. When he stalked down the aisle at Riverside Church with his Black Manifesto, he symbolized in unforgettable imagery the Black man's basic shift in tactics. It was one of the few truly beautiful moments in the Black man's dismal captivity in America.

A proud Black man defiantly challenging white church power at its very center without benefit of human-relations committees . . . beautiful as it was, both in conception and execution, it failed. The walls of Jericho did not come tumbling down. The white church did not respond in any significant fashion. It would be easy now for Black people to read back into the whole Black Manifesto incident the conclusion that somehow the Black churchmen failed to support James Forman, and for that reason he could not exert the pressure necessary to force the white church to respond. This is not true. Forman attacked the predominantly white denominations, and every Black caucus in a predominantly white denomination gave Forman and the Black Manifesto complete support. I attended all the early meetings in New York when total support for the Manifesto was being hammered out by denominational caucuses and leaders, and not a single Black caucus leader or Black interdenominational group failed to give complete endorsement and support to the Black Manifesto. I supported it then and I support it now. The white church failed to respond for the simple reason that it could not. The white church is not capable of independent action. It has only a limited ability to respond. It has very limited power. Four seventy-five Riverside Drive only appears to be a power center. When you talk to the denominational and National Council of Church officials there, you are still dealing with the office boy, who is powerless to make decisions. The white church has human-relations committee buffers to protect its executives in the exercise of their very limited powers, but the white church itself is only a buffer for the white power establishment. It does not exercise power, it merely protects and serves those who do. If we are to attack real centers of white power, we must look beyond the church to those who control the church and all white racist institutions. What the white church can do, it must be made to do, but let us remember that this will be pathetically little in terms of our needs.

We are learning only gradually how to deal with the institutional structures of the white community. One method Black people have developed for dealing with white institutional structures can be described, inasmuch as the white power group now understands it and is already taking elaborate steps to prevent its continued use. The method is based on the simple fact that the white structure always falls victim to its own thinking. When a human-relations buffer is set up to hold Blacks at arm's length, it eventually seems necessary to place some nice, safe, responsible Blacks on the committee to give it legitimacy and increase its effectiveness in dealing with Black people. The nice Black members usually sit around for a year or two until they find out how the committee works, and then they take the very committee—that the white folks created to serve as a buffer to keep Black people on the outside of the white racist institutional structure—and turn it around and use it to attack white centers of power. It is as though the outer defenses of a fort were captured and the cannons turned around and fired into the fort they were erected to protect. It is a beautiful tactic, capable of creating momentary panic and alarm, even if incapable of achieving a significant shift of power. It has happened in every Protestant denomination as well as in the Catholic Church. It has been much less effective in dealing with white racist political and economic institutions, for several reasons.

First, because the most effective and intelligent Black leadership is in the Church. Second, because white political and economic leaders do not feel constrained to legitimatize their oppression and exploitation of the Black community by pretending to share with Blacks. Third, because political and economic institutions exercise real power and therefore control substantial wealth, so they can afford to be more selective and pay a better price when picking a "house nigger" to sit by the door. The Church is naturally more vulnerable to this kind of attack, because it is a buffer institution and therefore must maintain a higher degree of legitimacy in the Black community. If the white church cannot keep Black people relatively happy and quiet, it is not efficiently serving the interests of the white power structure and will be restructured. Top white denominational executives are amazingly more intelligent and more liberal than the ignorant Middle American who sits in the pews and contributes the money which pays the bills. Top-level white religious leaders understand their function, which they dare not interpret even to ignorant parish ministers who are totally incapable of comprehending denominational strategy. White religious leaders are for the most part willing to go as far as necessary in meeting Black demands without actually effecting any real shift of power. This requires unusual skill and dexterity. The white executive must somehow make Black people feel that a real transference of power is taking place and at the same time assure white Middle America that he is actually shoring up the basic foundations of white supremacy and white power. If he fails, either Black rebellion breaks out or white contributions dry up. In either case the second line of white defense must be activated. Civil rights are suspended, repression is given a new hand, and the emergence of a police state becomes the response to public demand.

Most of the white people who attended the meeting to end repression did not have the slightest idea of the role they were playing. They were doing the things they had been trained to do. Everything is outlined in the sociology and psychology books. They followed standard community-organization procedures. They let Black folks air their grievances and they prepared to issue a statement. They did not understand that the process they were following would not affect the problem of growing repression—or if they understood, they were not authorized to move beyond this traditional procedure. I made my usual statement of protest (I ought to have it mimeographed and hand it out at the door at all such meetings):

> Repression is not something which will go away because we proclaim that we are against it. We are moving rapidly toward a repressive police state because the American people feel that it is necessary to protect their white supremacy and their white power. Your constituencies at home are demanding repression. Your own white members are the ones who are insisting upon repression. The police work for them, and for you, because you are a part of the system. They are doing what your people want done, and for you to join in the passage of a resolution denouncing it is the height of absurdity. White people want repression because they feel that they need it. No resolution is going to change this fact. It cannot be stopped by resolutions because we are dealing with the automatic reaction of white people rising to defend their racist institutions. White people are aroused. They feel threatened because Black people continue to attack their basic institutional structures. And if they feel that the maintenance of the *status quo* is essential to the preservation of white supremacy and white power, they have a right to feel threatened—because as disorganized as we are, we are seriously attacking the basic power institutions on which the preservation of white supremacy depends. The very shift of emphasis in the Black community from integration and nonviolence to community control, self-determination, Black Power, and self-defense constitutes a basic attack upon white supremacy. The Black Panthers, with their guns, sandbags, and symbolic resistance (evidencing more of a talent for dying than for killing), serve to bring this shift into sharp perspective. White people are afraid. They are even more frightened because their own white young people are also attacking the basic white institutions. They are attacking from a different perspective and for the ac-

complishment of different objectives, but this two-
pronged attack upon white institutions has triggered an
automatic defense mechanism. Only a fool could have
expected less. Repression will increase no matter how
many statements human-relations councils issue. Repression will not be confined to the Black Panthers. It will
not be confined to any particular group. It will quickly
seek to stamp out all dissent and to destroy anyone and
anything which threatens in any way the white power
structure and its basic institutions.

Black people are going to be forced to take the Liberation Struggle seriously if they are to survive. It is Nation
time for the Black community. We must begin the labori-
ous task of building a Black Nation here and now wherever we are. We have precipitously launched an attack.
Now we must begin to create the Black institutional
strength necessary for a life-and-death struggle. Every
institution in the Black community reflects our basic weakness, in that it was created out of our identification with
white people. They are pseudo-institutions, in that they
do not serve our interests and were structured only for the
interim in which we were waiting for the realization of
total integration. Our pseudo-institutions meet none of the
basic criteria for bona fide institutions. They do not seek
power to serve the interests of a people, but rather they
seek to participate in the destruction of a people through
integration. For a Black institution to accept integration
as a goal means that it also accepts the white man's
declaration of Black inferiority. White institutions exist to
preserve white supremacy. Black pseudo-institutions exist
to wipe out the identity of Black people. To seek integration with someone who hates and despises you and has
declared you to be inferior is certainly some strange kind
of group insanity. To love your oppressor and seek to
persuade him to love you is certainly the acceptance of
inferiority. We cannot engage realistically in a Black Lib-

eration Struggle thinking that Black liberation means integration.

Institutions that were created to realize the Black man's dream of integration can only contribute to his continued enslavement. At this time those of us who are seriously engaged in a Black Liberation Struggle must transform our institutions. We can understand the white man's institutions, how they work, the mechanism by which he defends them, and why they are important to him. By the same logic we must understand why the creation of Black institutions is essential to our Liberation Struggle. We cannot long continue to function with *ad hoc* committees and disorganized groups trying to carry out institutional functions, because we have no real institutions. We must begin to build structures that reflect the realities of the Black Liberation Struggle. These will be separatist structures, because our basic reality is the fact of separatism which has been forced upon us. The Black man must build his future in terms of the reality of his separatism. We must begin to build separatist institutions as the only possible basis for power. We must restructure everything because everything Black people have is integrationist; our political organizations, our colleges and universities, our economic ventures, and our civil-rights organizations. We must restructure the total institutional fabric of the Black community.

White people are reacting to reality in the only way they know, because we are striking at the foundations of their power. The miserable fact is, we do not understand what we are doing. We are striking out emotionally without the philosophical and institutional foundations which are necessary for struggle. Black Christian Nationalists have the job of making understandable to Black people the only reasonable philosophy by which Black people can survive. We must do it because no other group is equipped to do it. We must co-opt and restructure the

Black church as the basic institution from which all other necessary Black institutions can be derived. We must move quickly because the oppression of Black people will increase. Unless we are building the power to withstand the repression of a police state, every Black organization, every Black leader, every vestige of Black struggle will be wiped out deliberately and brutally. The white man knows what he is doing, and the Black man's time is running out.

CHAPTER 10

Conflict:
The Struggle for Power

From the moment the institutional power structure of a group is challenged, conflict is inescapable. Any group acts to protect its power and the institutions upon which that power depends. The act of declaring those outside the group inferior and conditioning them to accept this declaration of inferiority is a part of the process by which a dominant group maintains both its power and its position. By virtue of its declared inferiority, the powerless subordinate group is systematically separated from the powerful dominant group. It is kept on the outside of the institutional power structure by which it is oppressed and exploited. The dominant group must brutally exercise its power as a part of the process of conditioning an enslaved people to accept their enslavement. The process is as simple as Pavlov's classical experiment with a dog, food, and a bell. A powerless oppressed people are taught that any rejection of subordination and inferiority will be immediately punished and that acceptance will be rewarded. In America the white man's life is lived within the framework of his institutional power structure. He struggles for status and power within the system. The Black man's life is lived outside the white man's institutional power structure. These comprise two different worlds totally separate and apart. The Black man is permitted to exist only if he will constantly reaffirm his inferiority by approaching the white man as a supplicant, with hat in hand.

Gunnar Myrdal's thesis outlined in *The American Dilemma* failed to realize that the *declaration of Black inferiority* and the separate Black world which it automatically brought into being precluded the possibility of the white man's feeling any genuine guilt about the logical contradiction inherent in the actual treatment of Black people, as opposed to the American Dream of equality, justice, and opportunity for all men. Black people are deliberately excluded from participation in the American Dream by the white man's *declaration of Black inferiority*. We are on the outside where we are supposed to be. We have been structured out of the white man's system. When we demand that American institutions be restructured to include us, or that they be destroyed as the instruments of our oppression, we are challenging the American way of life and ought to expect violence and conflict until the question of our position in American life is resolved. The white man can withdraw his *declaration of Black inferiority*, thereby permitting a restructuring of his institutions, or Black people can withdraw their challenge to the *status quo* and accept inferiority as a way of life. Unless one group is willing to alter its position, continuing conflict is inevitable. The Black man cannot naively assume that the white man is going to give up his privileged position without conflict. The Black man must therefore mobilize the total Black community in an attack upon repressive white institutional power. This is the emerging nature of the Black Liberation Struggle to which Black Christian Nationalism calls all Black people everywhere. We must escape from powerlessness through the building of Black counterinstitutions and attacking the white institutional power establishment upon every front.

Every organization and activity in the Black community must be evaluated in terms of whether or not it constitutes an attack upon the power institutions of the oppressor. Anything in the Black community which is not involved in an attack on these enemy institutions is irrelevant and meaningless. Thousands of Black people can gather in all seriousness to discuss the Black condition, as members of the NAACP and the Urban League do each year. But inasmuch as the things they are saying and the resolutions they are passing are in no way related to a basic attack upon white power institutions, they are totally insignificant and a waste of time and effort. Many Black people do not yet understand that Black oppression is maintained by the power of white institutions including the NAACP, the Urban League, and the negro church. Anything that diverts the Black man's attention and effort from an attack upon white institutions is counterrevolutionary because it is confusing his mind and dissipating his energies. No program can be valid for Black people that accepts the white man's *declaration of Black inferiority* and seeks only to help the Black man accommodate to the *status quo*. Neither legal victories nor better jobs can change the Black man's status in America. Only the power to define our own person and control our own condition can change our role in America. We are no longer begging for crumbs, we are demanding a full loaf. Organizations and leaders in the Black community must realize that we are not content to be either servants or slaves in the white man's house. We will no longer accept the inferior status accorded Black people in a white-dominated world.

We have one basic problem from which all of our other problems stem. We are powerless and we have been structured out of the dominant white institutional establishment where power resides. We waste our lives trying to pretend that we are on the inside and constitute a part of the white man's world. The dream of integration does not affect the reality of separation. Everything in the white man's world has been constructed to keep us on the outside. It makes no difference how much we long to be on the inside. It makes no difference how much we love white people or how much we try to look like them, talk like them—we are still on the outside. Our being on the outside was not our decision, but theirs. It makes no difference how long we go to school, how beautiful we are, how persuasively we talk, or how sweet we smell. All of this has nothing to do with our condition. We are on the outside because we are Black and the white man can exploit us more easily there. Perhaps even more important, his drive for status is realized by keeping us in a subordinate position. As Black people we have no choice; we must challenge the white man's institutional power structure from which we are excluded and by which we are oppressed. Only so long as we accept the white *declaration of Black inferiority* is it possible for us to accept the *status quo*. When we attack white institutional power we are attacking the total white group, because everyone in the group plays some part in strengthening the group and in turn depends on the group for personal status and security.

As a group or a nation comes into being, the individuals who make it up understand their roles and their responsibilities. They delegate authority, responsibility, and power. They know that they are going to get something from the group and that the group is going to demand something from them in return. Institutions are necessary, so they give institutions certain kinds of power to serve their needs and interests. But as the group matures, people tend to forget. Individuals rise to the top and begin to dominate institutions. The Church, the economic institution, the industrial complex, the Army and the Navy fall under the control of individuals who are torn between serving the interests of their group and serving their individual interests. Gradually they come to believe that the institutions belong to them. They become a power elite within the group. At the beginning no one is greatly concerned. Individuals have delegated authority; they expect leadership and they expect their institutions to serve their interests. It does not bother them that some individuals are putting together U. S. Steel, General Motors, and the railroads, or that Rockefeller has assembled an oil empire. They do not realize that basic control of the nation is coming to rest in the hands of a few families. The ordinary white man has limited vision and ambition. He is content to eat and sleep and not have to worry about Black people taking away his superior status. As long as his leaders give him this basic guarantee, they can fight among themselves about climbing to the top of the power elite within the white group. The little white man is not really worried until he notices that he is receiving less and less. Then he loses his job and begins to feel that he is really no better than the "nigger" on the outside. This he cannot accept, and he begins to look critically at his institutional establishment.

So the white group becomes two groups. There is a small group on top running everything, and there is a large mass of poor, disadvantaged white people on the bottom who don't have anything and who are beginning to feel resentful. They begin to articulate their dissatisfaction. "The interests of the wealthy and the interests of the poor are not the same. The poor must unite and fight." The power elite at the top has overreached and lost control of the masses of poor white people. Poor white people start to protest and organize. They split into two groups only because the poor want a larger slice of the pie. In this kind of racially homogeneous situation, socialism or communism offers the logical answer for the poor. Those at the top who control the means of production and the machinery of communication are naturally anti-communist. Socialism or communism offers a program for those at the bottom who are trying to take power away from those at the top. All of which has absolutely nothing to do with us as Black people, because we are outside of both the system and the struggles that take place on the inside. It would make little difference to us who won. We would still be on the outside. The communist fight is not our fight unless we are able to use the confusion and the division to launch our own attack upon white power. In short, we do not trust poor whites any more than we do rich whites. They are both on the inside and we are on the outside.

In every country in which there is not a large racial minority, only the threat of communism restrains the rich. In any country where Black people are a majority and there are just a few white people trying to keep power, communism or socialism can become a philosophy of libera-tion. But in America there is a totally different situation. When the white people at the bottom become seriously disturbed, the white people at the top become frightened because they can look out and see us watching and waiting to tear the whole system to bits. They feel compelled to make some kind of reconciliation with the poor, realizing that if they don't Black people are going to attack all of them while they are fighting each other. The pattern of relationships between white people in a country with a large racial minority which has been structured out of the system is entirely different from the way it would other-wise be. For this reason no place in the world is like the United States. White people always have one eye on us and the other on whatever they are doing. So everything is different. There will never be a communist revolution in America because of us. White people will be forced to design a totally new revolutionary pattern for America. Marxism does not suit the American condition.

The existence of thirty million more or less alienated Black people in America means that a framework for revo-lution with built-in protection for white supremacy is an essential prerequisite for any serious American revolution. The fact that the very nature of revolution makes this kind of built-in protection for white supremacy impossible serves to make the existence of the Black man the most important stabilizing force in American society. Poor whites will not revolt against a system which perpetuates their racial superiority unless driven to the wall, and intelligent whites who control the system are ever conscious of this point of no return. If all Black people in America must be supported at a subsistence level on public relief, we will be well worth it to the white power elite, who will pay little of the billions in cost but will reap all the benefits of the social stability forced upon the masses of poor whites by the constant threat of Black Revolution.

Members of the white group must consciously stay together to keep the Black group out. When they wrote the Declaration of Independence they meant, for white people. When they wrote the Constitution they meant, for white people. When they talk about democracy they mean, for white people. When they talk about educational equality they mean, for white people. We are structured out but most Black people do not understand this. We are still trying to function as if we were inside the system. We are still trying to pretend that it is possible for us to move into the white power establishment. We are on the outside and the integration dream is a mechanism of our continued enslavement. We can never come together as long as we feel that those nice white people in there are going to open the door one of these days and let us in. We spend our time waiting. Each one of us tries to get as close to the door as possible, so that if they open it at all, we will be the one who gets in. So we fight each other just trying to get close to the door, not realizing the simple fact that there is no door.

So in America there is little danger of serious class conflict. That's very hard for some radical white people to accept. They are always off in a corner somewhere trying to put a revolution together. They can't understand that they can't have one here. When we hear Black people trying to advocate a communist revolution, we have reached complete nonreality. How can Black people become involved in a struggle for control of a system from which we have been totally excluded? The exploitation of a powerless Black minority which has been declared inferior permits the white power elite to make concessions to the masses of white people on the bottom. They can always be conciliatory by taking just a little more away from us and giving it to them. The masses of poor whites are satisfied. Not only have they received a little more in the way of material things, but they have received a lot in the form of increased status. The distance between poor whites on the inside of the system and poor Blacks on the outside of the system has been increased. The value of being white has been increased. So we are a kind of safety valve for the power elite. They can always ease tension within the white institutional framework by depressing those outside of the institutional framework a little more. Whenever you hear poor white people hollering about how all people must get together, just understand that as soon as those in power hear them screaming they are going to take a little from you and give it to them and they are going to shut up. That is what happened to the labor unions.

When the labor unions were fighting for recognition they were "revolutionary." The CIO had all the revolutionary rhetoric. They talked about "the solidarity of the poor" and "Black and white together." That was when they were trying to get power. As they were given power they were reminded that they were inside of the white power establishment and Black people were outsiders. They forgot all about Black people. Gradually they even stopped using the words. They forgot about Black people in that they were not willing to attack the white institutional structures that excluded Black people and protected the white workers' privileged position within both labor and industry. Contract tricks such as building seniority instead of plant- and company-wide seniority were used to keep Black workers on the plantation within the ranks of labor. The disparity between where we are and where white people are is greater now than it was when the unions were first recognized. We were closer to where the poor masses of white people were then than we are now. They shut up the poor white people, maintained the power of the rich white people, and left us still on the outside, poorer and more powerless than we were before. Under these circumstances a communist revolution in America is an impossibility.

Since the beginning of America there has been little real social conflict. Basic white institutions can be challenged only by Black people who are outside the system. They have been seriously challenged just once, and that was by Black slaves. The only time white people have really felt that their basic power institution was actually endangered was when the slave insurrections swept the South. Slave insurrections could come out of no place and shake America to its foundations. White people recognized the danger. They felt threatened and they were afraid. Slave attacks on basic white institutions, however, only served to increase the stability of the white structure. They had not thought of Black people as capable of launching an attack. We were too ignorant. When the insurrections occurred they couldn't believe that they had happened. Then they wondered, "Where next?" They were frightened. The result was not the freeing of Black people (because the insurrections failed) but the solidification of the white dominant group. From the time of the insurrections the white group said that they could never permit Black people to have the slightest possibility of launching a real attack upon the white power structure. The development of the Klan following the Civil War reinstitutionalized the separation and oppression of Black people and was condoned by white people and their governmental units all over America. It was done deliberately, because all white people feared the possibility of Black revolt.

So fear served to increase the stability of the dominant

white group, guaranteed the perpetuation of the power elite, and shaped the character of white racist institutions. This white fear has never subsided. From the time of the first slave insurrection, when the first heroic handful of ragged, hungry, hopeless Black men banded together and struck out killing white people, white people have not had one night of fearless sleep. Not one day have they lived without a consciousness of the constant threat that Black people represent. This is a basic part of the American social structure and the conscious intent to keep Black people powerless. Conflict can be resolved within the white group because they have but to point at us. Internal pressures within the white group are always adjusted without disturbing the power base on which white supremacy rests. Sometimes we think of those as being attacks upon the system, and we are confused. The organization of white labor was not really an attack upon the structure. It was not an attack upon the white power establishment. Poor white people were merely exerting an internal pressure inside the dominant white group to get just a little bit more for themselves. As soon as they got it they were through.

Sometimes we think that there is a youth revolution. This again is not an attack upon the power establishment. It is merely an effort on the part of white young people within the white system to get a little more personal freedom for individuals within the white group. These pressures and adjustments serve to maintain and strengthen the white group. Youth will react eventually just as labor did. It will accept compromise and become a part of the establishment which is dedicated to keeping inferior Black people on the outside. We get confused when we see whites attacking whites within the white structure, and feel that we ought to be involved on one side or the other. Neither side is attacking the whole structure. They are both struggling within the structure. Internal pressures are in the process of forcing internal adjustments, and the power elite inside the white structure has a tremendous ability to make these adjustments—because they can always take a little more away from us and give it to any alienated white who needs a little more. So white conflict can always be resolved by the white power elite.

Abraham Lincoln played a key role in maintaining the white power establishment and its oppressive structure. The Civil War was an irrepressible conflict because a group of white working people felt threatened by the slave institution. The slave institution assured the power elite free labor and excessive profits. Wealthy white people on the top could eventually own enough slaves so that poor white workers would be unnecessary. When they were no longer necessary they would be eliminated. Poor white people were forced to destroy the institution of slavery, not to end the oppression of Black people, but to remove the threat that the institution of slavery posed for them. Abraham Lincoln said time and time again that he was not concerned about the slavery of Black people. If he could have maintained the dominant power of the white group by freeing some of the slaves, he would have done that. If he could have maintained the dominant power of the white group by freeing none of the slaves, he would have done that. He freed all the slaves only because it was necessary to preserve the dominant power and supremacy of the white group of which he was leader. Abraham Lincoln cared nothing about the condition of Black people. Black people are confused when they extol the "Great Emancipator." They have forgotten that his only concern was maintaining the white group and that he served white people well. He saved the white group. Without Abraham Lincoln, outraged white workers would have destroyed the group. If he had let them alone they would have torn it all up and we might have been really free. But he held it together.

In every crisis some intelligent white supremacist has stepped in and saved the white group from self-destruction. Abraham Lincoln saved the white group. He did not emancipate us. We are still on the outside. We are still denied the basic rights of citizenship. Down through the years we have been busy running back to Congress to get Black people included under another section of the Constitution. We never intended to be protected by the Constitution. We were outside at the beginning. We are still outside.

Many of the great white leaders Black people worship played important roles in maintaining the power and stability of the white group and its capacity to oppress us. Franklin Delano Roosevelt saved the white group from disintegration. The whole structure was falling apart. Wealthy white people were jumping out windows because they were losing their fortunes. When a white man has lost his fortune, it does not really mean a thing to the group. He loses only a piece of paper. The white group still owns whatever the paper represented. The mines, the railroads, the factories, the ship lines—those are not pieces of paper. White people who play the stock market trade little bits of paper representing tiny fragments of ownership. In a stock-market crash personal paper fortunes may be lost, but actual control of real wealth remains in the hands of the white group. The danger to the cohesion of the white group is real, however. Factory wheels grind to a stop. The system must be readjusted quickly before the poor and the hungry attack the system itself. Franklin Delano Roosevelt patched up the white system, put it back together, and made it work. Everything that he did was designed to prevent a real attack upon the system itself. Relief, WPA, NYA (National Youth Administration), NRA, every possible measure was adopted to pacify those who might attack the system. Those who controlled the real wealth screamed and protested, because Roosevelt found it necessary to take a little from them at the moment to protect their basic control of the system and its productive machinery. They were stupid. Roosevelt understood the system, how it works, and at what points it is vulnerable. He was willing to protect the white system at its vulnerable points no matter what the cost. White people could not be permitted foolishly to attack the system which maintained and preserved white supremacy. During Franklin Delano Roosevelt's administration we came no closer to getting into the white power structure than we had during the days of slavery. Actually we were closer during the days of slavery, because thousands of Black insurrectionists were attacking the power structure.

This is something we don't understand too clearly. We think that every time a white man puts the system back together he is our friend, because he alleviates a little of the personal discomfort incidental to economic dislocation. He is not our friend because he saves the white power establishment which is oppressing us. We must attack the white power structure from which we are excluded, because it is the basis of our oppression and exploitation. We have no choice. But to fight effectively we must become a group. Black people must become a Nation within a nation. It is not a matter of choice but of survival. We have no alternative. Unless we become a nation, we perish. The distance between what we have and what the white group has becomes greater day by day. We either become a Nation and confront the white group here and now or we perish. We hate even to contemplate it because as a people we hate conflict.

Anyone can tear up a Black group simply by creating conflict, raising issues, and arguing. Everyone leaves because he can't stand it. Confrontation and conflict are uncomfortable for Black people because we have been conditioned to believe that they are wrong. When we say that Black people must become a Nation and attack the institutional basis of white power, Black people draw back. All they see are dead Black Panthers on every corner. They start singing "We Shall Overcome." But there is no overcoming without an attack on the white structure.

There is no other way. And individuals cannot attack. We must come together as a group. We must become a Nation to attack the basis of white power. Look at the summers of '65, '66, and '67. We hoped that those eruptions would mark the beginning of an organized coming together of Black people across America in a unified liberation struggle. It was difficult to tell whether we were watching a mob of individuals rioting or the beginning of a nation in rebellion. We saw Black people throwing Molotov cocktails, breaking windows, and stealing liquor, washing machines, and TVs and we couldn't tell whether it was a riot or a rebellion. If it was just a group of individuals who were frustrated and angry and who suddenly erupted, it was a riot and not a revolution. There are certain prerequisites for revolution. There must be discipline and co-ordination of activities designed to accomplish a specific objective. The activities of individuals are co-ordinated by a central leadership. These things are necessary to change a mob riot into a group revolution. Those of you who were either observers or participants know that in most instances in most cities it was closer to a riot than to a revolution. The people were not organized. They had no discipline. They had no sense of leadership and they were not co-operating with one another. Black people all over town were calling the police to report what Black brothers and sisters were doing.

It was closer in many ways to a riot than to a rebellion, but it did mark the first real indication of a growing revolutionary spirit. When an oppressed people begin to come together as a group, it is difficult even for those who are in the group to know really what is happening from moment to moment. For this reason the racial conflicts of '65, '66, and '67 in New York, Watts, Newark, and Detroit were termed riots by the dominant white group, which sincerely hoped that the eruptions indicated nothing more than individual anger and frustration. They were eager to dismiss them as riots without meaning. They didn't know, but they hoped to God that they were just riots. They hoped that they were not a group attack upon basic white power institutions. They hoped that individual frustration and anger could be dealt with by giving Band-Aid treatment to the points of irritation, basketball courts for Twelfth Street, a few jobs for the "hard core" unemployed, and OEO jobs for potential riot leaders. It was not a serious social upheaval. It was just an individual thing, a few bad ones stirring up trouble. Certainly "good niggers" had not been involved. That was the white analysis, but it was more than an analysis—it was an explanation intended for us.

At the same time, these explosions were called rebellions by Black Nationalists (all of us who are trying to build a Black Nation). We said, "These are not riots, they are rebellions. It is the beginning of a Black Nation. The spontaneous coming together of an oppressed Black people into a self-conscious revolutionary group. The beginning of the process of Nation building." White people were more worried than they cared to admit. They spent millions of dollars trying to find out whether Black people were rioting or rebelling. They used the traditional criteria: find the conspiracy, who was behind it, who coordinated it, where was the central leadership. They could not find the conspiracy they were looking for because it did not exist. It was just the beginning! They could identify perhaps four or five looters who worked together. That was all they could find, and although it disturbed them a little, they finally concluded that there had been nothing more to it. The Kerner Commission launched hundreds of investigations, and they all concluded that there was no conspiracy. That was true. There was no conspiracy. But Black Nationalists were closer to the truth when we said it marked the birth pangs of the Black Nation. It actually did represent a new kind of Black attack upon the white power structure. White people sensed that it was more important than it appeared to be, and decided that it could not be permitted to happen again. They would increase the fire power of the police with sophisticated weaponry and up-to-date communication equipment. But they still were not certain whether or not it was a riot or a rebellion.

Poor ignorant white people knew that the attack was a rebellion. They didn't care what they read in the newspapers, what Moynihan said, or what anybody else said. They knew that it was a rebellion because they had sensed the difference in the attitude of Black people long before the first brick was thrown. They had seen it in our eyes and in the way we walked and the way we talked. They had recognized the new Black identity long before the sociologist and the psychologist had. Ignorant white people began to buy guns and get ready, saying, "This is a rebellion. Even if Black people don't understand it, we do. This is a rebellion and we are going to get ready for it." The big white folks smiled because they figured they knew how to control it. Perhaps Black people were moving toward nationhood, but it was a very slight movement. In a sense, the masses of Black people were moving as though according to plan, even though there was no plan. Individuals were responding to the same stimuli and to the same irritations. This is the beginning of a Nation, when a people begin to feel the same way and to respond in the same way. From the dream of integration and identification with the dominant white group, Black people were beginning to move toward a separate identity. If you identify and seek to integrate with white people, you don't throw bricks through their windows and set their buildings on fire. So in a sense these riot-rebellions marked the emergence of a new sense of Black identity separate and apart from the white group. This was an essential step in bringing a people together and preparing to attack white power institutions.

Somehow white people never seemed really to grasp the meaning of revolution. They misunderstood as usual. They think of revolution always in terms of terrorism, of

Black men running to the suburbs and killing white women and children. That would not be a revolution, or at best it would be a very primitive kind of revolution. Revolution is an attack on the power establishment and its institutions. This need not necessarily involve hand-to-hand fighting, bloodshed, and terrorism, although it may. The idea of Black people attacking white institutions disturbs white people, no matter what tactics are used. That is why the words "separatism" and "nationalism" are considered dangerous by white people and by many Black people. They know that inherent in the concepts of separatism and nationalism are confrontation and conflict with the oppressor and the total rejection of the white man's *declaration of Black inferiority*. A Nation cannot exist without attacking the source of its oppression.

The idea of Black separatism irritates and troubles white people. So they warn Black people to beware of separatists, and they induce national "leaders" like Roy Wilkins to issue statements that presume that separatism is bad. He denounced a plan which gave Black preachers in Massachusetts a million dollars to deal with urban problems in their own way. He said that it was bad because it indicated the acceptance of separatism by white people. He did everything possible to block it. He interprets Black separatism exactly as a white supremacist does. He knows that as soon as Black people accept separatism, they will attack every white institution which supports the white *declaration of Black inferiority*. Black people are becoming self-consciously a group. What began as individual frustration is becoming an attack upon the power institutions of the dominant white group. That is why the Black Panthers are receiving so much attention from the power structure. Their numbers are insignificant, but when they declare war upon the police they have launched an attack upon an institution which is a part of the white structure. Whether they shoot any police or not, their very declaration constitutes a threatening attack; and the power structure reacts to wipe out the Black Panthers, who represent the embryonic military power of an emerging Nation. Whether you like the Panthers or not, they represent a military vanguard of the Black Nation. Their murder is a part of the price of Nation building. White people recognize their significance more quickly than Black people. The Panthers make all kinds of mistakes because they were never in an army before and they must learn by trial and error. But they are an army, and it is trying to attack one of the institutions that is oppressing Black people. We will find as we go along that there will be Black people attacking white institutions in other ways on other fronts. Together they will give form and shape to the emerging Black Nation and its struggle to escape from powerlessness.

We must take power from the dominant white group. That is the only way we can get it. Power is not received as a free gift from heaven. If you want it you must take it. That is why we are concerned about Nation building and that is why group conflict is inevitable. A Black group seeks power and a white group fights to hold it. This is the basic cause of the repression which is sweeping America. The white group senses our Nation building and feels threatened, so every white institution is coming to its defense. If Black people don't recognize what is happening and don't come to the defense of the Black group just as if we had institutional foundations, we are going to be in serious trouble. Whether you joined voluntarily or not, all Black people are a part of the Black Nation. When white people start shooting down Black people they are not going to make fine distinctions. We can attack or wait until we are attacked. This is the nature of group conflict. Black Christian Nationalism calls the Black church to a position of central leadership in this conflict. When we say Black *Christian* Nationalism, we are not modifying the basic nature of nationalism nor are we minimizing the necessity for struggle. We are saying that the struggle in which we are engaged is the will of God as revealed by the Black Messiah.

PART 4

We Define Our Program

CHAPTER 11

The Gospel of
Black Liberation

A revolutionary Black church that seeks to explore new directions cannot hope to take everyone along on the journey. But certainly in a world in which people are dissatisfied with the church—as most Black people are, because they are finding less and less relevance in both its message and its program—there ought to be an increasing number of Black people willing to make the sacrifices necessary to structure a revolutionary church totally committed to the Black Liberation Struggle. We begin with the basic premise that the Black church is essential to the Liberation Struggle, because it is controlled by Black people and is capable of being restructured to serve the Black Revolution. We also assume that a Black Revolution is impossible unless Black people are able to build an entire system of counterinstitutions, created and designed to serve the interests of Black people as all American institutions now serve the white-supremacy interests of white people. To build a system of counterinstitutions we must

first build one basic Black institution which has the acceptance of the masses of Black people, facilities and economic
stability not directly dependent on the hostile white world,
and the capacity to spin off all the other institutions needed
for the establishment of a Black Nation within a nation.

These basic concepts are a source of general confusion
to many young Black revolutionaries who have rejected
religion in general and the Christian religion in particular
—because it is a white man's religion, is counterrevolutionary, and serves to perpetuate the Black man's enslavement
by teaching otherworldly escapism and distracting his
attention from his powerlessness, exploitation, and oppression. The Christian Church has served the Black man
poorly, and certainly a white Christ sitting in heaven at
the right hand of a white Father God could not be expected to champion the Black man's cause against the
cause of his own people, who owe their present white
supremacy at least in some measure to the inspiration of
his divine whiteness. White Christianity is a bastard religion without a Messiah and without a God. Jesus was
not white and God is not white. Jesus was a Black Messiah, the son of a Black woman, a son of the Black Nation
Israel. Historical and anthropological evidence abounds to
prove the Blackness of Jesus, so let us not waste time whipping a dead horse (or a nonexistent white Messiah).

Historically Christianity is a Black man's religion created
out of the experiences of Black people in Africa. This is
not to say that Christianity was the one and only Black
man's religion. It was the religion of a small, numerically
insignificant, mongrel tribe of nomads who wandered for
centuries mixing, intermingling, and intermarrying with all
the peoples of Africa and the Fertile Crescent. They were
a Black people racially, culturally, and religiously. All
Black people in America do not derive from these Israelite
tribes, but some do. Neither do all the Black people in
America derive from any other African tribal or religious
group. The ruthless white slavers took slaves wherever

they could find them. All the great religions of the world came from the deep spirituality of Black people. Black Coptic Christians kept Islam from moving below the Sahara for more than two hundred years. Black Jews scattered throughout the world after the fall of Jerusalem and the fort of Masada. White European and Russian converts to Judaism still bear the marks of their African blood in their physical features and hair textures, as many white Jews will admit. Only one point is really important. Black people have a legitimate right to be Christian or Jewish if they wish. Historically both religions belong to us. A Black man in America can follow any of the historic religions of the world and be confident that he worships as his Black forefathers in Africa worshipped at some time in the Black man's past.

Christianity is not a white man's religion. He has only distorted it, used it for his selfish purposes, and for a time concealed from us its true origins. We have now reclaimed our covenant as God's Chosen People and our revolutionary Black Messiah, Jesus. Slave Christianity which we learned from our white masters is counterrevolutionary and has served to perpetuate our enslavement. The revolutionary teachings of the Black Messiah commit us to revolution and Nation building. Today our task is clear. We must free the Black church from slave Christianity and call it back to the original teachings of Jesus, and we must liberate the Black church as an institution and restructure it so that it can become the center of the Black Liberation Struggle. Young Black revolutionaries who cannot put aside their ideological hangups (largely inherited from white people) and be about this very serious business must stand accused of frivolity and of playing games with liberation. Elderly, middle-of-the-road, integrationist Black Christians—who cannot put aside their love for a nonexistent blue-eyed white Jesus, the dream of a heaven off somewhere in the wide blue yonder, and their identification with their white oppressors, to follow a revolutionary Black Messiah, the Jesus of history—obviously love whiteness more than truth and are willing to accept the white man's *declaration of Black inferiority*. Neither of these segments of the Black community will play a significant role in the Black Liberation Struggle, because neither realizes that it is Nation-building time and we struggle for our very survival. Neither is willing to accept historical, philosophical, theological, or pragmatic truth. Neither is willing to submerge his individualism in the emerging Black Nation, accepting discipline, accountability, and the simple faith that nothing is more sacred than the liberation of Black people. Neither is willing to pursue liberation for Black people by any means necessary.

There is a difference in the conditions under which a white man lives in America and the conditions under which a Black man lives anywhere in the world. The white man has power. Existing institutions belong to him. Communications systems belong to him. Everything belongs to him and functions to serve his interests. Everything in the world is now being used to serve the white man's needs. It was set up to serve him and if it fails to serve him adequately he can change it, patch it up, turn it around anyway he likes until it does serve his needs. The Army, the police, the National Guard, the industrial complex—all of these things exist to serve the white man's interests. It is reasonable that Black people live in old inner-city houses while white people live in new houses in the suburbs, because they control all of it. If we controlled it, we would live in the new houses and they would live in the old houses. This is not an accidental thing. The white man controls the system so he uses it for his benefit. We are not a part of the control group and receive what is left. Not only do we get only what is left, but deliberately, consciously, and systematically we are kept powerless so that we cannot seriously threaten his control. He deliberately keeps our children ignorant so that they will not be too competitive. In a computerized age, he designs the educational system so that we do not learn about computers. In the twentieth century, we are still being taught horse-and-buggy skills and ideas. This is by design. We must understand that we live in a world in which we are disadvantaged in ways that are not always obvious.

If you are down and out and broke, you don't have any place to live, and you are hungry, you know that you are disadvantaged. But when you are riding around in a Cadillac, have a split-level home, three or four silk suits, and are wearing fifty-dollar shoes, it is difficult to believe that you are really disadvantaged. It is hard to add it all up and say that you are really disadvantaged. You own too much. You have things. Your house looks good, you keep your wife looking good or you keep your husband looking good, whichever the case may be. It is hard to think of yourself as disadvantaged. When you see other Black people who don't have anything, who are getting beaten up by the police, who are out of work and being sent to Vietnam, you say to yourself that there must be something wrong with them. You're making it, why can't they? You are working two jobs and everything else you can on the side, but you are making it, so you say, "I just don't feel like the white man can be as bad as they say or he wouldn't be letting me get by." It is difficult to feel disadvantaged when you have a few material things.

But being disadvantaged or advantaged really does not depend on what you have. You can be free and not enjoy any of the material luxuries. But if you are free you know that you can control the system which determines who is to have material things. If you don't have things you have dignity, because you have power. You don't have to bow down to anyone, because it is your system. It all belongs to you. In a sense you own everything. You are a man. But the man who has material things without power doesn't have anything. He is being permitted to exist in the midst of a system which is controlled by someone else.

He is dependent absolutely for every nickel that he receives. He can drive the Cadillac only so long as the man permits him to drive it. He can have the suits, the shoes, the house, only until the man decides that he doesn't want him to have them anymore. Some Black people possess things but do not have any system by which they can create things for themselves. So they are dependent.

All Black people are disadvantaged because we are powerless. We don't really own anything. We are just like the slave on the plantation in his rags. He didn't own anything. He wore what the man let him wear. Today the man is letting some of us wear slightly better clothes than he let us wear on the plantation. His enlightened self-interest dictates how much he is willing to let us have from day to day, and this has nothing whatever to do with either our ability or his goodness. He has found that it pays to let a few Black people have decent houses, nice clothes, and good cars. It is a control mechanism and it serves to confuse other Black people. But it is still a plantation situation because we don't own anything. We don't control anything. We are still living on the plantation as long as old master is making all the decisions.

On the plantation old master could have let us live in a nice house. He could have built slave quarters just like the big house (we did the building anyway). He could have said, "Build me some pretty slave quarters. I want one hundred houses out there just like the big house. Get out there and build them." We would have been out there building and singing because we were going to live just like old master. When we finished he could have said, "These are your new slave quarters. You can move in now and live." When we moved into the fancy slave quarters they were still slave quarters because he still controlled them and us. And if he could tell us when to build them and when to move in, he could tell us when to move out. So we were still slaves. He could have moved us into the big house and moved himself into a slave hut. But he was still giving the orders; he wouldn't have been a slave because he lived in a little house. He was the master because he controlled the system and he gave the orders and we did what he said. We would have been more confused in the big house than we were in the slave cabin, because we would have walked around in the big house thinking that somehow the situation had changed, without realizing that only a shift of power could change the basic situation. Either you have power or you don't, and if you don't and you are not trying to get it, you are a natural-born slave. If you don't have power and you are satisfied in your powerless condition, you are even worse off than you think. When old master put you in the big house and you didn't have any power but you enjoyed the things, you were worse off than you were in the slave cabin. In the slave cabin you knew that you were helpless and powerless, and you were dissatisfied. In the slave cabin you were trying to figure how in the world you were going to kill old master and take his power. You were better off in the slave cabin. For a man to be enslaved and not know that he is enslaved and not to struggle to end his enslavement means that he is not only physically enslaved, but his mind has been enslaved.

That is the problem we face today. Our physical enslavement we could endure. Even getting beaten up once in a while we could endure, because we do that to each other regularly. It is our mental enslavement that keeps us confused. We do whatever the man says, because everything we have comes from him; but more pathetic is the fact that we accept this condition and try to pretend that we are a part of his power structure. We play that it belongs to us, too. "It is not his, it is ours," we think, and that is the basis of our confusion. That is why Black folks act foolish in so many situations. Many Black teachers think that they are teaching in our school system and whatever is there is good for Black children. Once they realize that it is not our school system but their school system, designed to keep Black people in chains, they will begin to fight against the system. In every classroom they will realize that it is not what they are supposed to be teaching that should be the lesson of the day, but what they are not supposed to teach because they are fighting an enemy system. You are fighting hostile power and you must seek to subvert it at every opportunity. A Black lawyer who goes into court thinking that the court is blind and established for the maintenance of justice is a fool. The court is not color-blind and is not established to secure justice but to perpetuate the enslavement of Black people. If he goes into court thinking that he is just arguing an objective case he is going to lose every case that involves the maintenance of white supremacy, because the court is not designed to be either equitable or just. To see Black judges sitting on the bench deciding cases as if they were white is enough to make a Black man cry. Many times they are so happy just to be on the bench that they make more white-racist decisions than a white judge would dare to make. They are confused by their very presence on the bench.

This is the framework within which we seek to build a revolutionary Black church. Black people everywhere feel that they are really a part of the white man's system. When they ride down the street they feel that America belongs to them. They take visitors from out of town around and show them *our* city. This is *our* new art center. This is *our* General Motors building. A Black individual with this attitude cannot possibly face reality. However much you would like it all to be yours, it is not. You don't own it, you don't control it, and it is part of a system which has been designed and constructed to keep you on the outside. You can ride around and look at it but it does not belong to you. Look, but don't touch. The feeling that it belongs to you corrupts your whole life. Everything you do is corrupted by this unconscious feeling that the world around you belongs to you. You can't talk about a Black church until you realize that you are Black and that all Black people are outside of a system that the white man controls. Only then will we realize the necessity for the creation of power designed to serve the interests of Black people. As long as we are satisfied with thinking that we are part of the white man's system we cannot deal with the creation of power institutions. This is the basic weakness of the existing Black church.

The Black church is a white institution ministering to Black people with no awareness of the fact that it is not a part of the white church and that it must lead Black people in a liberation struggle for power. So the existing Black church proceeds to preach, teach, and program as though Black people are a part of the white man's system. Look at any Black church you know or think back to the ones you grew up in. Ninety-nine percent of everything they do is predicated upon the proposition that we live in a world in which white and Black people share power, justice, freedom, and opportunity equally. So the whole program of the Black church is unrealistic. When we seek new directions for the Black church, we must understand the basic framework within which Black people live in America. As Black people we exist outside the white man's power structure. It is his system, he controls it, we are outside of it.

We must begin to put together Black institutions to serve Black people. Black institutions must be prepared to seek power, which means that they must inevitably face confrontation and conflict with the white power structure, because no one gives up power easily, quietly, or happily. The only way that power is transferred is through confrontation and conflict. The church is no exception. The Black church exists in a world in which the conditions of Black people will not be changed until Black people are willing to confront and accept the inescapability of conflict. The existing Black church is opposed to conflict. It teaches that conflict is opposed to the will of God and that we must love everyone and turn the other cheek. This is a basic lie which the church preaches Sunday after Sunday. The whole life of Jesus was a life of conflict. If we reject conflict, then we must find a Messiah who did not deal in conflict. Jesus was in constant opposition to the established power structure. The course of his ministry was determined by his flights to avoid assassination. Jesus was a threat to the establishment. He sought to lead the Black Nation Israel in opposition to the establishment. The establishment intended to stop him by any means necessary and finally he was lynched. When we seek new directions for the Black church, then, we are facing the necessity of bringing the church back to its historic roots. Not to the roots that the old slave master gave it during slavery days, but back to the historic roots of a Black Messiah who was concerned with the liberation of Black people.

Any liberation struggle must involve confrontation and conflict. There is no such thing as a peaceful, calm, quiet liberation struggle. Even Dr. King's nonviolent phase of our liberation struggle involved conflict. Every time he went into a city and organized a mass demonstration and brought Black folks out to protest in the streets, white people confronted them and there was conflict. The fact that they kept marching and protesting day after day made it conflict in spite of the fact that they did not strike back. This not striking back was an early phase of our struggle. We had not yet learned that you cannot fight effectively without striking back. It takes time to learn. We had not yet learned that you can't fight a war with the enemy in key positions of leadership in your army. You cannot win if the enemy is directing his army and yours as well. All our organizations and institutions had white folks running them. We thought we had picked good white folks and therefore they were on our side. Their position was impossible because they were a part of the system of oppression under which we suffered and from which we were excluded. But we were learning, and the conflict and the struggle were essential to the learning process. In seeking new directions for the Black church, we are not unaware of the simple fact that the day will come when Black people who are seriously engaged in the Liberation Struggle can no longer tolerate a Black church which is preaching a counterrevolutionary message and exerting a counterrevolutionary influence. In some way it must be redirected and its programs reoriented so that it can begin to deal with the realities of the Black man's existence.

The Black church must face the simple fact that its basic problem is a theological one. Young Black people and a large segment of the total Black community criticize the Black church because of its irrelevance to the problems of the Black community, without realizing that the Black church is acting and programming in terms of its individualistic otherworldly conception of salvation— preaching that salvation is the free gift of God, made available to those who believe by the sacrifice of Jesus on Calvary, and that we are saved by faith and not by work. The Black church cannot theologically justify participation in a Black Liberation Struggle designed to transform the world into a heaven on earth. Most Black people who criticize the church unconsciously share its otherworldly individualistic theology, even though they reject it consciously and emotionally. Black people suffer from a theological split personality just as the Black church does. Most of the things Black preachers use to answer charges of irrelevance cannot be justified within the framework of traditional Black theology. The Black church is trying to move in response to the growing clamor of the Black community without facing its theological obsolescence. Dr. King and the Southern Christian Leadership Conference had little theology to justify their involvement in the process of trying to change the world rather than preparing people for heaven. At some point we are going to be forced to decide whether we want heaven in the sky or here on earth, and which is compatible with the teachings of Jesus.

For a number of years new directions for the Black church have been implicit in the theology, philosophy, and program of the Shrine of the Black Madonna, and were implied in the initial call issued by the Black Christian Nationalist movement. Our first Black Christian Nationalist Convention offered us an opportunity to reaffirm our Black Protestant Reformation and begin the task of restructuring both our ritual and our program. A serious seeking for new directions demands new program ideas and restructuring of the church. And that is difficult for any people who are accustomed to particular ways of doing things. We must consider such seemingly trivial matters as whether or not it will be desirable for the Black church to continue as an eleven-o'clock Sunday-morning operation. If we honestly believe that nothing is more sacred than the liberation of Black people, we have made a basic theological statement to which ritual and program must conform. The idea that the church must function at a certain hour on Sunday morning was not derived from the Black Liberation Struggle. Many people are never going to come to church on Sunday morning. Even the use of the word "church" must be examined. Perhaps more and more we ought to stop saying "church" at all and say "Nation" all the time. The very word "church" has limiting connotations. It always calls to mind some little church back in Georgia or Alabama or somewhere, and your conception of what a church is and what a preacher is is defined by this memory. When church does not fit into this pattern it makes you uncomfortable even though you don't know why. The church ought not be forced into the mold of childhood memories that are unrelated to the Black Liberation Struggle. The connotation of "Black Nation" is entirely different from the connotation of "Black church." Just by the new label we imply that we are talking about all Black people and that we recognize the simple fact that a Nation has a right to struggle for freedom, whereas in the minds of most people a church is a kind of escapist institution and has a right to concern itself only with individual salvation. Perhaps we ought to begin to deal with the concept of nation as opposed to the concept of church and not use the two interchangeably. One is concerned with individual salvation and the other with Black liberation. For us, church is a small unit of the nation in which a group of people are working together for the liberation of the Nation, not a little group of individuals engaged in the task of assisting each other find their way to heaven.

Finding your way to heaven can be a very time-consuming occupation. You organize a thousand people, and if they are all committed to helping one another get to heaven their program is cut out for them. They go to church on Sunday morning and the preacher tells them about heaven. He makes it sound both attractive and attainable so that they will come back to listen again. All activities are geared to preparation for heaven. Everything is worship-centered, so you have three hundred people singing in the choir and another hundred ushering. Everybody seeks to participate in the central worship experience. Program areas that are unrelated to heaven are hard to find. Some modern churches are building housing projects, but these are really designed to endow and undergird the going-to-heaven programs. The housing is hardly intended to help anybody because most of the houses are built with government financing, and government restrictions are too expensive for anybody who cannot afford another house anyway. This kind of activity does not constitute a program but a church endowment. It is also a matter of image. If Reverend X has a housing project then Reverend Z must also have one, or people will say that Reverend X has a more effective relationship with God—which brings us back to the preparation-for-heaven process. Deliverance is a very competitive field. It is difficult to find a program that relates to Black liberation in a Black church.

The traditional Black church preaches a gospel of salvation. If you are saved from sin you can go to heaven, because that is what salvation means. To be saved you must put aside the sins of the world or come out from the world. Saints gather together in the church in order that they may be kept pure and go to heaven when they die. The whole program is geared to otherworldly salvation. The message is the good news of what Jesus did for us on Calvary. What Jesus did on Calvary makes our salvation possible, not anything that we can do for ourselves. God has already done it through Jesus because God was in Jesus reconciling the world unto Himself. If Jesus had not been nailed to the cross we could never have bridged the chasm which separates us from God. We are evil. We were conceived in sin. The very act of procreation is sinful. We were conceived in sin. We live in sin. We are a depraved and fallen people because Eve was tempted and revolted against God when she ate the apple. Only God could bridge this chasm of sin. So Jesus came into the world in order that we might be reconciled to the perfection of God through faith. We are saved while we are yet sinners, if we believe. We are saved by grace and not by works. If you seek this kind of salvation in the name of Jesus, a total church program is implicit in your theology.

A gospel of salvation carries with it a preparation-for-heaven process which is a complete church program. It is concerned with petty personal sins rather than collective social guilt. You resent it if anyone suggests that heaven is not out there. The whole gospel of salvation is a vicious circle. You run around trying to be saved so you don't do anything else. You neglect the problems and oppression which are destroying you because you are concentrating on your personal otherworldly salvation. Heaven is a state of being. No man ever went to heaven in chains, I am sure of that. No Uncle Tom ever sneaked into heaven, I know that. No one who spent his life trying to be accepted by white people ever got into heaven. However you define heaven, you can't get in acting a fool and reducing your life to a selfish absurdity. You will be held responsible for the collective social, economic, political, educational, and cultural sins of your particular nation. God will not judge you as an individual but as a member of a group.

An individualistic gospel of otherworldly salvation has a universal appeal, because we are all guilty and we are all afraid to die. We do not know what is on the other side of death, but everyone is afraid to die. On the other hand, we do not want to be held accountable for the social sins of the group of which we are a part. Every white man would rather stand trial for his individual sins of sensualism and materialism than for his collective sin of racism. So the gospel of salvation serves to protect us from our group guilt. What German wants to face God charged with the sins of the Third Reich? What white American wants to face God charged with the collective guilt of slavery and four hundred years of systematic oppression and exploitation of Black people? The gospel of individual salvation offers men a way out, an escape. We must move from a gospel of individual salvation and begin preaching and programming for a gospel of liberation, and we must make it plain. People have come to the Shrine of the Black Madonna for years without really understanding that we are preaching a gospel of liberation which is diametrically opposed to the gospel of individual salvation. They hear the gospel of liberation and transpose it in their minds into the traditional gospel of individual salvation. The Black Liberation Struggle is being held up by our inability to mount an effective Black theological revolution. As a new Black Protestant Reformation sweeps across America, unshackling the hands and minds of Black people and releasing the Black church from its Babylonian captivity, the Black Revolution will begin. Power for Black people will not come from the barrel of a gun but from liberated minds willing to accept the theology of here and now expressed in the Black Christian Nationalist Creed.

There are basic differences between a gospel of liberation and the gospel of salvation. The two are not the same and we cannot build a Black Nation without rejecting the gospel of salvation. You are either trying to do one thing or the other. With the gospel of liberation everything is defined in terms of the Black Liberation Struggle. That which supports the Struggle is good. That which advances the Struggle of Black people is moral. The Black church must find its new direction in the acceptance of a new theology which holds that nothing is more sacred than the liberation of Black people.

The theological basis for the gospel of liberation can be found in the life and teachings of Jesus. Not in his death, but in his life and in his willingness to die for the Black Nation. To say that God was in Jesus reconciling the world unto Himself at a particular moment on Calvary when Jesus died upon the cross is not the same as saying that God reconciled men unto Himself in the life and teachings of Jesus, which gave men a new conception of human dignity and inspired them to fight to be men instead of slaves. God was in Jesus and He can be in anyone who is willing to dedicate his life to the Liberation Struggle. There is no unbridgeable chasm which man cannot cross if he but shakes off fear and individualism and enters into the Struggle. The chasm which separates us from God is our own selfishness and individualism, which makes us more concerned about our individual salvation than we are about the liberation of all Black people. The liberation of all Black people is salvation for each of us. In seeking after individual salvation, each individual is struggling to get to heaven through something which God can do for him. In struggling for the liberation of the Black Nation, we submerge our individualism and struggle together to realize the will of God for all Black people in our everyday lives right here on earth. We would make of this earth a heaven in which Black people can live with dignity, a world in which we are not ashamed to die and leave our children. The gospel of liberation is not a gospel of salvation. We work to liberate the Black man's mind so that he can liberate himself and help his Black brothers and sisters liberate themselves. More Black people are ready to die in the "glorious revolution" which has not the slightest chance of success than are ready to study, think, analyze, plan, and organize a realistic liberation struggle. Our first and most difficult task is to liberate the Black man's mind—even though it is much simpler to promise him personal salvation and eternal life in heaven with God and ask only that he wait patiently upon the Lord and remember that God never gives us more than we can bear.

The first task of the Black church is to liberate the Black man's mind. It must be willing to deal with truth and stop telling fairy tales to men and women. If the Black church is to move in new directions it must learn the nature of reality and become committed to truth. The Black church must become a teaching church. It cannot be a church that says what people want to hear. It must help Black people begin to think realistically about everyday problems. This is the process by which we will move from a gospel of salvation to a gospel of liberation. We must define liberation, define struggle, analyze tactics, and develop methods for the struggle. We must look at history to find out what works and what does not work. The Black church must define liberation in terms of reality. Then we must put together the organization and structure to make it effective. We must learn to deal with individuals. We seek to bring all Black people together in one Black Nation so that we can struggle together for liberation. We will not all start at the same stage of development; some of us will be more emancipated from our white identification than others. But no prizes will be given for the kind of individualistic personal pride and arrogance which uses a little knowledge to destroy the unity of a group. The submergence of intellectual pride is difficult, but the individual who uses his knowledge and skills to destroy the Nation will, as Jesus suggests, be put out of the Nation and treated as a Gentile. The Nation must become a group working, thinking, and planning together. One of our basic problems is the development of a process which will make this possible.

Only gradually will individuals begin to understand and feel the relationships that must exist within the Nation. The willingness to submerge individualism means more than just saying that we must unite because we are all Black, or even that we must unite to protect ourselves from genocide. These are valid reasons for uniting but will not in themselves make a Black Nation come into being. We must deliberately reject the values and thought patterns of the white Western world. We must consciously create a new Black mentality and value system which recognizes the equal worth of every Black brother and sister. This will be the power of the Black Nation, and nothing can be permitted to relegate it to a secondary position.

Black unity must mean that we are willing to bear with one another's weaknesses and share with one another ideas as well as dollars. The new Black church will not ask for faith in Jesus, a mystical Saviour, but for faith in one another and commitment to walk in the footsteps of Jesus, as we join in the Black Liberation Struggle as defined by the Black Christian Nationalist movement.

CHAPTER 12

Building a Promised Land

We do not understand the struggle in which we are engaged. We identify with the enemy. This is true of Black people everywhere. It was true during the days of slavery. It was not as Brother Malcolm said. The "field negro" also identified with the slave master. That was one of Brother Malcolm's mistakes. He thought that because a Black man was out in the field he had less of a sense of identification with the white man than the "house negro." That was not true. It does not make too much difference whether you are a field negro or a house negro. You can identify as easily with two thousand dollars as you can with forty thousand dollars. You identify with two thousand dollars because you hope that someday the white man is going to let you get forty thousand dollars. Identification does not have any real relationship with where you are or the depths of the degradation to which you have been driven. If you are oppressed you identify with your oppressor, unless you can understand the process by which you are being enslaved.

Serious commitment to the Black struggle involves an intellectual understanding. It is not entirely an emotional thing. You can be emotionally aroused and your emotions may drive you to seek intellectual understanding, but emotional involvement is not enough to keep you committed to the struggle. Your emotional response is little more than angry frustration because the white man refuses to integrate with you. It does not indicate a rational understanding of your relationship with your oppressor. You can become very angry and proceed to run up and down the street with a rifle shooting white people. That does not indicate any profound understanding or comprehension of reality. You are being driven by emotional Black rage, but you are not thinking and you do not understand. If you shoot one hundred white people this act does not make you a Black hero. You are just a confused individual without a program reacting emotionally to your individual frustration. There could be a situation in which shooting one hundred people might be a very necessary thing, but it would have to be related to a rational program and certainly would not be used unless all other possibilities had failed. By identifying with the enemy we accept his *declaration of Black inferiority*. We see his power, and we recognize our powerlessness. So we cry out in protest. Crying out in protest is the basic program of Black people. It is the general program of any people who are powerless and do not understand the basis of their powerlessness.

When Moses returned from Midian, Israel was not in Egypt trying to put together a program for liberation. The people were hurt, they were filled with anguish because there had come "a Pharaoh who knew not Joseph." They were saying, "We used to be a people and we were accepted like everyone else; now we are slaves, and someone else tells us what we can do and what we cannot do. Someone else takes the profit from our endeavors. Now we are slaves and we cry out in anguish." But that is not a program. Crying out in protest is not a rational liberation program, even though Dr. Martin Luther King did it for years. No oppressor ever went into hiding because an oppressed people were crying out in protest. If I were an oppressor I would be happy when the oppressed were crying out, because I would know that as long as they confined themselves to crying out in protest they were not going to do anything meaningful. I might even send people among them to encourage them to cry out louder, as white people obviously did in marching with Dr. King and supporting his cries of protest. There is no understanding involved, only physical suffering and mental anguish. The Southern Christian Leadership Conference is still hung up at this infantile level of operation because they are afraid to move beyond the position where Dr. King left them. When we cry out in protest because we want so much to be with white people, our very cry of protest is a cry of love.

We do not understand the social dynamics so we cry out in protest. That was the basic reality of Dr. King's movement. Individuals who had been crying out by themselves came together and cried out as a group. Individuals who had been pleading with God by themselves came together and Dr. King prayed for them. Those who had been singing the old spirituals and hoping that God would hear came together and sang "We Shall Overcome," but there was no basic difference, they were still only frustrated individuals crying out in protest. What kind of rational program was involved in the whole movement? What rational basis even existed for the development of a liberation program? They held meetings, but these were merely "crying out" meetings. They marched in the street, but this was just another way of crying out. What were they demanding when they marched in the street? "Please set us up an interracial committee so that we can integrate! Accept us, please." Then Bull Connor turned the fire hoses and the dogs on them and put the cattle prods to them, and they suffered happily because by suffering they would redeem Bull Connor. "Eventually, even as he puts the cattle prods to our women and to our children, he will be redeemed and he will love us and he will not be able to do it any longer." That was the program. We can say that it was a beautiful program. It was only beautiful for people who have no understanding of process, social analysis, or program. It was a pseudo-program, a sham program.

Dr. King was doing the best he could within the framework and limitations of his understanding of the problem. We can say that it was beautiful to believe that God would do the kind of things he asked God to do. Certainly he had faith, and we can say that it was beautiful that in this kind of world any man in his right mind could believe that God would act that way. However beautiful it was, there was no way in the world that it could have worked. It was unrealistic. Neither God nor man could have been expected to respond to that kind of irrational behavior. It was fantasy. We think that we have moved a long way from Dr. King's position today. We have given up nonviolence and protest, but we *have not moved* very far. We never really were nonviolent. It was a clever tactic. We believed that if we were going to redeem the white man we had to be nonviolent. But before every demonstration Dr. King would send his lieutenants through the Black community trying to talk the Black brothers out of their guns, saying, "At least give nonviolence a chance." Fortunately the brothers with the guns had no more program than did Dr. King. They had no more of a program for guns than Dr. King did for his dream. It was not too hard to talk them into giving them up because they didn't know what they were going to do with them anyway.

Dr. King's dream sounded more like a program than individuals sitting around poolrooms and barbershops with guns, so they were persuaded to give them up. Classes in nonviolent self-defense were a big part of the movement. You lay down, curled up, and put your hands over your head to protect your vulnerable parts, so that you could stay alive and come back again to have another try at redeeming Bull Connor. We haven't moved very far from this nonprogram stage of development today. We must understand that there is no possibility for the development of a rational program until a people can accept the fact that they are dealing with an enemy who will do anything to preserve his power and privilege. Across America today we have an almost total absence of a Black program. Black people are not fully convinced that they have an enemy. They know that many painful things are happening and they cry out in anguish. Then we strike out in anger, frustration, and hostility. This is the second stage. We strike out blindly at the nearest point of frustration and irritation, whatever that is: the corner grocer, the slum landlord, the police, anyone. Black rage is usually blind rage. "I must do something, take some kind of action, hit somebody, make somebody pay because I've been hurt." We can strike out at the nearest point of irritation, but unless we have defined the enemy we are fighting paper tigers. We are burning down things that have little to do with the real power of the enemy. The enemy has not been defined. This is a part of our own frustration. We know that our actions are not changing our condition. The pain continues and we still have a deep hurting sense of self-hatred and inferiority. This also is a part of our Black rage. When we strike out in blind rage we strike out against other Black people much of the time. We cannot identify the enemy, so we hate ourselves. It must be our fault. It must be the things that we are doing. It must be the bad things that the Black brothers and sisters are doing that are causing the problems. We feel the hostile power everywhere around us but we cannot see it, we don't know where it is coming from, we cannot define it, we cannot identify it—we can only fear it.

The third stage involves defining the enemy, and here Black Christian Nationalism has difficulty communicating with many Black people. When Brother Malcolm said that the white man is our enemy Black people were frightened and they have not yet recovered from that fear. Even today we do not want to admit that the white man is an enemy who must be dealt with as an enemy. We do not want to admit that he is an enemy who has declared us inferior and who has set up an elaborate institutionalized system to oppress and exploit us. Tell Black people that we are fighting for survival and that concentration camps and genocide are not impossible in America and they will turn nervously away, protesting that the white man is not that bad. Sometimes you wonder just how bad they think he is. He took us from Africa packed on slave ships like animals. He killed more than one hundred million Black people just bringing us across. He raped a continent and destroyed a civilization. He made us work for nothing to build a country for him and make him wealthy. He raped our women and made "niggers" out of our men. How can we say, "He ain't that bad!" What else can he do? Today he is taking Black men to Vietnam to fight yellow men for a cause that is opposed to the interest of Black men in every way. Twenty percent of the front-line troops in Vietnam are Black.

Until we define the enemy we are not prepared to move to the fourth stage, which consists of program development. How are we going to program to deal with our problems of exploitation, brutality, and repression unless we know who the enemy is? We might as well be sitting in churches praying to go to heaven. We might as well say that the enemy is the devil and pray against him, unless we are willing to face the simple fact that the white man is the enemy. We run around fighting all kinds of mythical enemies. We end up saying, "You know, the thing wrong with Black people is the fact that we won't get together." Then we make not getting together the enemy. Not getting together is not the enemy. The enemy is the white man, who deliberately and systematically oppresses and exploits us. We don't get together because we have been programmed to mistrust each other by the white man. We don't get together because we have no basic philosophy on which we can get together. Upon what basis are Black people going to get together? Being Black is a condition, not a program, and we can't make a program out of being Black. Why do we go around saying that our basic problem is unity? You hear it everywhere. "The thing that is wrong with us is we won't get together. The man would treat us right if we just got together." We are speaking out of the depths of our self-hatred. Our problem is not one of getting together.

First we must find out who the enemy is and then we must come together in a program designed to deal with a specific enemy. If we don't know who the enemy is, what difference does it make whether we are together or apart? If we know who we are fighting, then we can become a people because the enemy is fighting all of us, and the enemy will drive us together. But as long as we do not know who the enemy is we will think that our problem has nothing to do with white people. We will decide that it must be a matter of personal worth. The white man rewards us and punishes us in terms of our personal worth. If we don't have anything it is because we are not worth anything—because if we were, the white man would give it to us. So what can we do? Let's try to improve ourselves. Let's take our children and make them exceptional so the white man will have to recognize them. We cannot see that the white man does not have to recognize anything we put together. The white man does not recognize Black genius unless it serves his interests. You can be the best engineer in the world, but why must the white man recognize you? This is the strange never-never land of Black fantasy. Bill Matney is certainly not the best radio-television announcer in the world, but NBC white folks drag him around the country as though he were the last "nigger" in captivity. It suits their interests to have one Black announcer on display, and they get their money's worth out of him.

We cannot begin to program anything until we know who the enemy is. And when we know who the enemy is, we know that it is not just my enemy and it is not just your enemy, it is our enemy. And if we are fighting a common enemy we must come together. If we believed that the white man was out to destroy us, there would be nothing that could keep us apart. All of us in America, Latin America, the West Indies, and Africa would come together. Pan-Africanism would be an inescapable reality. As soon as Black people identify the enemy we will unite with every Black person in the world who is fighting the same enemy.

How ought the Black church to be functioning in the world today? What ought the Black church to be doing? What ought the program of the Black church to be? Our long-term goal is Pan-Africanism, the bringing together of Black people across artificial national boundaries as one people, realizing that we are an African people. No matter where we were taken by the slave ship, we are still an African people. In a very real sense the Black church must substitute the ultimate goal of Pan-Africanism for the white man's ultimate goal of individual salvation in heaven with God. Pan-Africanism is the objective toward which we struggle. It is the Promised Land for Black people, a Promised Land which includes all Black people in all countries. In addition to the struggle for liberation as Black people wherever we happen to be, it also includes the faith that someday we will reassemble in our homeland, Africa. We project Pan-Africanism realizing that there are certain things which must be done here on the corner of Linwood and Hogarth in the city of Detroit. If we are ineffective here it is very doubtful that we would be more effective in the Congo, or in Ghana. What would increase our effectiveness in dealing with Black people in

Africa? Methods, techniques, and programs can be used anywhere if they are realistic and sound. Many times we criticize Black people for not running headlong to support anything we announce, when we really don't have anything to announce in the first place. We just announce that we would like all Black people to come together behind our banner. Then we look back to see who is coming. Black people have listened to that kind of nonsense for more than a hundred years. We are tired of someone calling us together to help him work something out. More and more we are saying, "If you don't have anything worked out, Brother, we don't have time to be standing there behind you while you try to put something together." Work it out, create a program, point a direction, define methods, define objectives, and then call us. If the Black church is going to turn its attention from heaven to earth, it faces the same problem. To be effective it must develop a rational program. This is difficult for Black preachers who have spent their lives dispensing the free gift of God's salvation with little serious thought or effort.

If we come into the Black church and say that we are gathered together in the name of God, we must believe that God created us equal to any other people on the face of the earth. If God created us equal, it is up to us to secure and maintain an equal status. If the church offers less than this to Black people it is not speaking for God. "Created in the image of God" means that we are willing to stand up like men, to defend our own people like men, and to defend our communities like men. The church must program for power. It must. The Black church must help us take as much power as we are able to take and help us utilize that power for the benefit of Black people. Many Black people are unable to face the question of power. They caution, "Power will make us just as bad as the white man." So what? There is a big difference in being just as bad as white people and being on top, and being just as bad as they are and being unable to do anything about it. We are even worse than they are in the sight of God. God is more disgusted with us for accepting our oppression than He is with white people for oppressing us. I know that God doesn't want me to let people walk over me and He does not want me to let anyone walk over my people, if I can help it. The kind of church BCN is trying to build is a church capable of putting together a power base for Black people. When we suggest building a power base we raise questions of morality for many people. Is it moral for us to be building a power base? There is no other way to exist.

We are trying to build Black institutions and our only possible point of beginning is the Black church. As wrong as it is, as bad as it is, as weak as it is, as corrupt as it is, as counterrevolutionary as it is, as Uncle Tom as it is, it is the only starting point we have. We have churches on every corner housed in buildings of every size, shape, and description. We have nominal control over it, but because of our confusion and psychological sickness it does not serve our interests. We have billions of dollars tied up in church buildings. If we are seriously interested in Black liberation we cannot realistically afford just to turn and walk away and leave this huge capital investment in the hands of the enemy. We must devise a way to co-opt it, restructure it, and make it the heart and center of the Black Revolution. The Black church must be programmed for Black liberation. That is why the things we are doing at the Shrine of the Black Madonna are of crucial importance. We are seriously attempting to restructure a Black church upon the basis of a Black theology. Upon this restructured institutional base we can build anything else we need. We can spin off economic, educational, political, and cultural institutions as rapidly as we can train the necessary specialists. The Black church restructured as a power base can guarantee the success of any organized undertaking designed to serve the interests of Black people. Just think what Black churches could do

on the Sunday before any election. We could ask everyone to stay home from work on election day to work at
the polls. All Black folks would vote and cover the polls
the rest of the day. The church would be dealing with
political power. The Black church must program for
power, realizing that you cannot use power until you get
it. Only the Black church has the potential capacity to
mobilize the total Black community.

As the Black church begins to conceive of its basic task
as liberation here on earth rather than salvation in preparation for heaven, it will be forced to re-evaluate critically a
total organizational structure designed to inspire rather
than to teach. The basic teaching method used by the
church is the Sunday service of worship which depends
on the sermon for its very limited content. Obviously the
sermon is a very clumsy teaching method, as is the so-
called church school. They continue to be used because
the church is not expected to teach. The development of
training methods is basic to a new Black church. It is
not enough to come down front and say, "I believe in
liberation and I want to be a part of the movement." You
must participate in a training program involving lectures,
discussions, and reading. You must come to understand
the position of the church and the nature of the Liberation Struggle. You must learn a point of view, a philosophy, and a theology before you can participate
meaningfully in the life of the church. You cannot learn
it all on Sunday morning! Sunday worship is a festive
occasion, a celebration. We celebrate the Black Nation
on Sunday morning. If there were but ten of us we would
be celebrating the fact that ten of us constituted the Black
Nation. The church must teach, and members must learn
if we are to build a Black Nation. We must learn how to
influence the Black community and how to organize the
Black community if we are going to confront the enemy
who is our oppressor from a power base. We must build
centers where people can come to be trained and go out

to work. Until we can build this kind of institutional structure, the Black church will be insignificant and the condition of Black people will be hopeless. The Black Church can lead Black people to the Promised Land.

The Promised Land symbolizes man's eternal dream of a heaven on earth. Our Biblical account begins with Abraham. God spoke to Abraham and sent him out to found a nation. "I will be your God and you will be my people." Abraham was in Chaldea and God said, "This is not where you belong; separate yourself from these people, establish a nation." The concept of separatism as opposed to integration is a recurring theme in the Old Testament, and God is always on the side of separation. "You must separate from people who are wrong, who are against you, who are corrupting you, and set up a nation in which you can control your own institutions." He told Abraham to go out and found a Nation. What does it mean to found a Nation? It means to go somewhere and begin to set up institutions on which a Nation depends. And when God says, "I will be your God," He means that He will support your efforts with power. This is the history of the Black Nation Israel. God supported the Nation-building process. The existing nation was corrupt, so God sent a man out to establish a new Nation. Israel began with the search for a Promised Land, a place to build a Nation. Moses continued the search when he led Israel out of bondage. A Nation's search for a Promised Land flowing with milk and honey, where every man can sit with dignity under his own vine and fig tree, is a basic part of the religious experience. A Nation has a right to expect its religious institution to be engaged in the task of building a Promised Land. A religious institution which is not so engaged serves no valid institutional purpose. The search for a Promised Land is basic in the Old Testament and in the teachings of Jesus. But men did not always clearly understand what they were doing. They would get confused and interpret the Promised Land in purely geographic terms. They would get possession of a piece of land and think they had it. Then they would degenerate and start fighting and exploiting each other and they would lose the Promised Land, because they had identified with it geographically. The Promised Land is a group of people living together and sharing a communal way of life with love for each other. It is not a place but a way of life.

I remember talking with Brother Malcolm and his brother Wilfred. Someone was complaining about how bad conditions in the Black community were. Wilfred laughed and said, "The way niggers are today I wouldn't want to be in a Nation with them. If we can't change them, you can count me out." This is basically true. Most Black people would not care to be in a Nation with "niggers." But a Nation with Black brothers and sisters would be another thing! If we can again become human beings with a sense of dignity and decency, everyone will want to enter the Promised Land with us. But a Promised Land is more than geography. During the Egyptian captivity there were people who wanted to stay in slavery. During the Babylonian captivity there were those who did not want to leave Babylon. When they finally were given their freedom, some stayed behind. They were no longer seeking a Promised Land. People get confused about what it is they are trying to do. The Black church has the task of trying to lead Black people to a Promised Land of which many cannot even conceive. This is the first step. Black people must be able to dream of living together with love and dignity, and desire this kind of world for themselves and their children. If we can accept the possibility and desirability of this kind of Black communal living, then we can begin to program for its realization. We have only to determine realistically what we must do to build here on earth the dream which already exists in our minds.

Black Christian Nationalism calls Black people to commit themselves to the possibility of building a Black communal society here on earth by accepting the BCN training and discipline necessary to free the mind from individualism and materialism and by laboring to restructure the Black church to provide a power base for the systematic building of the Black Nation.

CHAPTER 13

Programming for Liberation

The theology, philosophy, and program of Black Christian Nationalism has been developed at the Shrine of the Black Madonna in Detroit. We realize that everything we are trying to do requires the coming together of Black people everywhere, so our ultimate goal is Pan-Africanism. We are Pan-Africanists and our basic loyalty is to the worldwide unity of Black people and to the liberation of our motherland, Africa. We support the Black African, West Indian, and Latin American liberation movements. We support the Malcolm X Liberation University in Durham, North Carolina, which is training American Black people for settlement in Africa. We support the growing independent African Christian movements which are developing along lines similar to those of Black Christian Nationalism, and we seek to establish ties with them. We support cultural nationalism, which serves to focus attention on African history and culture and motivates Black creative artists to find inspiration both in the Black man's glorious past and in his heroic struggle to be free. This is the direction in which we move and the framework within which we work. We accept the basic truth that whatever we do on a local level has validity only if it contributes to the development of international Black unity, power, and liberation. We do not project Pan-Africanism as a distant goal which will someday require our support in one great battle for the liberation of Africa.

Pan-Africanism calls us to involvement in the liberation struggles of all Black people now! We cannot participate meaningfully in the liberation of Africa until we understand that we are oppressed by an enemy who maintains his power throughout the world by a simple white *declaration of Black inferiority*. Black people everywhere must attack the institutional power structure by which we are oppressed. Black people must attack this single structure wherever they are. We must build Black counterinstitutions as a basis for Black unity and power. We must decide the points of enemy weakness at which united attacks will be most effective. These carefully selected and constantly shifting points of confrontation and conflict must have the support of Black people everywhere. Having selected a target, Black people must make available whatever resources are required without diminishing aggressive confrontation on all other fronts. Co-ordinated worldwide attacks on the white power establishment are inescapable prerequisites to the climactic battle for the liberation of Africa. The unity, discipline, and power necessary for the liberation of Africa must be put together in Black communities across the world. Only a Black Nation which exists in the hearts and minds of Black people everywhere can battle sacrificially for the liberation of its homeland, Africa. Black Christian Nationalism calls Black people to join together in this struggle. Our program can only be understood in this Pan-African context.

The Bible is the history of man's struggle for liberation —real people confronting the everyday problems of life. Abraham, Moses, the prophets, and Jesus were all trying to program for freedom. Israel would not listen to Jesus define the enemy in terms of the Roman power structure, including the Temple in Jerusalem, the Jewish tax collectors, and the wealthy Black Israelites who supported the power system of the oppressor. Israel did not enter the Promised Land without the development of a liberation program. At first Israel failed because of poor organization, ideological confusion, and inadequate program development. It took forty years in the wilderness to develop a viable liberation program with the basic educational emphasis upon those under twenty years of age who had not been psychologically destroyed by the experience and conditioning of slavery. The story of the Promised Land did not begin with Moses and it did not end when Israel fought its way into Canaan. The Promised Land is a state of being in which people achieve the kind of existence God intended men to have. God created men in His own image, and therefore we are dissatisfied when we are enslaved. But our reaction to enslavement can be either effective or ineffective depending on whether or not it contributes to changing our condition of powerlessness by attacking the institutional power establishment from which we have been systematically excluded. Black Christian Nationalism defines seven stages of Black response to enslavement in America:

SEVEN STEPS TO BLACK LIBERATION
(Stages of Black Response to Enslavement)

1 *To seek integration.* An effort to become a non-people (characterized by self-hatred, identification with the oppressor, and "niggerization"). A period dominated by the NAACP, the Urban League, and the slave church.

2 *To cry out in protest.* Still seeking integration (characterized by sit-ins, freedom rides, mass demonstrations, freedom marches, and civil-rights legislation). A period dominated by Dr. Martin Luther King and his "dream."

3 *To strike out in violent rage.* Striking at points of irritation with neither organization nor fully developed philosophy (characterized by the breaking of identification with the oppressor; the development of Black consciousness, Black identity, and "Black Power"; and the spontaneous eruption of ghetto rebellions). A period dominated by Malcolm X, Stokely Carmichael, and Rap Brown.

4 *To analyze the nature of our oppression.* In order correctly to define the enemy and the institutional basis of oppression (characterized by the emergence of Black Christian Nationalism and the new Black theology). *The Black Messiah* by Albert B. Cleage, Jr., published in November, 1968, by Sheed and Ward, New York.

5 *To develop an educational process.* Including new methods and techniques for the mass dissemination of information in the Black community (characterized by the development of BCN educational research and BCN training programs).

6 *To restructure the Black church.* As a Black institutional power base serving the interests of Black people.

7 *To confront the enemy.* Attack the white institutional basis of Black oppression and build Black counterinstitutions.

Many Black groups are loyally following programs which are no longer aiding Black liberation. The NAACP started out years ago committed to integration. In spite of ideological confusion it accomplished some good. Now its total program is irrelevant but its present leadership cannot come to a national convention, admit that integration is impossible and undesirable, and recommend a shift to a program designed to recognize the Black man's separate existence. Instead they waste time and energy denouncing separatism. It seems that the Black man is programmed to self-destruct at the word "integration." Organizationally and individually Black people fall apart when the white man says, "O.K., I'll integrate." He doesn't have to do anything, he just says, "O.K., I'll integrate," and our protests collapse—because we have no position beyond the futile dream of integration!

National Black organizations, including the Black church, reflect the inescapable fact that Black people are psychologically sick. For four hundred years we have lived with powerlessness and the white man's *declaration of Black inferiority*. We have been conditioned by oppression, brutality, and exploitation. We have been systematically structured out of white institutions and the white power establishment. We have become a nonpeople seeking to disappear into the "superior" white group through integration. We have accepted the white man's *declaration of Black inferiority* and, seeing ourselves through the white man's eyes, we have come to hate ourselves and to identify with our white oppressor. We have accepted his materialistic, individualistic value system, and in every way we have contributed to our own enslavement. Our powerlessness has been perpetuated by our inability to build genuine Black institutions and our refusal to accept genuine Black leadership. Black pseudo-institutions existing in the Black community (such as the Black church) have actually served the interests of the white oppressor. So-called Black leaders have been selected by the white oppressor. These Black leaders have been accepted by Black people only in a limited interim capacity, while they waited for integration. Black people have been prepared to delegate only limited powers to Black leaders who shared their Black inferiority. Only Marcus Garvey and Elijah Muhammad were given genuine leadership with power and authority prior to the emergence of Black Christian Nationalism with its centralized authority, rigid discipline, and fixed body of truth.

We must restructure the minds of Black people. We

must make a total change. Nothing constructive can be accomplished until Black men's minds are transformed. Let it be clearly understood that we are not talking about traditional education and training. For many years Black people placed great emphasis on the white man's educational process. Du Bois stated our faith in education beautifully with his concept of the "talented tenth." He believed that ten percent of Black people who were educated and really committed to the Black struggle could lead the Black masses to liberation. It was a naive concept which did not take into account the psychological sickness of Black people. The talented tenth used their education to exploit not lead the Black masses. Dr. Du Bois did not realize that the kind of education which white people gave Black people only served to strengthen and reinforce the white man's control. The white man's education serves to support his *declaration of Black inferiority* and to train Black people to reject everything Black and seek total identification with the white world. We cannot honestly expect white education ever to do anything more. This serves the white man's interests, and the schools—all of them—make up his educational institution. We have all been conditioned by the same process, both in the white man's schools and in the white man's world. Place a group of educated Black people in one room and a group of uneducated illiterate Black people in another room. Ask both groups to discuss the problem of Black liberation, and both will express the same trite, superficial ideas and speak from the same false premise. If either group is able to break through the chains of mental bondage it will be the uneducated group. They both believe that white people are essentially good and can be persuaded to change their evil ways. Both believe that much of the fault for our condition stems from our own shortcomings. We just have not measured up! We really are a little inferior. Both groups believe the same things. A group of college presidents, professors, doctors, lawyers, and preachers are going to come out with exactly the same program as the one put together by a group of uneducated Black people. On election day they will vote in exactly the same way, if the members of either group happen to vote. The methods which the white oppressor uses to miseducate Black people are ninety percent effective. Our situation is hopeless until we are willing to face the facts: (1) We are psychologically sick; (2) we are systematically conditioned to support the mechanics of our own enslavement; and (3) we are being systematically miseducated by the white man's educational system and mass-communications media.

Black Christian Nationalism approaches Black liberation realistically. First we must restructure the minds of Black people. We have developed a complicated training program (a Black educational process) incorporating the ideas in Chapter 4, "Salvation: A Group Experience." We have rediscovered the concept of Nation and African communalism, uniting all aspects of life in one total experience with power to heal and transform. We use the three processes by which the individual is able to submerge his individualism and become a part of the Black Nation: (1) The individual is transformed through a rational group experience in which he must face reality as mirrored in group confrontation, criticism, and love; (2) the individual is transformed through the emotional experience of a rhythmic religious ceremony deliberately designed to break down the walls of individualism; and (3) the individual is transformed by the sudden Pentecostal experience which occurs unexpectedly after the walls of individualism have been eroded quietly through sustained, deeply emotional group experiences over an extended period of time. Regular classes in yoga and gungfu (karate) are offered because their emphasis on meditation, discipline, and physical fitness help counteract the white man's "niggerization" process. Step by step the old brain which the white man has ruined must be replaced by a new brain capable of absorbing new information, building a new self-image, and rejecting individualism and materialism. The old brain cannot accept new information because whatever is taught becomes a part of the old lies involving the acceptance of Black inferiority and a sense of self-hatred.

Because there are three phases in our training program (creating the motivation to change, unlearning the old, and learning the new), we place great emphasis on our school of Black studies (Alkebu-Lan Academy), which replaces the traditional church school and works with elementary and junior-high children and young people. If we can start with five-year-old children it doesn't take so long to untrain, and the task of training is greatly simplified. But even so, a great deal must be unlearned because a five-year-old has already begun to learn from his parents and to catch their psychological sickness. High-school and college-age young people who come into our student groups are partially motivated to change by a general alienation from both white society and their parents.

Everyone who joins the Black Christian Nationalist movement must go through a twelve-month training program before formal initiation into full membership. Two additional years of advanced leadership training are recommended. When an individual walks down front and says, "I want to join the Black Nation," he publicly admits that he desires to be changed. In accepting him we agree to assist in his transformation. If he has too much arrogance to admit that the white man's oppression has messed up his mind, the Black Nation can do little for him. The total Black Christian Nationalist program is founded upon training. This is our basic contribution to the Black struggle. No other Black group in America (other than the Black Muslims) is willing to face seriously the fact that Black people are psychologically sick and have been systematically conditioned to hate themselves and love their oppressor. Every other Black group tries to program with Black people the way they are (which is obviously an impossibility) or to readjust prejudices and misconceptions (which is equally impossible). Our basic twelve-month training program starts with Kuanza,* the act of beginning, and is called Kua, the process of growing.

BCN TRAINING OUTLINE

KUANZA   (The act of beginning). Acceptance of BCN creed, covenant, pledge of loyalty. Baptism into the Black Nation.

KUA   (The process of growing).
            (Basic orientation—"G training," three months—Black group dynamics.
            Moja—First level—three months—BCN theology.
            Mbile—Second level—three months—BCN philosophy.
            Tatu—Third level—three months—BCN program (introduction to Information Center—"Seven Steps to Understanding").

KUANZISHA   (The initiation into full membership).
            Nne—Fourth level—Assignment of program responsibilities.

ADVANCED LEADERSHIP TRAINING 1

Tano—Fifth level—required for Shrine officers and ministerial training groups. (Eligible for BCN Central Committee).

ADVANCED LEADERSHIP TRAINING 2

Sita—Sixth level—required for ordained ministers and program specialists.

Saba—Seventh level—BCN Central Committee.

* Names are taken from Swahili, a Bantu language.

Members who complete the basic twelve months of training are initiated into full membership with the solemn ceremony of Kuanzisha. Those who cannot participate fully because of age, health, hours of employment, or out-of-town residence may be designated either contributing or associate members.

Membership Classification

Membership in all Shrines is divided into three classifications:

> A Participating Member (with vote)
> B Contributing Member
> C Associate Member

Members in each category indicate their intentions as follows:

PARTICIPATING MEMBER (with vote)

I commit my life to the Black Christian Nationalist Movement, and accept the discipline which this commitment places upon me. I will support its total program by attending services and activities regularly. I will participate in the action group to which I am assigned and will seek other opportunities for service. I will contribute the basic pledge of ten dollars per week or more when I am employed. I will accept such leadership responsibilities as may be given to me.

CONTRIBUTING MEMBER

I support the Black Christian Nationalist movement. I will attend services of worship regularly and will contribute sacrificially. I am unable to participate in an action group or to accept organizational or leadership responsibilities.

ASSOCIATE MEMBER

I accept the Black Christian Nationalist philosophy. I will attend services of worship whenever possible and will contribute regularly to its financial support.

The basic BCN unit of organization is the action group to which all participating members are assigned following

Kuanzisha. In a local Shrine, action groups have seven important functions which determine their agenda and program:

1 To perform assigned tasks, to support the total BCN program, and to involve members in Nation-building which is the program of BCN at work in the community.

2 To help members grow in their understanding of the theology, philosophy, and program of BCN through group discussion which leads to increased commitment and participation, and to help members grow in the development of necessary skills through attendance at training workshops, classes, and cultural-center activities and programs.

3 To recruit program specialists from the Nation as needed.

4 To provide opportunities for group fellowship which foster unity and the friendly spirit of African communalism.

5 To participate actively in the action council and its related community organizations.

6 To recruit new members for the Black Nation through a planned program of community outreach designed systematically to touch the total Black community.

7 To develop a leadership cadre of seven capable of organizing a BCN Information Center, a BCN Shrine, and a BCN cultural center in another community, city, or country. This program should be developed in co-operation with the Ministerial Training Group.

All BCN training programs utilize the resources of the BCN Information Center, which offers a standard one-hour multimedia presentation of graphs, maps, tapes, films, slides, speakers, books, and leaflets combined for maximum impact. The Information Center is used to train and re-train BCN members, and is incorporated into the curriculum of the training laboratory for the Ministerial Training Groups and action group cadres preparing to be sent into the field on extended assignments. In addition, the Information Center serves to introduce members of the Black community to Black Christian Nationalism. A cadre beginning a mission in a new community or city will open a BCN Information and Training Center as its headquarters. The Information Center is standardized and, with the exception of minor adjustments dictated by the size and shape of the building in which it is housed, will be the same anywhere in the world. Residents of the Black community are invited to attend the basic multimedia presentation which is offered at regular hours daily. They may also attend classes if sufficiently interested. Books, posters, buttons, and African art objects are sold to help defray expenses. BCN memberships will be solicited and when a base has been established a Shrine of the Black Madonna will be opened with regular services and activities. This will be followed by the opening of a cultural center offering additional events. The new Shrine will be a replica of the Shrine of the Black Madonna in Detroit.

The BCN Information Center's "Seven Steps to Understanding" can be simply summarized:

1. The white man has declared all Black people to be inferior (the rights of Black people were not considered in either the Declaration of Independence or the Constitution of the United States, as evidenced by the fact that they were written and signed by slave owners).

2. All American institutions are racist and serve to maintain white supremacy.

    a. All white people are controlled by white racist institutions.

b. All white institutions exist to serve the interest of white people.

c. All Black people are oppressed and rendered powerless by exclusion from white power institutions.

3. The Black man has been programmed systematically to accept the white man's *declaration of Black inferiority* (this is the process of "niggerization" and the basis of the Black man's dream of integration).

a. Black pseudo-institutions are controlled by the white power structure and serve the interests of white people and not the interests of Black people.

b. Black people have been programmed for individualism and self-hatred.

c. Black people have been programmed for materialism which takes the form of an obsession with trinkets, trivialities, fads, and conspicuous expenditure. This is "niggerization."

4. Black people were not always enslaved. In Africa we were a proud and beautiful people.

a. We recount the glories of the Black man's past. (All major religions came from Africa.)

b. Christianity is historically a Black man's religion.

c. We outline the white man's degradation of Africa (and the co-optation of Christianity).

5. BCN must "de-niggerize" Black people in order that they can love themselves and unite to build Black counter-institutions which serve their interests.

6. The Black church is potentially the most powerful institution in the Black community.

a. It is irrelevant and counterrevolutionary.

b. It is the only base from which Black people can

begin the building of Black counterinstitutions.

c. The actual building of a Black Nation depends
on the building of Black counterinstitutions.

7. It is Nation time. We must act now!

a. There is growing repression and the threat of
genocide (McCarran Act, "no knock," pre-
ventive detention).

b. We must co-opt the Black church now!

c. Pan-Africanism is our goal. We must stress international co-operation. (We are an African
people and our oppression is international).

BCN Information Centers are also engaged:

1. In maintaining a library of books and publications
relevant to the Black Liberation Struggle and in maintaining a national and international communications network
with Black leaders and organizations.

2. In researching, editing, publishing, and producing
educational materials (books, films, tapes, slides, and posters) for use in the Black church.

3. In sponsoring workshops in community organization,
communication techniques, economic development, Black
studies, and community control.

4. In sponsoring classes in African history, geography,
and religion.

5. In the development of new teaching techniques utilizing modern electronic equipment essential for any serious
effort to transmit ideas to masses of Black people through
the Black church. These techniques include tape-recorded
lessons, filmstrips with sound track, 16 mm. sound films,
and electronic video recordings (cassettes).

6. In researching the effects of news stories on the Black
community and the possibility of systematically counter-
acting the white news slant by building in "resistance"
(programming the Black community to resist news which

has not been processed to conform to the reality of the Black experience).

7. In developing new methods for the dissemination of corrected (processed) information so that gradually built-in resistance to unprocessed information is developed throughout the Black community.

Black Christian Nationalism is a movement and we demand serious commitment as Jesus, the Black Messiah, demanded serious commitment when he called his Disciples. He expected men to leave everything to come and follow him with complete loyalty, discipline, and devotion to the liberation of Black people. We have only fragmentary information about the organization of the Disciples of Jesus. We know that there was a central committee of twelve closely associated with Jesus, and that there were Disciples in Bethany, Jerusalem, Galilee, Judea, and throughout Israel. We also know that the Zealots functioned as a revolutionary underground part of the same movement and that the movement had enough support to enable the Disciples of Jesus to move freely about the country without money or any visible means of support.

Since the discovery of the ancient Dead Sea Scrolls in 1947 we know more about the monastic life of the Essene order than we do about the organization of the Disciples of Jesus.* The Manual of the Essene Order is much more explicit than the Gospels, because the Pauline emphasis of the early Church shifted attention from the things that

---

* Editor's Note: Scholars do not agree that the "Dead Sea people," commonly referred to as the Qumrân sect, were Essenes. André Dupont-Sommer and other leading authorities, however, consider such identification inevitable, and Albert B. Cleage, Jr.'s own belief is best expressed by himself: "Despite the reluctance of some scholars to identify the Qumrân sect with the Essenes, I am convinced that the sect was at least a branch of the Essenes and that the Dead Sea Scrolls bring a new dimension to our understanding of Jesus, the Black Messiah, and the early Christian community."

Jesus had done to the mystical significance of his sacrifice on Calvary. Undoubtedly the Essenes influenced Jesus, but the short duration of his ministry precluded the possibility of his following the Manual of the Essene Order. Black Christian Nationalism does not hesitate to borrow from the carefully developed organizational structure and procedures of the Essenes, discarding that which is not relevant to our twentieth-century condition. We have adopted their procedure for accepting new members into the movement. No longer do we accept a brother who comes down front as totally committed. He has only indicated a desire to be transformed. Like the Essenes we accept him as a neophyte or beginner. After a year of careful serious training he is initiated into a full membership, but for two additional years he is considered a novice, and is expected to pursue advanced leadership training and to accept program responsibilities under supervision.

It would be easier and more effective if we lived together in a commune as the Essenes did. We could help, support, and strengthen each other if we lived together. We are moving in that direction and our annual Camp Karamu is the first step. As soon as possible we must operate our own year-round camp and housing communes. It is demoralizing to be forced to leave the Black Nation, scatter in all directions, and mix with people who are still psychologically sick and confused. The strength of the Essenes was in large measure due to the fact that they lived together. The neophytes and the novices came into a community and they spent time each day seeking understanding. They would talk. They would be instructed. The Essenes tried to make sure that each individual who came in was properly instructed and if he was uncooperative they put him out. It is just as important to put out as it is to take in, and we often forget this. A great weakness of the church is its reluctance to let anybody go. In most churches you can do anything but bomb the building and people will fight to "keep you in the fellow-ship." That is a mistake. If an individual is not trying to build a Black Nation, dropping him ought to be a very simple matter without emotional overtones. The Essenes had it all worked out and it was a beautiful system. When Jesus talked to fishermen by the Sea of Galilee, he was talking to men who understood this kind of movement. That is why he could say, "Come and follow me." John the Baptist had been killed and he was assuming leadership of the movement. When they followed Jesus they knew what it meant to join a movement and to be committed.

In military language Jesus was building a cadre. The building of a cadre involves the training of officers essential to a regiment or larger unit. It itself is not a regiment. It can be just a half-dozen people, but they have all the basic skills necessary to lead a regiment. So you can merely add a thousand people to the cadre and you have a regiment ready to function because the leadership has been trained. The cadre has all the skills necessary to train and lead the thousand. Jesus did not expect to move multitudes of people to make basic changes. He picked individuals who seemed to be capable of becoming a cadre for the Nation he was building. He selected individuals who were committed to the revolution and asked them to leave whatever they were doing then and devote themselves to the liberation of Black people. Jesus trained many cadres other than the twelve Disciples. At one point in his ministry Jesus sent out seventy disciples two by two into all parts of the nation talking, preaching, and organizing. This is the meaning of cadre—individuals trained to organize, teach, and proclaim the same message which Jesus taught.

BCN defines SEVEN BASIC PROGRAM AREAS in its attack on oppressive white institutions and in its building of Black counterinstitutions:

1 NIA (purpose)—Research and Training
2 IMANI (faith in Blackness)—Communication

3 UMOJA (unity)—Community Organization and Action

4 KUUMBA (creativity)—Cultural Development

5 KUJICHAGULIA (self-determination)—Political Education and Action

6 UJAMAA (co-operative economics)—Commune Development and Consumer Organization

7 UJIMA (collective work and responsibility)— Development of Medical and Social Service Institutions

Program specialists in each of these seven areas are being trained, and an ideal organizational cadre will contain at least one program specialist in each area.

Jesus worked hard training the twelve. This was his central committee. We can see the difficulties he had getting them to understand. They made all the mistakes that human beings could make. He talked to them, he prayed with them, he preached to them, and they still came back and said the wrong things. The sons of Zebedee could still ask, "Lord, when you come into power may I sit on your right hand and my brother on your left hand?" Individualism! All that they had heard they did not understand. At the Last Supper Jesus was still trying to get his Disciples to understand what had to be done. When he entered Jerusalem on Palm Sunday the Disciples were waiting. On the Wednesday of Holy Week he went to Bethany to meet with a larger group of his followers. He preached to multitudes but he did not count on the great crowds, but on the small cadres with whom he worked. Black Christian Nationalism seeks to use the methods of the Essene order to train cadres capable of going out and organizing Shrines, Information Centers, and cultural centers in the Black urban ghettos and rural areas of America and throughout the world. The Black Nation will be built around small well-trained cadres who go out from our central commune and training center to organize and train

Black people everywhere. Because Black Christian Nationalist cadres will of necessity be widely separated across the world, rigid discipline during training, highly centralized control, and carefully standardized organizational structures are mandatory. There can be no place in the movement for individualistic improvisation.

Our basic contribution is our willingness to accept reality in the liberation of Black people and to reinterpret our Christian faith in the light of reality. This makes us different. For nineteen years we have been in the vanguard of the Black Revolution. We did not leave the Black church to participate in the Black Revolution; we discovered that the Black church has the philosophy, the institutional strength, and the stability to lead the Black Revolution. So for years, nineteen years, we have been in the vanguard of both the Black Revolution and the Black church. We have managed to stay at least five years ahead of national Black leadership. It has been a lonely and thankless role we have played but a very necessary one. There have been moments during the nineteen years when we became almost popular. That was when we had slowed up and others had begun to catch up with us. But for the most part a vanguard organization is not destined to be popular because it is ahead of the position which most people accept as normal for the period. Today it is interesting to watch Black people and Black leadership embrace the positions which we developed years ago, even as they avoid the more logical positions to which we have now evolved. It is interesting to hear ideas which we advanced years ago proclaimed today as new discoveries. As we move forward with the development of Black Christian Nationalism, a rational philosophy of Black separatism, we know that Black people have no choice but to follow where we lead, because there is no realistic alternative for this time and in this place.

The first anniversary of the Shrine of the Black Madonna in 1954, one year after our organization, was celebrated approximately at the same time that the Supreme Court was issuing its historic decision outlawing racial segregation in public education. The history of the Shrine of the Black Madonna is inextricably one with the struggles of Black people during this crucial period. We have offered leadership to the Black vanguard which has moved Black people from integration toward separatism. As Black people have moved from a complete unthinking acceptance of integration, the white man has unmasked himself, revealing the depths of his racial hatred. As we have come to understand the white man more fully, we have tended to move toward separatism. There are, of course, many Black people who still cannot face reality and who still dream of integration. But the movement away from integration cannot be stopped because the reality of the white man's hatred is now visible everywhere. *Newsweek* magazine did a study of the Middle American, describing how he feels frustrated, betrayed, and threatened by Black people, and how he is becoming more and more open with his hatred. It took one of the largest samplings ever made of white opinion and reported that the average white person is more and more willing to admit his hatred for Black people. That may sound strange to a few white people and to many Black people. But it is merely the confirmation of a fact which we have long recognized. White people hate Black people. White people are afraid of Black people. White people fight to maintain racial separation even as they give lip service to integration.

Much of this era which has now drawn to a close was dominated by Dr. Martin Luther King and was characterized by a complete acceptance of the white man's definition of reality. The white man defined our existence. He defined us as inferior and himself as superior. Black people accepted this white definition of reality. Dr. King's struggle was not against this white definition of Black inferiority, but rather an attempt to persuade the white man to accept us, to let us into his world. This constituted in fact a total acceptance of the white man's definition. Few Black leaders have dared question the white man's right to define both our identity and our condition. Not fear but lack of understanding silenced them. Marcus Garvey challenged the white man's right to define the Black man's life because of his superior intellect and his arrogant assumption that all authority for the Black man must be derived from the Black experience and the Black Liberation Struggle. Black people have had the white man's definition forced upon them. The books we read and the things we learn in school reflect the white man's definition of reality. There is no such thing as an objective book, an objective psychology, an objective sociology, an objective history, or an objective theology. Everything that the white man says or writes is an expression of his conviction that Black people are inferior. This is his definition of reality. If we accept his definition we cannot but accept Black inferiority. The struggle for integration reflects a total acceptance of the white man's definition of our inferiority. Why else would we want to integrate? Why would we want to lose our identity and our culture unless we hoped to escape inferiority by integrating with the "superior" white man?

Black Christian Nationalists affirm the fact that Black people have the right to define their own existence. We have a right to define our own religion, our own theology, our own science, our own history, and our own culture. We do not have to accept any definition which the white man gives us because his only authority is the white experience and the white struggle to maintain white supremacy. If the white man can define what is true and what is false; if the white man can define what is good and what is bad; if the white man can define what is superior and what is inferior—then we are chained to powerlessness and oppression. He will tell us about law and order if we rise up in the name of justice. If we demand equal education he will tell us about our innate genetic inferiority. If we say that we have a right to fight for freedom, he will tell us that violence is bad and nonviolence is good. But if we dare to make our own definitions just as the white man does, then we live in our own world and we have created the foundation for a separate and equal existence. To say that Black is beautiful is easy. To put a bumper sticker on your car saying BLACK IS BEAUTIFUL is easy. But to believe it is difficult. To believe it is difficult because the white man has conditioned us to hate ourselves and to love him. We say, "Wouldn't it be nice if Black were beautiful?" But that is not the same as saying, "Black is beautiful!" We must define for ourselves the things in life which are true. We must create our own psychology, our own sociology, our own history, and our own theology. We must realize that the white man's definitions are not valid for us. Black Christian Nationalists accept only one basis for authority: the Black experience as it is shaped by the Black Liberation Struggle. This is the cornerstone of Black Christian Nationalism.

BCN Orientation Reading List

Political

1. *Philosophy and Opinions of Marcus Garvey*, Cass, London 1967 — Marcus Garvey
2. *Garvey and Garveyism*, Collier (Macmillan), N.Y. 1963 — Amy J. Garvey
3. *Towards Colonial Freedom*, Heinemann, London 1963 — Kwame Nkrumah
4. *Africa Must Unite*, New World (International), N.Y. 1970 — " "
5. *Neo-Colonialism*, New World (International), N.Y. 1969 — " "
6. *Axioms*, Nelson, London 1967 — " "
7. *Dark Days in Ghana*, International, N.Y. 1968 — " "
8. *Handbook of Revolutionary Warfare*, International, N.Y. 1969 — " "

9. *Consciencism*, Modern Reader, N.Y. 1970 — Kwame Nkrumah

10. *Class Struggle in Africa*, International, N.Y. 1970 — " "

11. *The Wretched of the Earth*, Grove, N.Y. 1963 — Franz Fanon

12. *Studies in a Dying Colonialism*, Grove, N.Y. 1965 — " "

13. *Towards the African Revolution*, Grove, N. Y. 1967 — " "

14. *Black Skins, White Masks*, Grove, N.Y. 1967 — " "

15. *The Crisis of the Negro Intellectual*, Morrow, N.Y., 1967 — Harold Cruse

16. *Rebellion or Revolution?*, Morrow, N.Y. 1968 — " "

17. *The Black Power Revolt*, Sargent, Boston 1968. Edited by — Floyd B. Barbour

18. *By Any Means Necessary*, Merit (Pathfinder Press), N.Y. 1970 — Malcolm X

19. *David Walker's Appeal*, Hill & Wang, N.Y. 1965 — David Walker

20. *The Choice: The Issue of Black Survival in America*, Putnam, N.Y. 1971 — Samuel F. Yette

21. *Racism and the Class Struggle*, Monthly Review, N.Y. 1970 — James Boggs

22. *Revolution in Guinea*, Monthly Review, N.Y. 1969 — Amlcar Cabral

23. *Caste, Class, & Race*, Modern Reader, N.Y. 1970 — Oliver C. Cox

24. *Malcolm X: The End of White World Supremacy*, Merlin House, N.Y. 1971. Four speeches edited by — Benjamin Goodman

25. *The Political Economy of the Black Ghetto*, Norton, N.Y. 1970 — William K. Tabb

Historical

1. *Introduction to African Civilizations*, University, N.Y. 1970 — John G. Jackson
2. *African Glory*, Walker, N.Y. 1956 — J. C. Degraft-Johnson
3. *Race: The History of An Idea*, Schocken, N.Y. 1965 — Thomas F. Gossett
4. *African Life and Customs*, Humanities, N.Y. 1967 — Edward Blyden
5. *Africa and Unity: The Evolution of Pan-Africanism*, Humanities, N.Y. 1969 — Vincent B. Thompson
6. *Rebellion in Black Africa*, Oxford, N.Y. 1971. Edited by — Robert Rotberg
7. *Africa's Gift to America*, Rogers, N.Y. 1961 — J. A. Rogers
8. *Black Man of the Nile*, Alkebu-Lan, N.Y. 1970 — Dr. Yosef ben-Jochannan
9. *African Origins of the Major "Western Religions,"* Alkebu-Lan, N.Y. 1970 — Dr. Yosef ben-Jochannan
10. *Marcus Garvey 1887-1940*, New Beacon, 1969 — Adolph Edwards
11. *Black Protest*, Fawcett, N.Y. Edited by — Joanne Grant
12. *The Race War*, Bantam, N.Y. 1967 — Ronald Segal
13. *The Black Man's Burden*, Modern Reader, N.Y. 1969 — E. D. Morel
14. *We Charge Genocide*, New World (International), N.Y. 1970. Edited by — William Patterson
15. *Africa: Mother of Western Civilization*, Alkebu-Lan, N.Y. 1971 — Dr. Yosef ben-Jochannan
16. *The Chronological History of the Negro in America*, Mentor, N.Y. 1969 — Peter Bergman

Religious

1. *African Religion and Philosophy*,
   Praeger, N.Y. 1969   John S. Mbiti
2. *Concepts of God in Africa*, Praeger,
   N.Y. 1970   „   „   „
3. *Muntu: The New African Culture*,
   Grove, N.Y. 1961   Janheinz Jahu
4. *Christianity, Islam and the Negro
   Race*, Grove, N.Y. 1967   Edward Blyden
5. *The Black Messiah*, Sheed & Ward,   Rev. Albert B.
   N.Y. 1968   Cleage, Jr.
6. *Black Christian Nationalism*, Mor-   Rev. Albert B.
   row, N.Y. 1972   Cleage, Jr.

CHAPTER 14

A Nation within a Nation

In defining our program it is necessary to state clearly what Black Christian Nationalism means by a "Black Nation." We are not seeking five states in the South for Black people, or seven states, nor are we advocating a "Back-to-Africa" movement, although we have no objection to any of these. But it does not seem realistic to think that white people are going to give us anything that we are not prepared to take! We are concerned with "Nation" in a different sense. We seek to create a *Nation within a Nation*, uniting Black people in such a way that we have the basic benefits of nationhood in the interim while we prepare for the liberation of our homeland, Africa.

This concept does not immediately require one geographic place in which we can all reside. Most urban centers in which we now live are becoming predominantly Black and in many counties of the South we are already a majority. In this sense Black Nation means a real unity of all Black people in both urban centers and in the rural counties of the South. The Black people of Harlem will feel a kinship with the Black people of Alabama, Louisi-

ana, and Mississippi, and Black people in Chicago will feel
a kinship with Black people in Los Angeles, Philadelphia,
and Detroit—a kinship which is more than an emotional
feeling, because it also has the tangible attributes of Nationhood. We will be in communication with one another.
We will support one another. We will be related through
one co-operative economic movement which will enable us
to distribute goods raised in the rural counties of the
South on Black farms in northern urban centers where
Black people are now dependent on white merchants for
their produce; we will establish regional canneries and
wholesalers to distribute the food that Black people grow.
In many rural counties in the South there are systematic
efforts to starve Black people and to force Black people
off land they have owned and farmed for generations.
Black farmers need outlets in the North. They need the
support of Black brothers and sisters throughout America.
BCN proposes to mobilize and co-ordinate this kind of
national Black co-operative economic program.

Only the concept of Nation which recognizes that we
are a people can give us the strength and motivate the
necessary organization to make this possible. Even as Black
people are being forced off the land in the South, Black
people are being starved in the North, and we have no
system for the transference of goods. We have no truck-
ing lines, no canneries, and no wholesale houses. The only
groups in America that are beginning to move in these
economic areas are the Black Muslims and Black Christian
Nationalists. But because the Black Muslims lack the necessary growth potential to organize more than an insignificant percentage of American Black people, only the
Black church can build a Black Nation upon the foundation of the theology, philosophy, and program of Black
Christian Nationalism. The Black church either follows
where we lead, or it dies and seriously endangers the
survival of Black people.

When we say "Black Nation," we are not talking about

going anywhere. We are talking about fully utilizing the potentialities that already exist where we are. We must utilize the ghettos in which we live as a basis for power, training, and preparation for participation in the liberation of our homeland, Africa.

"Black Nation" is the concept of an emerging Black church that considers itself related to Black people as the Temple at Jerusalem was related to Israel. It considers all Black people a part of the Nation to which it ministers. It ministers not to a congregation but to the Pan-African Black community, the Black Nation. Then the Black Revolution becomes a part of the ongoing theology, preaching, and program of the Black church. What does this mean in terms of program development and the outreach of the Black church? How can the Black church begin to put together national economic co-operatives, a national political movement, and a national cultural revolution? How can the Black church do these things?

Many of the things that the Black church must do are already beginning to happen in the Black community, but the Black community lacks the institutional stability which the Black church can give. It lacks the resources which the Black church has frittered away because it has been subservient to the white church and has failed to realize its central importance in the Black community. But if the Black church is to move, it must understand the temper, the mood, and the thinking of the Black community. No longer can a Black preacher think that his total inspiration can come out of his denominational connection, out of the stale atmosphere in which he associates with other like-minded nonthinking individuals. He must find basic reality in the Black experience of the total Black community. The Black church faces a crucial moment of testing. Either it becomes relevant to the Black Revolution or it dies.

Many things indicate the changing temper of the Black

community. Black people have come a long way since 1954. We have come by many paths from many different directions. Today in most churches there is a feeling that we would like our church to be a part of the Black Liberation Struggle. A few years ago, Black people would move from place to place seeking better schools for their children, paying from two thousand dollars to six thousand dollars more than a house was worth to get into an integrated (changing) community. By "better schools" they meant schools which were not all Black. They sought an integrated school where white people were still trying to teach. They felt that the only way to get a school where the teachers, principal, and administrator were still trying to teach the children was to find a school where there were so many white children that the teachers, principal, and administrator would be afraid to stop teaching. So they tried to keep ahead of the Black masses so their children could get an education. Much of this has changed. Not that Black people do not still want an education for their children; but no longer do most Black people feel that they must flee to a mixed school in order to get an education. Many Black people are now willing to fight to make Black schools good schools. That is a big change in thinking for most Black people. Many Black parents realize that the Black school isn't a bad school because it is Black, but because white people have stopped putting money into it. White people have stopped trying to teach, white administrators have stopped maintaining standards. That is not the fault of either Black parents or children, but the fault of a white system which does not intend to educate Black children. Today most Black people are willing to accept the Black school if the Black community can control it. We want to make it a Black school recognizing the culture and traditions of Black people. We want Black people in positions of power so that Black children may have Black power symbols. Black schools must transmit the culture, history, and value system of Black people. BCN seeks community control of schools as a basic objective.*

A few years ago Black students went to college to learn how not to be Black. You unlearned your speech patterns and your life style. You learned how white people dressed and the trivialities they talked about. You tried to memorize all these important things so that you could appear to have taken on the refinements of white civilization. For this the white man was willing to give you a slightly better job than you could have gotten if you had come right out of the ghetto with your Black speech patterns and your Black life style. So college seemed to be a way of escaping being Black. But they didn't escape very far, however non-Black they learned to act. Even Ralph Bunche couldn't get away from being Black with all his international acclaim. The same prejudice and discrimination other Black people faced, he faced. The same is true of other Black "leaders." They face the same problems that other Black people face; the only difference is that they can have cocktails with white people from time to time on certain special occasions set apart for that kind of activity. The organization of BCN college chapters to help Black students stay Black and devote their lives to the liberation of Black people has high priority in the BCN program.

Colleges are no longer places where Black students go to escape the ghetto, but places where Black students go to prepare for leadership in the Black ghetto. Of course there are still sophisticated Uncle Toms on every college campus who consider it a tremendous opportunity to act

* The 1971 Supreme Court decision by the new Nixon Court seems to reaffirm and strengthen the 1954 decision outlawing segregation in public education. The original decision launched the Black Revolution. The 1971 decision attempts to cut the ground from under Black separatism and Black power by strengthening the illusion that integration is possible of attainment.

white and talk white and convince white people that they
know how to put down the revolution and keep Black
people quiet and in their place. There is a tremendous
market for "good niggers." During slavery days you could
work in the big house, eat the garbage off old master's
table, and wear his old castoff clothes. Today the reward
is even greater. A "very good nigger" can move into the
thirty-thousand-dollar bracket. This is a temptation for
a young Black graduate who has had difficulty all his
life getting thirty dollars together. He must decide, however, that he cannot earn thirty thousand dollars *and* serve
the Black ghetto. You can work as a personnel manager
and your job will be to keep Black folks out of the plant
and in the dirtiest lowest-paying jobs. If I were a white
man running a plant, I'd have five Black personnel men
sitting right by the front door. Every Black person who
came in would have to get by them. Not many would
make it because the managers would know their job. In
most plants the key Black man is paid to prevent Black
people from getting anywhere. Most large universities are
now looking for good Black men to keep Black students
under control. They must be men of many talents,
but some try. It is difficult to deliver in the thirty-
thousand-dollar bracket because it is hard to control people who really don't want anything you have to offer.

In the midst of all this, most Black preachers are still
preaching about a white Jesus taking Black people to
heaven when they die. A few years ago we wanted the
right to vote. We thought that if we got the right to
vote, that in itself would in some magic way make us
American citizens. The Federal government passed all
kinds of civil-rights laws and made token gestures designed
to permit Black people to register and vote. Gradually in
the South Black people registered. Now we are no longer
concerned about registering to vote, or voting, as magic
symbols that we have arrived. Black people now want to
vote in order to control Black communities. This is a

tremendous leap forward. In the middle of all this—Black people organizing, registering, trying to "vote Black" to control Black communities—the Black preacher is still talking about deliverance and going to heaven when you die. A few years ago we fought for public accommodations, just to be able to go anywhere, to use the same toilets that white people used, and to eat a hot dog where white people ate hot dogs. Now we are not really concerned about public accommodations except as a statement of the fact that we are entitled to everything that exists in America. If anyone tried to keep us out of a place we would burn it down. But if no one tries to keep us out we are not bothered, because who really wants to eat a hot dog with white people? Our attitude has changed. Now we want our own motels, hotels, and dining rooms. And while Black people are trying to get their own thing together, Black preachers are still talking about going to heaven with white people when they die. The Black church will either become relevant to what Black people are doing or the Black church is dead. BCN is committed to the organization of independent Black political power designed to give Black people control of Black communities, and BCN is dedicated to the building of Black agencies and institutions to serve the total needs of Black people.

Black writers were once the darlings of white people. They wrote for white publications and white readers. Poets wrote beautiful little poems that white people could read and marvel that "niggers" could write. Dramatists wrote plays for white people. We didn't have any Black writers who wrote for Black people. Today we have a cultural renaissance of Black writers who write plays, books, and poems for Black people. The whole concept of Black literature has changed. Black men of genius no longer care whether white people read what they write or not. Sometimes significant Black work is not formally published at all. It is mimeographed and distributed. Imamu

Amiri Baraka circulated a book of poems in mimeographed form for years—not because no one would publish it, but because he didn't consider it important to have it formally published, and he is one of the outstanding Black writers of this century. The new Black concept holds that Black writers ought to write plays that can be performed on a street corner. His plays ought not to require a big theater and one hundred thousand dollars to produce. If he can't write a play for the ghetto that can be performed on a street corner, he ought to forget it.

Black writers are working within a totally new concept of relevance. To perform a Black play on a street corner in a Black community means that the author writes only one-half of the play, and brothers and sisters will add the rest and become an informal part of the cast. This is the emerging new Black art. Street-corner plays and poetry readings are a part of the new Black experience. Black poetry is written for Black people where they are. Don Lee writes beautiful poems and the white man does not have to give them his seal of approval. You can go into a poolroom or a bar and read his poems and Black people will say, "That's right." Now that's literature! And while Don Lee is writing beautiful poems and Imamu Amiri Baraka is writing beautiful plays, Black preachers are still talking about Black folks going to an integrated heaven with white folks and putting their hands into the hands of a white Jesus—"he'll wipe away every tear and heal every sorrow." The Black church is out of it, Black preachers are out of it, and a number of young Black seminarians are out of it, because they are out of touch with the Black community. They still wonder how much money they are going to make and who must die before they can get a big church. BCN considers the cultural revolution which is taking place in Black America an important part of the Liberation Struggle of Black people. Imamu Amiri Baraka, Don Lee, Sonia Sanchez, and a thousand other Black poets, writers, and artists preach more relevant sermons than the most eloquent Black preachers with their slave theology, integrationist philosophy, and individualistic psychology. Black cultural development constitutes one of the seven basic program areas to which Black Christian Nationalism calls the Black church.

Black people are engaged in a struggle for survival and everything in the Black community must contribute to this struggle. A serious question is, Can Black people survive in this country, or will white people ultimately destroy us all? In a struggle for survival all Black people must be brought together, and the only institution which can bring Black people together is the Black church. In restructuring the Black church we must remember that it cannot be done in a superficial fashion. We cannot make the church a little bit Black because Black people are developing a Black identity. Either we are going to build a Black church, or we are not going to build a Black church. You cannot tack a little Black onto the old white structure. The new Black church must be basically concerned with building a Black Nation. It must do everything possible to make the church a part of the Black Nation. Everything that is done in the church must be programmed to strengthen the Liberation Struggle, to support it, and to train Black people for the revolution. We cannot have fish fries in the church which are not connected with the revolution because it is a waste of time and a waste of energy. We can't have women's groups sitting around talking about foolishness week after week. "What will our women's fellowship do next week? Let's have a speaker talk on hat-making." That kind of programming is all right in a white church because white churches do not have anything else to do. If their women want to waste time making hats or learning how to make hats, that is a perfectly respectable activity for them. But for a women's group in a Black church to be sitting around trying to learn how to put a hat together (and it not even an

African hat) is a total negation of the seriousness of the Black Liberation Struggle. The same is true of a men's group. I've seen men's groups waste hours trying to plan a program for the following month. "What shall we do? Let's invite Mr. Jones to speak. Who is Mr. Jones? He speaks around the city a lot. What does he talk about? He'll report on a book or modern art or something." This is total absurdity in a Black church. If there is a men's club it ought to be a part of the revolution, and any speaker ought to be telling Black people about the revolutionary struggle. The total program ought to be relevant to the Black Revolution. Most Sunday schools are enough to make you cry. Old ladies teaching because they love children are without the slightest conception of what is happening in the Black world. They sit with their outmoded little quarterly running through their white-folks lesson for Black children who can't even read. They could at least use the hour to teach a Black child how to read so that he could go home and read about revolution for himself. But there they sit with their little pictures of a white Jesus and their golden verse. Nothing belongs in a Black church unless it is a part of the Black Revolution, and anything that is a part of the Black Revolution belongs in the Black church. But still Black preachers preach about a white Jesus and going to heaven when you die.

We are God's Chosen People. I don't debate it, I declare it! Black people are God's Chosen People. God supports his Chosen People. We have the witness of the Old Testament. When we fight a battle, God fights with us. In the Old Testament, when the prophet held up his arms, God held the sun still so that the enemies of Black Israel could be killed. That is the kind of God the Old Testament talks about. That is the kind of God who supports the Black Nation. At the Shrine of the Black Madonna we have a Committee Against Racist Wars and we counsel young Black men who are opposed to the war in Vietnam. Anything we can do to help young Black men stay out of Vietnam we are willing to do. The Shrine of the Black Madonna and BCN are on record in opposition to the participation of any member in the war in Vietnam or in any white racist war. Members of any Shrine or BCN group who do not refuse to participate as conscientious objectors on religious grounds will be excommunicated. We do not oppose all war and conflict. We are willing to fight to establish God's will on earth. We will not participate in a white racist war. We will not fight to oppress helpless people. We will not bomb children and women as America is doing in Vietnam. We will not fight to strengthen the white's man's domination of Asia, as America is trying to do in Vietnam. We oppose that kind of war. We support wars for the liberation of Black people and nonwhite people. Our role is defined by our concept of Nation. We want to keep young Black men out of racist white wars, but we will not tell young Black men that war is wrong, because there will be many times when we must fight. The Black church may be forced to send young Black people out to fight a holy war. We reject nonviolence. We believe in the defense of the Black community and of Black people everywhere. At any time young Black men may have to defend the Black ghetto with the blessing and support of the Black church. This is a part of the concept of Nation which must be built into the Black church.

The Black church can be described by the Swahili word *Karamu*, which is the festival place at the center of the village, the festival place to which people can come in moments of happiness and joy and in times of trouble and crisis. The Black church must become this kind of center for the Black community. For the white church this would not be realistic because the white church is not the center of the white world. Wall Street, the downtown business district, and the shopping mall are centers for white people. For Black people the church can be the center because we are not a commercial people. We will engage in commerce only because it is necessary to live, but the church is the festival place where we can come to do the things which are necessary for our survival. Black Christian Nationalists think of each Shrine of the Black Madonna as the festival place in the center of the Black community, our *Karamu.*

As Black Christian Nationalists we seek to build a Black value system. We reject American values. The Black church must do this conscientiously, deliberately, and openly. We reject the white man's values, the values of the Western world. Many white people feel that they also reject these values, but as a matter of fact they cannot. The white value system is a very simple one to understand. Whatever suits the white man's purpose is right. He follows this without deviation. Slavery was right because it was necessary. When it was no longer necessary, he changed it. Law and order are necessary for the white man when he is in power. The preservation of law and order justifies anything. Within the framework of law and order the white man will discuss differences of opinion. I heard a white labor leader get up at a mass meeting shortly after the 1967 rebellion in Detroit and talk for forty-five minutes on the sanctity of law and order. "You can't just run out and fight to get things. You must work within the framework of law and order. You can't just run out and fight. That's basic. That's the foundation of civilization—law and order." I could remember when labor was organizing. Law and order were the last things considered. They were as ruthless as any group of people who ever fought for power. They killed, they robbed, they stole, they beat people half to death. Anything was acceptable because labor was fighting for power. Now labor is established as a part of the structure, and a labor leader stands up without any conscious hypocrisy and defends law and order. The same is true of any people. When you get what you want, you need law and order to keep it. When America was fighting a revolutionary war, anything was good that supported the revolution. Anything was acceptable which led to victory. Only when you win do you need law and order. As Black people we are not on top. Our struggle is not over. In terms of what we are trying to do, law and order are much less important to us than securing power and equality for Black people. The Black church must re-examine its total position. With Black people in a powerless position and structured out of the power establishment, law and order designed to maintain the *status quo* cannot possibly serve our interests. The Black church must support whatever Black people are doing to secure liberation. We are concerned with justice, not law and order.

We must develop a new value system. The white man says killing is wrong. He drafts you into the Army and sends you to camp, spends six months teaching you how to kill, takes you halfway around the world, points out a stranger, and tells you to kill him. "Do it until I say stop!" Then he brings you home and says, "Killing is now over until I need you again." The morality of the white man's Western world has no foundations. Do not steal, if you are poor. If you own a big factory, though, you are permitted to steal every day from everyone who buys your products. What you steal is called profit. You steal every day from thousands and that's legitimate. But if you are poor and you steal a loaf of bread because you are hungry, that is both sinful and illegal. Racism is theoretically wrong on Brotherhood Sunday, but society in the Western world is racist because it is necessary to preserve the *status quo*. The Black church must develop a new value system for Black people. We can no longer function within the framework of the white man's value system.

Our values as Black people must be derived from the Black experience as that experience has been shaped by our continuing struggle for liberation and survival. Everything in the Black community must relate to this struggle, so it offers the only basis for a Black value system. If it supports our struggle for liberation and survival, it is good. If it separates us from each other and weakens us, it is bad. This fact the Black church must understand. It must be the yardstick by which we interpret the message of Jesus which we preach to Black people. If it separates us, if it takes from us power, it is bad. If it brings us together, if it unites us and gives us power, it is good. We can build a new value system for Black people on this simple premise.

You may well ask, "How can we get all of this into a real church?" Recently I visited a church in Milwaukee. They didn't call it a church, they called it the Panther Den. It preceded the Black Panthers and was not related to them. It was a youth organization with large storefront headquarters. Its adviser was a young Black Episcopalian minister. He was called to an "integrated" church as assistant minister. The only thing integrated about the church was the white pastor. The members were Black because the white members had fled, as white people always do in a changing community. There has never, to my knowledge, been an integrated Christian church. There are only churches in transition, where white people are in the process of getting out and Black people are in the process of coming in. I have never seen an integrated church that was stable. But this was an integrated church because they had a stable white pastor who was determined to stay. He needed a visible symbol of integration in the pulpit on Sunday so the bishop sent a young Black man to work with young people and be visible. The young assistant began working with young people in the community. This wasn't really what the church had in mind. They expected him to work with the fifteen young people they had in the church. But he insisted upon working with the young people in the community. There were hundreds of them and they started coming into the church to attend youth meetings. The middle-class Black members said,

"They are tearing up our building." This is what most adults say at some point or other when young people start using a church building. The young assistant said, "They are not really tearing up the building, but we will try to take care of it, if that is what you mean." Most ghetto churches do not have real janitor service. We are good janitors for everyone but ourselves. So the young people began to try to take care of the building and they found no cleaning supplies and no buffer for the floors. So they bought the things they needed to take care of the building. Finally the members said, "Even though they are taking care of the building, we still think that there is something wrong with young people running in and out of the church all of the time, and somehow they don't have a Christian look." So the young man went to the bishop and asked if he could rent a store front a few blocks from the church, be reassigned to neighborhood youth work, and leave the church where everything he was doing was running counter to what the members thought the church ought to be doing. The bishop agreed. Everyone was happy, including the middle-class Black members, who liked having a lone white symbol up front with their white Jesus. The young Black assistant had served only to confuse the picture.

The young Black assistant moved up the street with his community kids. At first it was just a recreation program, which was natural. They had Ping-Pong tables and pool tables and on weekends they sponsored dances. Then they began to have spontaneous "rap sessions." They would talk and the minister would bring in books and Black papers. Gradually they arrived at the stage where *they* thought that the Black Revolution was too important for them to be wasting time playing pool and Ping-Pong, so they took the pool tables and the Ping-Pong tables out and sold them to buy other things which were relevant to their program. They worked for more than a year with "rap sessions," discussions, classes, and forums. Gradually they developed what they called a "liberation dinner." It began as just a dinner and then they decided that if it was a liberation dinner they ought to serve "survival food." Everything was built around the struggle Black people have had to survive in America. Grits, because they are cheap, helped Black people survive; greens, because Black people could take weeds out of the field and make a tasty meal. So what we usually call soul food they called survival food, because they understood why Black people began to eat these particular things. They had wine, not as a sacrament at first, but because it had been a crutch on which Black people had leaned in times of trouble. So they had wine on the table to say that many times when we might have been doing something constructive we took the wine instead. It was a survival meal and it became a ritual, a sacrament of commitment to the Black Liberation Struggle. It started in darkness and the minister would read from Black poets in addition to the Bible. Their building was on a main street and Black people would be walking up and down the street, their voices, laughter, and profanity a part of the service, because they were a part of the Black experience. So the liberation dinner became a ritual, a sacrament.

The community kids developed formal conferences, bringing in out-of-town speakers. Then one of the young men who was a leader suggested that they ought to have something on Sundays when other people were going to church. He didn't want to say that they ought to have church services on Sunday, but something ought to be going on; so they set up something for Sunday morning, at about the same time other people were in church. They talked about the Black experience, Black culture, and the Black Struggle. In their own way they had gone out the front door of the church and come in through the back door. They had created their own ritual and program out of the Black experience. It is one of the few meaningful Black churches in America. They are recreating the sym-

bolism and rituals of the church, but it is a Black symbolism and Black ritualism created out of the Black
experience. I use this to illustrate the simple fact that even
if Black people leave the church, they will build it anew
out of the deep spiritual depth of the Black experience.

I participated in workshops for Black pastors in California. We had come together to experiment with worship. We wanted to find out how many of the symbols
of African culture we could use in Christian worship and
make meaningful to Black people. We were able to use
drums, carvings, pictures, songs, and many other things.
It was a deeply spiritual service of worship. A group of
ministers were experimenting in order to return to their
churches and begin to deepen the worship experience for
their congregations. There will be many different approaches involved in making the Black church and its
rituals, its organization, its program, and its sacraments
relevant to the Black experience. It is important to remember that the new Black church is coming into being
all across America. I visited a small church in Muncie,
Indiana, which is doing significant experimentation in new
forms of worship. They have a "Soul Sunday" service
once a month. Eventually every Sunday will be Soul Sunday, but you have to start slowly with Black people because they don't want to get too far away from white
people too quickly. So they have it once a month now.
Everyone wears African dress of one kind or another,
and they have a soul dinner following the Service. They
build the service around African culture and the important
things that can be learned from African culture.

As the Black church moves toward becoming the Black
Nation, it is engaged in a very difficult task. It is much
easier for a white seminarian to graduate, go into a suburban church, and do what everyone has been doing for
hundreds of years. He doesn't really need to think. He
can go through the motions with a little marriage counsel-
ing and youth work to make him feel relevant. A Black

seminarian going into a Black church must deal with the basic issues involved in building a sense of Nation. He must take all the things in the Black community that make up the Black experience and bring them together in such a way that Black people get a sense of Nation. Black people in a Black ghetto are ashamed of the things which make a Black ghetto beautiful. You can recognize a Black ghetto even if you are blindfolded, because you can smell fried chicken, shrimp, and french fries. You can smell the ghetto, and it is a beautiful smell if you are not afraid of the ghetto. The sounds you can hear, the music, the laughter, the anger of the ghetto, the frustration—even with the horrors of white exploitation the ghetto has a beauty that white America does not have. There is the sense of people being together, the sense of fellowship, and even the bond of common misery. It is a beautiful thing. But a Black preacher has always felt that his church was somehow in opposition to the beauty of the Black ghetto. His church was a little white oasis in the middle of a Black desert and he was fighting to keep *it* pure and white even when he personally sinned. This must change. The Black ghetto must come into the church and the church must build in terms of the Black experience. The church must build a sense of Black Nation by breaking down barriers which separate Black people from one another. All kinds of Black people must find that they are one people when they come into the church.

The church must organize politically—not behind the scenes in some quiet hypocritical way but openly and publicly. The church must fight for community control of schools. White people can no longer be permitted to destroy the minds of Black children. The church must fight for community control of the police. The Black community must control the police who patrol the Black ghetto. The church must educate Black people to understand the importance of community control. Black people can understand that we must control the Black ghettos in which we live. The Black church must fight for economic power, forcing white merchants in the Black ghetto to hire Black people and building Black co-operatives. The church must become a teaching institution, the fountainhead of an emerging cultural and creative experience for Black people. Every member must be involved. He must learn to do but also to teach, so that as the institution grows each member becomes a teacher in an expanding ministry. Eventually he must be able to go out and set up institutions. This concept of an expanding church is essential in the Black community. We radicalize Black people by involving them in the struggle. They realize their full potentiality as they submerge their individualism and become involved in the life of the Black community. People want to escape from the weakness and loneliness of individualism. They want to find a place where they are important and where there is something on which they can depend. The Black church can offer Black people the fellowship and support of the Black Nation.

CHAPTER 15

Let's Not Waste
the Holy Spirit

When Jesus came down from Nazareth and was baptized by John in the Jordan River, the heavens opened and the Holy Spirit descended upon him in the form of a dove and he received power. After spending forty days in the wilderness he walked by the Sea of Galilee and called his Disciples, who left their nets and fishing boats and followed him. He went into the synagogue at Capernaum and the people were astonished, because he taught them as one who had authority and not as the scribes. When John was in prison he sent his disciples to ask, "Are you the Messiah who is to lead the movement or shall we look for another?" Jesus could reply, "Tell John what you see and hear." The Holy Spirit is the revolutionary power which comes to an exploited people as they struggle to escape from powerlessness and to end the institutional oppression forced upon them by an enemy.

At Pentecost the Disciples were together as usual, eating, drinking, talking, and trying to remember and to understand the things Jesus had said and the things he had done. Suddenly it seemed that the room was filled with the rush of a mighty wind. It seemed as though tongues of fire came and rested over each head. The writer was trying to describe a deeply moving inner experience. Another person might have described the experience in a different way. There need not necessarily have been tongues of fire and the rush of a mighty wind, but there was the feeling that some great power was there, and that the Disciples had suddenly been caught up and were being acted upon by a force outside themselves. Each individual was touched and they began to talk. Galileans could not understand what they were saying. Yet visitors from other countries could understand them. Here again we have the symbolic language of the Bible. Suddenly caught up in the power of the Holy Spirit, they began to speak in such a way that people from everywhere except Galilee could understand them. Whether they were speaking strange languages in a literal sense, or whether the simple message of the Black Messiah calling men to struggle against oppression could be understood by the exploited and despised from every land, we do not know. This is the same simple message that oppressed nonwhite peoples understand everywhere in today's world.

You don't have to speak Swahili to understand the struggle of the people of Africa. You didn't have to speak French to understand *The Battle of Algiers*. You didn't have to speak Chinese to understand the suffering that created the revolution in China. In a sense, the common experience of suffering and misery creates a universal language of rebellion, struggle, and revolution, and in our kind of world the language of the Holy Spirit cannot but be the language of revolt. This is true in Vietnam. We do not speak Vietnamese, but we can clearly understand the voices of suffering and defiance. We can understand the words of a Vietnamese mother who sees her children consumed by napalm dropped from American bombers.

We can understand the words of a Vietnamese man who sees his entire food supply being destroyed by flame-throwers in the hands of American soldiers. We can understand the words of Vietnamese children being tortured by American interrogation teams. The Holy Spirit gives us a sense of identification with the rage of suffering oppressed people everywhere, and so at Pentecost the remnant of the Nation Israel, so soon to be humiliated and dispersed by the fall of Jerusalem and Masada, could be understood by all. It is rage, anger, hatred, commitment. It is divine discontent. It is the mystery of a magic moment when we are touched by a power which we cannot understand.

Only a people can feel the Holy Spirit. God does not speak to individuals. Ordinary Black men and women came together in Montgomery, Alabama, and decided that they could no longer sit in the back of the bus. We wonder what at that moment made the back of the bus so much more irksome than it was a week before or a decade before. Why did Black people suddenly decide to walk? What happened? The most reasonable explanation is the simple one. In this time and in this place, these Black people were touched by the Holy Spirit. The conviction that God had created them equal gave them a new sense of dignity. They were no longer able to ride in the back of the bus. They had been touched by the Holy Spirit. They were forced to walk, and so they walked for more than a year. How can we say what touched a Black mother, whose child had been going to an inferior segregated school, who suddenly decided that she would take her child to an integrated school where the child could get a decent education? Where did she get the courage to face a mob? It was the Holy Spirit. How can we explain the rage of Black people in cities all across America in 1965, '66, and '67, Black people who were accustomed to being oppressed and exploited, who had grown calloused to brutality by white police officers, to injustice in white courts, to misinterpretations by white newspapers and the mass-communications media, and who were accustomed to the hostility of white people? Why did all these things suddenly become unbearable? Black people in city after city rose up against oppression, saying, "We will no longer tolerate these conditions." Why the sudden violence and the upheaval which still shake America? It was as though the cities were filled with the rush of a mighty wind and tongues of fire rested over each Black head. We can't say it any better than the Bible says it. Why have Black college students suddenly decided that college is not a place to play and prepare for the exploitation of their Black brothers and sisters, but a place to prepare for participation in the Black Revolution? Why now? Why are students willing to face tanks and guns? We saw the pictures of the invasion of a campus in North Carolina: a handful of students practically unarmed, facing all the armed might of America on a Black college campus. Why are students in this day different? The power of the Holy Spirit. Why, at Howard University, would those who traditionally have been middle-class individuals trying to escape from their Black heritage and their Black identity, trying to absorb the life style of white people, suddenly decide that the university belonged to the Black community and ought to serve Black people?

When the power of the Holy Spirit came at Pentecost, a little group of Black Israelites who were disorganized, who had recently been discouraged, despondent, and separated because of the failure of Jesus, were together in one place. What did this little group do when the Holy Spirit came? It is not enough just to say that they suddenly felt as though the rush of a mighty wind had filled the room, and tongues of fire rested over each head. Everyone in the room felt that somehow life had new meaning and a new sense of direction. But what did they do? Sometimes you feel that the Holy Spirit has touched you. You feel power that you didn't know you had; you feel a commitment to do something that you didn't know you could feel. You want to move into areas of risk and sacrifice you didn't realize you had the courage even to dream of. These are moments when you have felt the Holy Spirit. The basic question is, What is your response to the Holy Spirit? If God can touch us, how do we respond? How did the Disciples respond two thousand years ago? It is not enough to say that one day a little handful of those who followed Jesus suddenly felt the power of God and went out into the world to change it. We cannot but ask, What did they do? It is not enough to say that they built the church, because to that we can simply reply, So what? The church has become the protector of oppression and institutional racism which constitutes the white man's world. The church has become a part of the machinery of oppression. If the church as we know it resulted from the Pentecostal experience, we can seriously question whether or not God had anything to do with it. The church of history does not commend itself to us as an act of God.

We accept Jesus as the Black Messiah sent by God to lead men in a revolutionary struggle for liberation because his life testifies to the validity of our faith. We can accept the beautiful mythology with which men have surrounded his birth because we can believe that the advent of a man like this, obviously sent by God, must have been attended by miraculous signs and wonders. Of course the heavens sang and a star came to rest over the lowly stable in which he lay. But we find it difficult to associate God with the church which bears the name of Jesus Christ. The institutional Christian church has never spoken for God nor mediated His spirit. Certainly God has tried through the person and teachings of Jesus and through the Holy Spirit made manifest at Pentecost. God was willing to become incarnate in the group of Disciples at Pentecost as He had become incarnate in Jesus at the moment of his baptism by John the Baptist in the Jordan River, as recorded in

Mark, the oldest Gospel. Following the Crucifixion, the incarnation was to have been a group experience, as Jesus had suggested. The arrogant Catholic position that God is incarnate in the Church—is Biblically and theologically correct, as opposed to the traditional Protestant heresy that salvation is an individual act accomplished by God on a one-to-one basis without the mediation of the church as Nation. The Catholic position is sound. The spirit of God came to followers of Jesus, *the church potential*, at Pentecost with power but found them apostate. They had lost contact with the life and teachings of Jesus. They wasted the Holy Spirit. To understand, we have but to turn back to the Disciples' own account of Pentecost and ask, What did the Disciples do with the Holy Spirit? They tell you, "We began to speak in tongues." They talked. "People listened so we told them about Jesus." Then what did you do? "We devoted ourselves to the Apostles' teaching and fellowship." That sounds like the church! They sat down together, listened to the Disciples preach, and enjoyed a beautiful fellowship. They wasted the Holy Spirit! They didn't really harness it to any kind of constructive program. The Holy Spirit comes. All God can do is give us a sense of togetherness, a sense of power, and a sense of commitment. If we waste it, it is gone.

Recently I spoke in Harlem at a mass meeting honoring Brother Malcolm. All through the meeting I was conscious of the fact that we were wasting the Holy Spirit. It was a beautiful program. It was one of those spectaculars which can only be gotten together in Harlem, which is still the artistic capital of Black America. There are so many talented people doing so many things and they come together once in a while for a spectacular, and this was that kind of occasion. There were people from Broadway; John O. Killens was there, John Henrik Clarke spoke, and Ossie Davis spoke. It was a beautiful program. There was a phenomenal dance group, with drummers who could jump seven feet in the air and never miss a beat going up or coming down. The Holy Spirit was there. The Disciples at Pentecost had no more spirit than we had that night in Harlem. Everybody was responsive. When the brother jumped and hit the drum, everyone was hitting it all the way up and all the way down with him. The spirit was there. It was beautiful. A group sang as an angelic choir might wish that it could sing. It was church! The National Black Theater put on a play. They had been rehearsing for a year, getting together, training people. It was beautifully done. The spirit was there. Let me describe their presentation.

A brother came out and walked down the aisle toward an empty stage, very dramatically. Music was coming through the amplifier right out of the Black experience: jazz, gospel, blues, and rock. They really had a sound-track. Everyone's mind was blown before the actor reached the stage. It was beautiful. There he was, walking down the aisle ever so coolly and up onto the stage. The spotlight followed him. He faced the audience, took off his coat, and carefully folded it over his arms. His voice cracked like a machine gun. "Damn niggers! Damn niggers! Damn niggers! Damn niggers!" And then "damn niggers" came from every direction. He said, "This is some garbage we picked up in Harlem." That's what he said. A "nigger" came down the aisle, beating a woman all the way. She'd stop and he would knock her down. He dragged her upon the stage. They came with dope and liquor, cussing, screaming, loving, fighting. Every Black stereotype known to white racist America was personified. It was beautifully done, like a scene from Dante's *Inferno*. The self-hate was frightening in its intensity. The National Black Theater is experimenting with a new kind of theater which has the bloodcurdling power of Voodoo. Finally a woman ran up on the stage and stabbed someone. He died for an eternity. In the middle of all of this, the back curtain opened and Brother Malcolm walked on the stage. The spotlight picked him up. He began to teach. "Don't be niggers, don't bring your dirt out into the street. Keep it at home. Lock your doors and get your business together." Everyone changed! The "niggers" faded into the shadows. Malcolm was talking and they were with him. He played his part well. He walked about talking about what Black people must do. While he was talking they were all huddled up in the shadows, and then they came out with their Muslim clothes on as though he had cleansed them by his words. Beautiful! Then more "niggers" ran down the aisle and shot him down on the stage. Sister Betty Shabazz was sitting near me in the front row. I don't know how she stood it. Then he fell down and died for another eternity. A new bedlam of grief rocked the theater. Everyone was crying and screaming. There must have been a hundred in the cast. People were standing, crying and screaming. The spirit was really there. People who weren't in the play were suddenly a part of the cast. They had just seen Malcolm killed before their eyes. Pallbearers came down the aisle carrying a casket. The spirit was there. They picked him up and put him in the casket and walked around with him, sobbing, crying, and screaming. A thousand people completely spirit-filled. Then suddenly Malcolm sat up in the casket. It was the Second Coming. People screamed, "He lives. He lives." He stood up and began to teach again as the lights were extinguished. We were not yet finished. There were poems about how beautiful it is to be Black, and how the time of the white devil is drawing to an end. Finally they said, "We will now hear from Reverend Albert Cleage from the Shrine of the Black Madonna in Detroit." I wondered what anyone could say after the two hours of emotional frenzy we had been through. We had wasted the Holy Spirit!

Everything had been beautiful, but we had wasted the Holy Spirit just as the early Christians had wasted it. We had gone through empty motions. We had not even recruited for the Black Muslims. No one had said anything about the problem. No one had identified the enemy. No one had mentioned a program. We had enjoyed the Holy Spirit. We had enjoyed ecstasy. No one had said anything about putting the Holy Spirit to work. We had burned it all up right there! There seemed nothing left to do but get drunk. Neither program nor direction had been either suggested or implied. It had been exactly like a Sunday-morning service of worship in a Black church. I said, "You are a funny people here in Harlem. I always thought I'd love to participate in a Malcolm memorial, here where you understood him best and loved him most. But I fear that you have forgotten the things he taught and the meaning of his life.

"This program has been all in honor of Brother Malcolm. Brother Malcolm taught us that the white man is the enemy. It is the white man's system of oppression that is destroying us. While we are here screaming that Black is beautiful, our brothers are starving to death in Mississippi and being driven off farms in Georgia and Alabama. Black people are being beaten to death in Detroit, and Black children are being denied a decent education all over this land. We are 'niggers' because the white man has deliberately and systematically 'niggerized' us. Let's not waste the Holy Spirit in a poem, a song, or a dance of self-hate. The day of the 'nigger' is drawing to a close. The era of the Black man has already begun to dawn. Let us look not backward but forward into our new day. Black culture must be an expression of our Liberation Struggle. It must express our hope and determination in poem, song, dance, and drama. It must express our total commitment to the liberation of Black people. There can be no Black art apart from the revolution in which we are engaged. Everything in the Black community must serve the Black Liberation Struggle. The white man is the enemy, yet everything we buy we buy from him. Black farmers in Georgia, Alabama, and Mississippi can't sell their produce because the white man is determined to drive them off the land. All we need is a truck and a driver to bring the food from Mississippi, Georgia, and Alabama to the people of Harlem. But we must know who the enemy is and we must develop a program and an organization designed to confront him.

"We can't use power until we get it, and we can't get it until we become a people. We must build a movement with power. Every organization we had has fallen apart because it had no program designed to meet our basic problem. BCN is building an organization which can unite Black people and secure the power necessary to deal with our oppression. A restructured national Black church could raise enough money on any single Sunday to save Black southern farmers. Black people would contribute for Black liberation if they had leadership. The African liberation movements are fighting to liberate our motherland, Africa! They are fighting white racists in Guinea, Zimbabwe, South Africa, Mozambique, and Angola, but they need support. A restructured national Black church could raise enough money on any Sunday to support the present African liberation movements for a month. There are critical battlefronts in America. The Cairo United Front and the Black struggle in North Carolina need support. A restructured national Black church could raise the funds necessary to support these critical battlefronts. BCN calls Black people to join such a movement. Today we train. Tomorrow we mobilize the power necessary to liberate Black people everywhere in the world.

"The revolution is about confronting an enemy and destroying his system of oppression. If the white man is oppressing you, then you must deal with him. We ought to be figuring out the things that have to be done. James Forman's Black Manifesto points out a direction for a national program. White people will never provide the money. But if white people refuse to pay reparations, the money still must be secured from somewhere! Two hundred million dollars for a land bank in the South is necessary. If white people don't put it up, we still need two hundred million dollars for a land bank in the South. We still need publishing houses, television stations, and everything else that James Forman suggested will enable a people to live. If we don't get it from one source, we must get it from another. That is what we ought to be talking about. That ought to be our agenda. That ought to be our top priority. We cannot afford the luxury of just having a good time. Black folks can enjoy being together better than anyone else in the world, but we waste the feeling of togetherness. Just think how many Black churches waste the Holy Spirit every Sunday morning, because they fail to tie it to any real, down-to-earth program. Salvation is saying, 'I believe in the revolutionary struggle which Jesus, the Black Messiah, inaugurated. I believe in the sacrifice he was willing to make. I believe that it is necessary for me to involve my total life in the struggle of Black people against the oppression of a white enemy establishment. I believe that I must become totally immersed in that struggle.' There is no other way to be saved.

"As Black people we live in an eternal Pentecost. Every moment of every day our ears are filled with the rush of a mighty wind until we almost cannot bear it, and we cannot rest for the tongues of flame which scorch us and drive us and will not let us be, until at last we lie bleeding and still and free."

BCN COVENANT

Declaring ourselves to be God's Chosen People, created in His image, the living remnant of the lost Black Nation, Israel, we come together as brothers and sisters in the Black Christian Nationalist movement. We are disciples of the Black Messiah, Jesus of Nazareth, who by his life, and by his death upon the cross, teaches us that nothing is more sacred than the liberation of Black people.

We covenant together, and pledge our total commitment to the task of rebuilding a Black Nation with power, here on earth. We will do whatever is necessary to achieve self-determination for Black people. We will fight the injustice, oppression, and exploitation of all Black people. As members of the Black Nation, we are bound together in an inseparable sacred brotherhood. To the service of this sacred brotherhood, we pledge our lives.

PART 5

We Define Our History

APPENDICES

Papers presented to the First Black Christian Nationalist Convention at the Shrine of the Black Madonna, Detroit, Michigan. Edited by George Bell, National Co-ordinator.

Africa and the Bible

Rabbi Hilu Paris

Rabbi Hilu Paris is a native of Ethiopia. A graduate of Yeshiva University in New York City, he is presently Instructor in African Studies at the State Urban Education Center, Brooklyn, New York, Religious Director of Education at Congregation Mount Horeb, a member of the African Historical Heritage Association, and Chairman of the American Pro-Falasha Committee.

In their universal religion all Africans believed in the one God, the Great Ancestor or the Eternal Being of the universe. Africans of today who have not been disturbed by the religions of Judaism, Christianity, or Islam still worship the one great God and still have many deities to worship and to ceremonize over. We would like to show the connection between that which many people think is Egyptian or Hebraic religion and its African antecedents.

The Hebrews had gotten much of their history, custom, and religion—one may say even their god—from the ancient Egyptians. In predynastic Egypt we see that the Egyptians had certain family clans and tribes that had their own emblem, a beast or bird whose unique powers were accredited to the social unit. Such designations as "the lion people," "the hippo people," and "the harpoon people" were properly used to identify these units. It appears that at least some of these emblems were carried over from an earlier hunting tradition whereby sympathetic magic—animal qualities of strength, speed, and cunning—was bestowed on the hunter. When agriculture became the dominant pursuit of most of the Egyptian people, these emblems were given more functional qualities, familiar to history in such forms as Annibus, the jackal-headed god of embalming; Sikmet, the warlike, lioness goddess; Ophof, the ibis-headed god of wisdom. From this we can see a similarity in the Old Testament in that the ancient Israelites, when they came into the land of Canaan and made it the land of Israel, divided their tribes into twelve units, or peoples, or clans, and those twelve units or clans were designated also by an emblem and a symbol.

Some of the traditions that we know the Egyptians had followed for over three thousand years of dynastic rule are found not only in Africa to this day, but are the same traditions found in the Old Testament. These Egyptian traditions are similar to the cultural history of the Hebrews, the Israelites, and those who were designated as Jews. For instance, as we said before, the tradition of the belief in one God was not unknown to the people of African descent. People of African descent always believed in the one God. That God they called the Great Ancestor or the Great Being. In the Bible we see the transition of this thought in the history of Moses. When he fled Egypt and went into the mountains, he came up to that marvelous site of the Burning Bush. There he made contact with the Great God, the Great Ancestor of Abraham and Isaac and Jacob. The name comes unto

Moses as *Eyeya asher eyeya*, I am that I am. "Tell them, Moses," said the God Jehovah, "When they ask thee who sent thee, tell them, Moses, that I am sent thee." And so we see that historical experience of the Hebrew people came out of Africa and out of an African civilization.

Another comparison is the Africans' way of life as seen in their rites of passage. The concept of the rites of passage embodies the Africans' belief that man comes into this world from the Great Beyond. The rite of circumcision spoken of in the Bible was not new to the African. It was a concept of purity and cleanliness in the physical area that is the seat of procreation in mankind. Circumcision was looked upon in the African concept not only as a means of cleanliness in the male but also the female. The tradition was handed down to both male and female that they should be circumcised as early as physically possible. One then passed through initiation periods at the ages of thirteen, eighteen, and twenty-five, which sanctified these age levels. The rites and ceremonies were dedicated to the God of the universe, who enabled one to reach these ages. Then one passed through the marriage rite, eventually coming to the rite of childbirth. This process was repeated until one finally reached the end of life, which brought the death rite. With the last rite of passage, one left this world. It is believed by most Africans that the soul leaves the body and goes back to the Great Paradise. We see this in both the African tradition and the Egyptian tradition. We know the Egyptians created their great monuments in order to immortalize the great kings. Everything that belonged to the kings was buried in the Pyramids, even the possessions of their servants. We also know that the Egyptians took the concept of the death ritual and made it the last rite of passage, the final great ceremony. It was believed that the pharaohs would be remembered for all time by all Egyptians.

The Egyptians also had the rites of prohibition of foods, the eating or not eating of certain foods. In the Luxor

Schools of Mystery the devotées would abstain from meat so that they would be purer spiritually and mentally and be able to grasp the god-force of the universe. In the Old Testament this was carried over in the prohibition of that which is called nonkosher—that which is called *tref*, or undesirable meat, in Hebrew. So the history of the Hebrews once again shows the continuation of an Egyptian past.

The Hebrews also borrowed the cubit, a basic mathematical system for the construction of Egyptian temples. We find in the Book of Leviticus—and also in the Book of Kings—that David, king of Israel, gave a blueprint to Solomon, his son, so that Solomon would build a tremendous and great and magnificent temple to the Jehovah God for Israel. We know from the records of Kings that Solomon had a great Egyptian architect, Harim, who came from Egypt to help build the temple. We must assume that Harim was one of the great builders of the Luxor temple. The cubit system was created by the Egyptians. The cubit system was also the mathematical basis for the temples in Jerusalem.

The Bible talks about the fact that the Israelites set up their commonwealth in the land of Canaan. The twelve tribes each had designated living areas. Most of them were agriculturalists. The Levites, who were the priestly caste, had their own land. Their inheritance was different from that of the Israelite tribes or nations. They also incorporated many Canaanite traditions, including religion. They eliminated a lot of common names and gods, but other gods were assimilated into the society. Starting from Joshua's time, the Levites continued to have relationships with Egypt and with the African continent. Although the Book of Deuteronomy indicates that the Israelites were commanded never to return to Egypt, it is certain that not many centuries elapsed before some of them found their way back to that empire. The traders who transacted sales of horses for Solomon may have been the first to resettle there. In the tenth century, in the time of Solomon's reign before the Christian era, Jewish captives were probably borne off to Africa. We see in the Bible that Israel forgot God and didn't do the things that were right in His eyes. Thus Israel under this new cultural commonwealth did not last one-tenth the time that the Egyptian empire lasted. We notice that the Jews kept returning to Africa, back to the roots of mankind itself. They also went to Babylon. In Babylon there was a tribe called the Elamites, a fact which is recorded in the Bible. This tribe was basically of African origin, and it had African links with ancient Ethiopia. The Israelites were never far away from their roots, the roots that lie in Africa.

The kings of Libya and the kings of Ethiopia welcomed Jewish captives in their empires. Necho took Jehoahaz captive in 607 B.C.E. He undoubtedly brought a number of the supporters of the Judean king with him to Egypt. After the destruction of the First Temple in 586 B.C.E. and the murder of Gidalia, the governor of Jerusalem, a large portion of the Jewish population migrated to Egypt again. (They took with them the prophet Jeremiah, who, according to an Abyssinian legend, drove out the noxious reptiles and crocodiles of that country.) Many of these Jews became mercenaries under the pharaohs and later under the Persian rulers. They settled in large, autonomous colonies, such as those of the Elephantine and Aswan on the Nile River, where we now have Lake Nasser and the Aswan Dam. Others penetrated into Ethiopia, where a Jewish kingdom is said to have existed up to the fourth century C.E. We know for a fact that a Jewish kingdom did exist as early as the time of Jeremiah's captivity, and up to the fourth century C.E., when Ethiopia became the first Christian country in the world.

I will deal with the Ethiopian Jews after discussing the background of the Jews' re-entry into Africa, particularly North Africa. Jewish settlements along the African coast of the Mediterranean also began at an early period. The legends by European historians concerning the African exploits of Joshua, of David's General Joab, and of the colonies said to have been founded by Solomon may be disregarded. It can be stated, however, that Jews accompanied the Phoenicians on their commercial expeditions and formed a part of the population of Carthage, the great metropolis founded in North Africa in the ninth century B.C.E. A seal bearing the name Joab was found in the ruins of Carthage, and Phoenician inscriptions record such typical Hebrew names as Joaz and Jehoahaz.

It must be remembered that the Jewish festival of Hanukkah, symbolizing the confrontation between Judaism and Hellenism, took place in Alexandria. The major battle took place in Jerusalem near the temple of Solomon, where the Hasmonaeon priestly caste of the ancient Jews defeated the Syrian Hellenists and rededicated the temple of Solomon to the worship of Jehovah.

The largest Jewish emigration to Africa occurred during the Greek period. Jews came in large numbers to Alexandria, which was founded in the fourth century B.C.E., attracted by a full grant of the rights of citizenship. Ptolemy I is said to have distributed some thirty thousand Jews over his kingdom in military colonies. These Jews rapidly adopted the Greek language and Greek ways, and their numbers were increased by new emigrations from Palestine. During the disturbances in Palestine in the second century B.C.E., the high priest Onassis fled to Egypt and set up a temple at Leontopoulos which lasted until the first century C.E.

What were these disturbances in Palestine? They were caused by the expansion and conquering of Alexander the Great. This expansion caused confusion in the Eastern world between the tradition of Moses and Judaism and that which came with Alexander the Great, Hellenism. At first, the Ptolemys of Egypt ruled and gave the Jews freedom of worship and political autonomy, demanding only payment of tribute. However, the rabbis and scribes of the Judaic tradition wanted to strengthen Jewish life under Greek rule. At the same time, the Hellenistic tradition was growing in Alexandria and in different parts of the East, particularly in North Africa where the Bible, the Old Hebrew Testament, had been translated. That translation was called the Septuagint translation, because seventy men in seventy days translated it independently of one other. This translation facilitated the understanding and acceptance of the Bible by other peoples in this part of the world. The part of Egypt which gave light unto the world three thousand years previously again created a new synthesis between Hellenism and Judaism. Some few hundred years after was the birth of Christianity. We must remember that these were African Jews. The African Jews in the empire of the Ptolemys produced the first translations of the Bible. A long list of religious and philosophical writings culminating in those of Philo-Judea launched the first great movement to win the non-Jewish elements of North Africa to Judaism. Africa also produced the first Jewish historian, known by the name of Jason of Cyrene, who wrote an account of the Maccabees.

Before the destruction of the Second Temple there were Jewish settlements in Tunis and Morocco. That destruction took place at 70 C.E. By the first century C.E. there were several thousand Jews in Alexandria and many thousands in Cyrenaica. When Egypt was annexed to the Roman Empire in 30 B.C.E., Alexandria lost most of its importance as a commercial center and the Greek population grew hostile toward the Jews. This is a possible explanation for the fact that Judaism never took hold in the Roman Empire. The reform of Judaism came out of this mixture of Greek, Judaic, and Egyptian tradition, especially that system later called Gnosticism, which gave fusion and force to both Hellenism and Judaism. This gave rise to what was later called Coptic Christianity.

The Jewish population of the time gradually diminished, many migrating to Europe, especially to Rome. Many of us feel that this was the beginning of the European Jew.

Riots occurred in Alexandria in 38 C.E. when Caligula attempted to force the Jews to worship him as a deity, and the situation did not improve until after his death. Following the destruction of the Second Temple in the year 70, the last embers of the Jewish revolt were ruthlessly extinguished. A tradition held by the Jews of Tripoli —that their ancestors were brought to that country by a general of Titus—is probably a reminiscence of the dispersion of the Jewish captives over Africa after the destruction of the Temple. The revolt of the Jews of Cyrenaica (in what is now Libya) from 115 to 117 was crushed by the Roman general Torbou, who deliberately turned a great part of that territory into a desert. The Jews of that region moved farther west among the Berbers, where they maintained their autonomy and established trading routes as far south as the Sudan. According to their tradition, the Berbers were part of the ancient Lost Tribes of Israel. When these new Jewish immigrants came in, the Berbers readily adapted to the new form of Israeli culture called Judaism, which was formed by the rabbinical authorities of the academies of Babylonia and of Palestine-Jerusalem. The Jews in the mountainous zones of North Africa—the Jebel—were well organized into tribes. The distinguishing feature was the division into separate communities of Israelites and priests—a distinction which still exists in some parts of Africa down to the present day. These tribes of Yoruwa, under the leadership of Dahia-al-Kahina, who has been called the Joan of Arc of Northern Africa, at first successfully opposed the Arab invasion but were defeated in the attack, and Kahina was slain about 703 C.E. Following this, many of the Jewish tribes became converted to Islam and participated in the Moslem conquest of the rest of the coast. Berber Jews also took part in the conquest of Spain.

Now we will leave North Africa and return to Egypt and Northeast Africa, where we know from the Bible that Moses married a Kushite woman. It is plainly detailed that Moses married her, and that the Kushites did not recognize any difference between a Hebrew and an Egyptian. Again we have evidence that the Hebrews, the Egyptians, the Midianites, and the Ethiopians were of one racial stock and background.

In Ethiopian tradition we also have the legends that not all of the Israelites went into the Sinai Desert to the land of Israel. Many of the Israelites went to Libya and were ancestors of the Berbers. Many of them came to the south and many of them settled in the land of Kush, which is today the Sudan. Some also settled in the land of the present Ethiopian empire, which was situated in those days on both sides of the Red Sea. Yemen, the land situated on the southwestern tip of the Arabian Peninsula, was in ancient times a part of the greater Ethiopian empire. The ancient Jews who came with Moses from the land of Egypt settled along the Red Sea. It is stated in Ethiopian tradition that over the hundreds of years when the confederation of Israeli states was consolidated under the rule of David and Solomon many of these Jews never lost their identity. In fact, after the beginning of the dispersion and breakup of the first commonwealth of ancient Israel in 586 B.C.E. and the second commonwealth of ancient Israel in the year 70 C.E. many Jews of the tribes of Judah and Benjamin who had remained in the ancient Palestinian empire came to the south and met Jews along the Arabian Peninsula. These Jews were found in both the western and eastern Sudan states. In fact, in the ancient kingdom of Ghana, which is now called the Republic of Mali, there were many Jews from the western Sudan who went through the Sahara Desert and settled in this ancient West African kingdom and became part of that society and tradition.

In Ethiopia there existed a track or path to the Ethiopian

highlands. In these highlands of Ethiopia there are a people called the Agaw, who have lived in the Hebraic tradition from ancient times. Their language is of the most ancient times. It is called *Karinya* in the Kushite dialect. These people with the Jews who came back to Africa created a new culture and new way of life. That way of life was called by the westerners *Falasha*, or Ethiopian Jewish life. In the eleventh century B.C.E., this land was called Abyssinia by the Europeans, a corruption of the Arabic term *habasha*, which means "a people of mixtures." The Ethiopians renamed the land Ethiopia when Haile Selassie first became emperor. To that area came a tribe from Yemen in 200 B.C.E., a tribe called the Ahgessahn. This ancient Sabean tribe—because Sabea was the ancient kingdom of South Arabia before the Arab conquest and before the Mohammedan religion had taken over—had migrated to the highlands of Ethiopia. They brought with them the writings, trades, arts, and crafts that were then current in Arabia. About the third century B.C.E., they formed a kingdom, the capital of which was known as Aksum. Why was Aksum important? The Ethiopians believed that the local kings of Ethiopia were descended from Solomon, King of Israel, and that the Tabernacle of the Law of God—that is, the Ark of the Covenant—had been brought from Jerusalem to Aksum by Menelik, Solomon's firstborn son. They believed that God had transferred his place of abode on earth from the ancient city of Jerusalem to Aksum, the ecclesiastical and political capital ot Ethiopia. The Book of Enoch (Ethiopian version) was used by the Christians for over three hundred years as their Bible, and is considered by some Jewish scholars to be the book par excellence of Messianic ideas in Ethiopia.

African Christianity and
the Black Madonna

Rabbi Hilu Paris

In this segment I shall speak about African Christianity, the Black Madonna and Child, and their influences on the world, past and present. In the magazine *Newsweek* dated May 9, 1966, there was an article dealing with the history of the Ethiopian Church. The article says this:

> The customs and beliefs . . . [of] the Ethiopian Church are a mixture of authentic African Christianity, Judaism, and traditional religion or, as they call it, animism. In addition to Sunday, Saturday is observed as the Sabbath, which is what all Jews throughout the world have observed as the Sabbath, for many thousands of years. Male and female children are circumcised and the Mosaic dietary laws are observed. The Ethiopians uniquely celebrate a feast in honor of Pontius Pilate, believing that he ultimately repented of his role in Jesus's passion and death. Western scholars have trouble establishing precisely what the Church believes, since there is no defined body of doctrine.

I would like to comment on two or three of these interpretations. First, Christianity traditionally came from Judaism; it came out of the Afro-Mediterranean world.

Second, the Ethiopians did not believe that they had to have a body of doctrine that would satisfy the Greek or Roman churches of their time. The Ethiopian Church did not believe in the interpretation of Christ that the Greek or Roman churches believed. The Ethiopian Church did not believe that it was contradictory to follow the laws of Moses and the teachings of Jesus. Therefore they, more than any other church in Christendom, continue the tradition of the Mosaic Law and the teachings of Jesus. Their rock-hewn churches and traditional interpretation of life showed that the original Patriarchs of the Bible, Abraham and Jacob, Solomon and David, Joshua and Ezekiel, and Jeremiah—even down to Matthew, Mark, Luke, and John —were of Ethiopian origin and part of the African tradition. They were what the American populace of today would call Black men. This church, isolated from European Christianity, was a blessing because it has retained the identity of the original Christians and the essence of what Christianity was. It also provides us with the missing link to the Judeo-Christian tradition.

From studying history we know that the question of the inferiority or superiority of men based on color began in earnest about four hundred years ago, when Europe went through its Renaissance and created a dogma of white supremacy and world imperialism—although in historical records that preceded the fifteenth and sixteenth centuries the Europeans have injected the concept of color. One of those records was the books of the Bible. We know that in ancient times there was no Biblical reference to a man's color, and there was no implied superiority or inferiority to the men of the ancient world. There was no question of Jesus Christ's color to the people of the ancient world. This question has arisen in our time because of the Western dogma of white racism. According to the literal descriptions in the Song of Solomon, written by the ancient Hebrews, and in Revelations, written by the later Hebrews, Jesus had a dark and ruddy complexion. I read from the text: "I am black and comely, O daughters of Israel." The poetic Biblical chapter Song of Solomon contains this love song written in poetry to glorify God. It gives us one of the few available clues to what color Jesus was when he walked this earth. Read further into this beautiful phrase in the Song of Solomon: "How graceful are your feet in sandals, O queenly maiden. Your rounded thighs are like jewels, the work of a master's hand. Your navel is a rounded bowl that never lacks mixed wine. . . . Your two breasts are like two fawns, twins of a gazelle. . . . Your head crowns you like the Mount Carmel, and your flowing locks are like purple. . . . My beloved is all radiant and ruddy, distinguished among ten thousand. His head is as of the finest gold. His locks are wavy, black as a raven." So much significance is placed on the Old Testament Song of Songs because King Solomon was the son of King David, and the Apostles wrote that Jesus was of the ancestry of David. If Solomon was really black, what then can be said about other ancestors of David, such as the parents of Jesus? The notion of race or color is practically nonexistent in Biblical history. We have, however, brief testimony from the Disciples of Jesus. John, for example, wrote in his Revelation: "A throne stood in heaven, with one seated on that throne! And he who sat there appeared like jasper and carnelian." Both of these we know are rare stones that are dark. It appears that the Disciples, when they spoke of Christ, had a picture in mind other than the white Romanist Jesus of present-day picture books. However, we of the twentieth century have forgotten what early Christians knew and did not forget. Early Christians should have best remembered what Christ looked like, and Jesus of early art was Black. In fact, you can still find murals and statues of the Mother and Child in chapels and even cathedrals today depicting Jesus and his Mother as Black. Many more examples of art featuring a Black Christ were painted over or moved out of the site as latter-day Christians decided to paint a God that resembled their image. The Cathedral of Millau in France, the Cathedral of Augsburg, Germany, the church of San Francisco at Pisa, Italy, the Borgia Chapel in Rome, Notre Dame des Halles in Belgium—all proudly display a Black Christ. About fifteen years ago *Life* magazine ran a photograph of the Pope in his private chapel. The Virgin and Child pictured on the wall of the chapel were Black. Panama today celebrates on October 21 every year the Festival of the Black Christ. In the port city of Porto Bello, eighty men carry a life-sized statue of Christ on a platform surrounded by flowers and candles. The dark face of Jesus on a crucifix is depicted with infinite piety and sadness. The procession continues until midnight. Then the Black Christ statue is returned to the local church and a gay celebration continues until dawn.

We know from history that the Moors (the North African Moslems) controlled the Iberian Peninsula for eight hundred years. During that time there was freedom of religion, until the conquest by El Cid, which marked the takeover of Spain by northern Christians. We know that there were eight hundred years of free intercourse among the Moslems, the Jews, and the Christians. We know that there was a certain freedom of thought and investigation of truth that the Aristotelian logic and the scientific inquiries of the Arab, Jewish, and Christian scholars had given to that period of Moorish civilization in Spain. We can still see in southern Spain, parts of France, and definitely southern Italy, that not only the portraits of the Madonna and Child are of African ancestry, but the people themselves are of African stock. This is one of the reasons that the Blackness of the Madonna and Child has continued to exist in that part of the world.

We also find the same thing existing in the Eastern Church and in areas of Russia and southern and central Asia. We recently have become aware of the Black Madonna of Kazan, Russia. This Madonna is also of African Blackness, of a complexion that one could never say is

European or Nordic. It is an ancient painting of the Madonna and the infant Jesus, only about ten or twelve inches high, done in a thin layer of gesso superimposed on a coarser, thicker layer, then placed over wood. Throughout its history this Black Virgin has been the source of alleged miracles, the inspiration of victorious armies, and the reason for at least two executions. Grateful pilgrims have adorned the Virgin with some 1,003 precious stones to thank the icon for its blessings. To the peasant girl and the Empress of Russia alike the painting has had profound meaning, and it is perhaps the most famous of all Russian relics. The Black Virgin of Kazan, also known as "the miracle icon of Holy Russia," was painted with this dark-skinned pigmentation in Constantinople during the twelfth century. Today the Black Virgin of Kazan is insured against loss for a half-million dollars. It lies in the steely silence of a bank vault in the small village of Mill Valley in northern California, thousands of miles from the site of the ancient civilization it once influenced.

We know that Byzantine artists created many Black Madonnas. We know that these Black Madonnas were created between the Fall of Rome and 1450—the last date before the onslaught of European imperialism and the interpretation of white supremacy fell upon the Afro-Asian world. These Eastern artists produced more Madonnas than all the Western European artists of the Renaissance combined. But the Madonnas the Byzantines painted, thanks to the Schism between Rome and Constantinople, were for Eastern churches and for missionaries who traveled east beyond the Black Sea and the Caspian south into Syria, Palestine, Mesopotamia, and the lands along the Persian Gulf. These missionaries also traveled north into the Balkans and the vast northeastern hinterlands reached by the great waterways such as the Volga and the Don. The people in these regions are by-and-large of a far darker complexion than those of western or northern Europe. In the twelfth century this was especially true of the area known as European Russia, or White Russia, the part that lies to the west of the Urals. At that time the Mongols were the ruling power. For hundreds of miles north of the Black and Caspian seas into the heart of Russia, the percentage of light-skinned inhabitants was small in relation to the numbers of Mongolian and other stocks, including people of black African origins. Even today there are large segments of dark-skinned people in Russia who reflect their mixed ancestry. Therefore we can say that for them the Black Madonna was really the first and only Madonna to be worshipped.

In conclusion, I would say that we are living in a very perilous time. We're living at a time in which technology has taken over, learned the duties of man. We're living at a time in which materialism has become a greater force than spirituality. We're living at a time in which man is still divided according to the pigmentation of skin. We're living at a time in which there are economic classes and institutions that control the great majority of mankind. The three universal faiths that had their birth in Africa and the Afro-Asian world—Judaism, Christianity, and Islam—are also going through a period of change and transition. But the religions of Black men in Africa and in the Americas—North America, Central and South America, and the Caribbean islands—regardless of what form they take in the twentieth century, must have the unifying force of Black redemption, unity, and victory gathered within them. The Feast of Ramadan, the Feast of Passover, and the Feast of Easter must in the twentieth century relate to the aspirations of the Black communities the world over. Now the traditional Christian tradition in Africa, the Coptic Church, is undergoing a revival. The religions superimposed by the European imperialists have been redefined in African terminology. The Church of England and the Church of Rome do not control many of these now independent churches in Africa, which are Africanizing the saints and reinterpreting the traditional religions of the African peoples into the new African Christianity, or African-Islamic faith. It would be my hope also that in the areas of the Middle East where the Sephardim—the Afro-Asian Jews—have once again become a powerful force, they will be able to reinterpret the tradition of Moses in the light of other reinterpretations of religions in that area, so that they will become part of the twentieth century. Hopefully they will relate to the history of the twentieth cenury and to the African peoples in the Afro-Asian world, in America, and in Europe. Christianity—the European version that is controlled by the European churches and institutions—will have to be redefined by Europeans for European usage and existence. In the African context, the Black American will redefine his Christianity, or Islam, or Judaism in light of the reinterpretations that are going on in Africa and in the greater Eastern world. With this, I believe, once again will arise the ascendancy of African heritage and tradition in these religions, and there will be a balanced world culture. This will not be an egocentric culture, but will basically be an Afro-Asian-centered culture, which I believe will lead all of us back to a more even and peaceful world. If not in our time, at least in the time of our children. Possibly the twenty-first-century man will truly be a part of a brotherhood, and all will live in peace. Amen.

African Origins of Western Religions: Antiquity to 1640 B.C.

Dr. Yosef ben-Jochannan

Dr. Josef ben-Jochannan was born in Ethiopia and received his Ph.D. at Cambridge. Presently an Instructor of History at Marymount College in Tarrytown, N. Y., Dr. ben-Jochannan also teaches at Pace College—New York City and Westchester. He is the author of *Black Man of the Nile, African Origins of the Major "Western" Religions*, and *Africa: Mother of Western Civilization.*

Reverend Albert Cleage, brothers and sisters assembled here at this historic first national conference of the Black Christian Nationalist movement in this Shrine of the Black Madonna, Detroit, Michigan: I am indeed grateful for the opportunity to share with you a few insights into the African origins of that which is popularly called "Western religions," namely, Judaism, Christianity, and Islam.

My lecture this morning will be an academic investigation of the origins of the religions I have named and a general history of the Africans' contributions to the world's high-culture civilizations. I will also include information about the history of our ancestors—the African (the Black man), his religion, and other aspects of his society.

For the last two to three thousand years Judaism, Christianity, and Islam have been presented to the African-Americans and other people of African origins in a manner suggesting exclusively European beginnings. Yet the beginnings of any of these religions did not involve one European. All three of them are of the creative genius of Africans, Asians, and African-Asians. European personalities entered them many generations following their establishment within Africa and Asia—and this does not mean solely around the so-called Middle East region.

It is not surprising to me that Israelites, Christians, Muslims, Yorubas, Voodooists, Spiritualists—both of the laity and clergy—of African peoples here in these United States of America would come together for the purpose of recapturing a common theological basis upon which we can again meet as honored sons and daughters of Mother Africa. But there is an overriding issue in this historic gathering: that is, our ability to recognize one another's right to hold separate, although basically similar, religious theories relating to our belief in that which we hold to be responsible for the world in which we live.

As we begin to examine the failure of lettered educators in the major institutions of higher learning—both Black and white—to deal with the African peoples' contribution to Judaism, Christianity, and Islam, we find that they had to suppress certain information—in some cases even entire sections of Biblical scriptures—in order to maintain the racist theory of the superiority of the European and European-American (the so-called Caucasian race) over all other peoples of the world. This is typical of the theory that *if you tell a lie often enough people will believe it.* But this theory must be extended to include the fact that *the liar* will also believe it. However, regardless of the liar or his lies, the truth of the African origins of Judaism, Christianity, Islam, and other religions not normally associated with Africa or people of African origin, still remains in the pages of the sacred scriptures of these teachings. It is upon this truth that I shall primarily base my entire presentation. So I now enter into the depth of our philosophical and spiritual teachings that made Judaism, Christianity, and Islam what they were at their creation, and what they have become today.

"In the beginning God made man from the earth." This is the manner in which certain versions of the Hebrew and Christian scriptures commence with regard to the creation of the world by God—Jehovah. To a great extent the same hypothesis is followed in the Moslem Koran. But one finds that this theory comes from the *Ta-urt*, which was taught by the indigenous Africans of Egypt. Ta-urt—the Great Mother Earth, the first form of the goddess Isis, the first known "Mother" in written history —preceded the Haribus (Hebrews or Jews), even the Garden of Eden, and the Christian's Mary (the Virgin Mary, mother of Jesus Christ) by thousands of years. Isis not only preceded Eve and Mary, she was the mother of many of the Gods before the creation of Jehovah (God), Jesus Christ, and Allah.

In regard to what I have said so far, one should examine Dr. E. A. Wallis Budge's *The Gods of the Egyptians*, Volume II, page 30, and Professor G. C. C. Maspero's *Dawn of Civilization*, page 99, for further details. But the Great Mother Earth, sometimes called "Great Mother" in other indigenous African religions of antiquity and of the present, bears other names, such as "Goddess Nzambi" (the Great Mother), and "Nkissi-Nsi" (The Mystery Power of Earth).

The Babylonians adopted the Great Mother Earth theory from the indigenous Africans, as seen on their totems under the title of *Omoroca*. Among the Greeks she became the goddess of Gae. In South America, to the indigenous people (the so-called Indians), the Moquis in particular, she became Mamapocha—the mysterious

Mother of Fertility. All of these names for Mother Earth preceded the Hebrew myths about the God Jehovahs (Yaweh, Yavh, Yva, etc.) creation of man (Adam) from the Earth (some say clay). The Great Mother was also represented by the Africans of many Nile Valley high cultures as the Goddess *Apt* or *Mut*.

Sut and *Horus*, the first-born twins of the Great Mother Earth, Apt, were taught by the Africans to be the primary elemental powers, Darkness and Light. Thus one sees Sut as the Power of Darkness and Horus as the Power of Light. One notes that the African Haribus also carried this birth theory into the creation myth after they left Egypt (Kimit or Sais) in the Book of Genesis (First Book of Moses). Thus they wrote: "And God said let there be light, and there was light out of the darkness. . . ." In this same regard Sut was often shown symbolically as a blackbird, whereas Horus was a white bird. These two symbols were depicted by the Africans of Egypt as the Black Vulture and the Golden Eagle. They were, in fact, the two most ancient types of elemental powers in the major mythological concepts of the known universe of antiquity. These symbols and their meanings related to the Haribus co-option in the First Book of Moses, Genesis, in which the following verse appears:

> . . . the sons of God saw the daughters of men that they were fair; and they took them wives of all which they chose.

This was followed by the reaction of the daughters in the same book:

> . . . the sons of God came in unto the daughters of men, and they bore children to them. . . .

The Hebrews' version of their fellow Africans of Egypt's Mysteries System teaching differs only with respect to the impregnators of the "daughters." In the lore of the African worshipers of the god Ra, the daughters were made pregnant by the intercession of the lesser gods, led by the God Ywh; the daughters became pregnant by man through the grace of God.

According to the teachings of the Stellar Cult people—the so-called Nilotic negroes (Africans who were the first to measure time and keep meticulous records of the movements of the seven pole stars), and the Twa (sarcastically called "pygmies" *), the Earth Goddess was used in their own Crucifixion resurrection myth thousands of years before the birth of the first Hebrew, Abraham, and before the birth of the Christians' Jesus Christ of Nazareth, son of two Hebrews—Joseph and Mary. The crucified god of the indigenous Mexicans, and the gods *Ptah* (the *Great I Am*, or Seeker) and *Ansar* of the Romiti † were supposedly sacrificed in the same manner as the crucified Great Mother Earth of the Twa people of central East Africa.

The Great Mother Earth sacrifice was highlighted by the slaughtering of the African god Sept, as shown in the Egyptian works dealing with the Stellar Mythos, which the European Christians adopted and corrupted to suit their own crucifix totem. Why was the cross used in this manner by the European Christians? Because the African "mystery of the cross" symbol and totem, for more than thirty thousand years before the birth of Jesus Christ of Nazareth, were used for burial of crucified victims who were shown staked to the totem in the manner Michelangelo later depicted with his northern blond, blue-eyed, Italian-model "Son of God." This type of totem is still evident on the inner walls of the Pyramid of Medam and others built about thirty thousand years ago. Strange as it

---

* The name *pygmy* is singular; *pygmies*, plural. It is a slave nomenclature placed upon the Twa people by European colonialists, Christian missionaries, and slavers euphemistically called entrepreneurs.

† *Romitu*, Egyptian: *Romiti*, Egyptians. *Egypt* is a name of Hebrew origin. *Kimit* was the African name.

may seem, even in the famous Tomb of Olham Fodhla of Ireland one can find a symbolic crucifix. The sacrifice or crucifix, as originally designated, is seen in the Hebrew version of the Lord's command to Moses. Thus Ywh said:

> "Take all the heads of the people and hang them up before the Lord against the sun, that the fierce anger of the Lord may be turned away from Israel."

Moses allegedly responded with the following to the judges of Israel, according to Num. 25: 4-5:

> "Slay ye every one his men that were joined unto Baal-peor. . . ."

The prime reason this information has been hidden from most Jews, Christians, and Moslems is to maintain the mythical concept, constantly perpetuated by rabbis, priests, ministers, and laymen, that their own respective brand of religious mythology, as well as their own history, was written by holy men inspired by God. This is followed by the theory that God is Ywh, if one is Hebrew; He is Jesus Christ, if one is Christian; and *Allah,* if one is Moslem. To these believers, no other God possessed the power of passing down holy inspiration; and, of course, there is no sacred book except the Hebrew *Torah*—Five Books of Moses (originally only four); the Christian *Holy Bible* (Old and New Testaments—all versions); and the Moslem Koran—that is, if one is conditioned in any of these so-called Western religions. Naturally God does not inspire men to write books that do not support religion à la European style; neither could He inspire the writings of the Africans, from whom all of these theories derive. The above command to Moses is similar to that which the Pharaoh * Rameses II (1298-1232 B.C.E.) received from his god Ra—though the contention that Yaweh did likewise to the Hebrews is not

---

* The word *pharaoh* means king or queen. It is not a proper name as used in the Bible.

supported by the Second Book of Moses in the Hebrew Torah. Yet the holy papyri of the Africans of Egypt show that the god, Horus, who existed for thousands of years before the Hebrew God Ywh, Christian God Jesus Christ, and Moslem God Allah, did state:

> "I am the one who presided over the pole of heaven, and the powers of all the gods are my powers. I am he whose names are hidden and whose abodes are mysterious for all eternity."

The most unfortunate tragedy in the education of Western man is the projection of Judeo-Christianity and Greek-Anglo-Saxon racism as concepts of the one and only Truth passed down to mankind from the one and only true God.

The above teachings remind one of the present use of the dove as a peace symbol. For with this image in use, it is not uncommon to hear the young, inexperienced, and immature expound their theory of its origin from the Soviet Union, while yet others place its origin with the Hebrews and Christians, none of them knowing that this symbol was used in the divination ritual of the Hathor dove, as the bird of Ra. It was used in this manner among the ancient Romiti of Kimit and other Nile Valley high cultures. The dove also represented "the God, Horus, risen from the dead," this even though Horus was also shown as the Hawk God. Horus, arising as both dove and hawk, proclaimed: "I am the dove! I am the dove!" as his spirit came forward from Amenta. (For further details one should examine the Ritual LXXXVI: I of the *Book of Free Masonry;* the ritual also appears in the *Book of the Dead.*) In the tomb of Rameses IX, the dove (Horus) replaces the hawk (Ra) completely as the commander of the Solar Boar that took the Holy Spirit. He was, for the most part, presented in his religious role in the form of a bird—mainly a dove or hawk—in Nile Valley symbolism. The dove is also represented in the Papyrus of Ani over the head of Maat (or Mati) and Osiris seated in the Dead Square (today called Masonic Square) in the Great Hall of Judgment. The same "squaring of the dead" has since been adopted by Masonic orders as the "squaring of the stones of the builders" and also as the "squaring of the conduct and morals of the Mason." Of course, these teachings have been attributed to Hebrew teachings from King Solomon's * temple. Nevertheless, scholars who have studied the origin of religions and their signs and symbols know that the latter teachings came from the ancient Africans of the Great Lakes region and Kimit. This is best depicted in the "creation of heaven" scene of the Egyptian Mysteries System. For it is the ideograph used by the Africans in this dramatic scene which became the present Mason's square. Therefore, it is obvious that the literal interpretation of the translation of the word "square" from the original hieroglyph into the English language is in error. The African usage of the word was in a metaphysical sense and not the geometrical right triangle used in modern Masonic signs and symbols. This is most noteworthy, as in the same documents we see that the god Ptah was believed to be the first architect of the universe thousands of years before the Haribus Jehovah, Christian Jesus Christ, and Moslem Allah were designated.

At this juncture one should have already observed that the Haribus and the Greeks were incompetent in perpetuating the original philosophical thoughts that the African sources so far revealed: so were the Romans and other Europeans who adopted their own version of the African's religion. For example, after the Romans seized control of the "Mother Church" (the North African Christian Church) they were forced to hide all papyri showing that the god Khensu was the first great Son of the God Amen; that he was able to make himself appear as a youth

* Solomon was not King of Israel until *c.* 970 B.C., which was thousands of years after the "squaring of the dead" was started by the Africans of central Africa and the Nile Valley.

in Thebes in the form of the God Ra; and that he became the son of the Goddess Nubit at night, converting
into a baby in the morning and an old man in the evening
—all teachings of Nile Valley Africans (the Mysteries
System's Grand Lodge). One needs to remember that the
god *Amen* is the same god which modern Jews, Christians,
and Moslems honor at the end of each prayer. And like
Jesus Christ of Nazareth, the god Khensu also renewed his
birth, arose from the dead, and appeared in the heavens
as the solar disk, thus gaining the title "The God of the
Dual Horizon." Among the many titles which Khensu
carried were "Aah Son of Hathor" (the Moon God or
Aah-Tehuti), "the Great God," "the King of the Gods,"
"the Lord of Heaven," and "Creator of Everlastingness."
All of these titles Khensu held before the Hebrew, Christian, or Moslem religion was created by allegedly God-
inspired men (prophets).

These teachings have become "pagan mythology" according to many bearing the title theologian, or professors of religion. But what is religion other than mythology? Is religion not the belief and teaching that the
spiritual nature of the human person is bound to a super-
human being called "God" (or its equivalent in many
other languages)? Strictly speaking, it is the belief in an
unknown, remotely separated from mankind, that is,
mortal man. This is nothing more than the earliest Africans had taught for thousands of years before the existence
of the first Haribu, much less a Moses.

Whether one follows a polytheistic or monotheistic
philosophy dealing with a godhead, it is still the so-called
pygmies of Central Africa—the Twa people—whom most
modern major anthropological and archaeological findings
have proved were the originators of the first religion and
its signs and symbols, most of which have been adopted,
co-opted, and/or plagiarized by modern religionists. The
following sign and/or symbol 뉴, called "the one great
Spirit," which is still the Twa peoples' most sacred, is

also most prominent as the "One Great One" among the Christians of the twentieth century c.e., and it is corrupted into what is now called the crucifix or Christ's cross: †
This sign or symbol has been proven by anthropological findings to be the first of ancient man's religious and scientific communication anywhere on the planet Earth. Earliest mankind, the indigenous people of the continent of Alkebu-Lan, which the Greeks and Romans labeled Africa, therefore, were in fact the one and only true creators of the first known God—One Great Spirit—and the first religion—sun and fire worship. The evolutionary growth of their religion permeated the Nile Valley and Great Lakes high cultures and all other African societies, including Kimit (Egypt), Kush (Ethiopia), Ghana (west Africa), Kongo (Congo), and Monomotopa (Union of South Africa) before the first European religion—the Druids'—was even conceived. Even the Europeans' most sacred signs and symbols are only very minor variations of those established by their African prototypes, which are today called "primitive" or "heathen," or even in some cases "cannibalistic." Hopefully, these facts should make us, as African people, sons and daughters of the original creators of the religious philosophical teachings which are today called Judaism, Christianity, Islam, etc., share a common communion. A communion based not upon the dreamer Haribu-turned-Roman, Paul, but one based upon the life style established by our forefathers at the shores of the African Great Lakes and Nile River valleys—both Blue and White. This brief presentation of the historical justification for the Black man's claim to the origin of the so-called Western religions cannot negate our thrust for further attempts to join hands with other African people who are still Paulist-European-oriented to the European-American Christian Church and its Caucasianized Jesus Christ, as depicted by Michelangelo under the commission of the Pope in Rome.

The African high cultures date back even to the days

of *Zinjanthropus boisei,* an apelike man the remains of which were unearthed at the Olduvai Gorge near the great Mwuanza Nyanza (which the European colonists called Lake Victoria), an African (not a Semite, Hamite or Caucasian) that predated Adam and Eve by more than 1,750,000 years. These historical facts are not based upon faith or dreams, they are archaeological and historical facts which have been verified by scientific data. However, we can go to *recorded* facts, signs, symbols, and totems in man's possession today, from as early as 25,000 years before the Christian Era (B.C.E. or B.C.) during the Sybillian II period.* The Africans of the Nile Valley high cultures had produced the first stellar calendar known to the world, this having been accomplished in the year ten thousand before the birth of Jesus Christ of Nazareth. The world's second calendar, or solar calendar, was established by the Africans in the year four thousand one hundred before the birth of Jesus. It is this latter calendar which the Hebrews used for dating their own history of Moses and others. These facts are thoroughly documented in the works listed in the extensive bibliography at the end of the paper entitled "African Origins of Judaism, Christianity and Islam." Many of these works you can examine at the end of this lecture and question period. Why? Because I am laying the indigenous-African, the so-called Black African foundation to show you that not only was the Hebrews' origin of Christianity of Black African creation, but that even before the Hebrews the indigenous Africans were teaching much of what the Hebrews still teach today as a direct result of their co-option of concepts and theories from the Africans' Mysteries System. I am also saying that the Hebrew religion is only a continuation of religious philosophical concepts and principles which the indigenous Africans (Negroes,

---

* The Sybillian I (25,000 B.C.E.), Sybillian II (12,000-8,000 B.C.E.), and Sybillian III (8,000-6,000 B.C.E.) periods ranged from twenty-five thousand to six thousand years before the Christian Era.

Bantus, "pygmies," even "niggers" and other such derogatory names they have been called by Western educators) had already started and developed to a very highly sophisticated degree.

We are told that the first Hebrew or Jew was a fellow by the name of Avram, or Abraham; and that "Abraham was a worshiper" of the existing national gods of a country called "Chaldea, in the city of Ur." Also, that "it came to pass that Abraham and his family were hungry in the desert where they were," so they decided to go down into Africa at a place called Kimit to get some food, clothing, shelter, and other forms of hospitality from the indigenous Africans, who were not yet labeled Negroes, Bantus, Hottentots, Bushmen, Semites, or Hamites, much less "Caucasoids" by so-called Western educators. These are very plain words: ". . . and they went down into Egyptland." Who went down into Africa? Abraham, the man from whom the Hebrews originate. All of this we find in the First Book of Moses, Genesis. In the Second Book of Moses, Exodus, we are also told that the Hebrews spent four hundred years of slavery building the pyramids of Egypt.* Let us closely examine this Biblical charge against the Africans of Egypt. If the Hebrews spent four hundred years in Egypt, up to the time when Moshe (Moses) was already ninety to ninety-five years old, then we must calculate the period in Egyptian dynastic history, which is hundreds of years before the birth of another Hebrew called Jesus Christ. If we add four hundred years to the time of Moses (remembering that Moses was supposed to have been driven out of Egypt by Pharaoh Rameses II, and that Rameses II died in 1230 B.C.E.) we must add four hundred to *c.*1235 and we will have 1635 B.C.E. In 1635 B.C.E. the Romiti of Egypt (not Semites or

---

* Kimit, or Sais, as this African land was originally called; Egypt being the name that the Hebrews labeled it; a name that resulted from their Noah-and-the-Flood drama in their own Holy Scriptures.

Hamites) were overpowered by the Hyksos, a group of Asians who had invaded Egypt from their homeland along the Oxus Riverbed (at what was earlier called Asia Minor—today's Middle East) in the general area where the present nation called Israel is located. But neither Israel (nor Palestine) existed during the period of history when the Hyksos invaded and occupied Egypt c.1675-1580 B.C.E. We are not going to have any "Promised Land" (Palestine or Israel) until years after Moses' disappearance. Why is this true? Because Moses, as the Hebrew history book or Torah tells us, did not see the Promised Land.

We must establish the period when Abraham came into Egypt. From the account in the Torah, he must have come into Egypt during the Hyksos occupation. The Hyksos had scourged the whole of the tip of northern Egypt and a section of Libya, and enslaved the indigenous African people. They destroyed because they did not know anything about the development of the African's Nile Valley high culture—and I mean "Nile Valley high culture," for many of us talk extensively about the Nile River, but we think of the Nile River only in terms of Egypt, even though only a short length of the Nile River flows through Egypt. The White Nile starts in central East Africa at the place today called Uganda, which was before called the Bunyoro States. There at the African Great Lakes, not only did the Africans develop their high cultures, but such African societies reached their zenith long before there was a Hebrew Book of Genesis and its story of Creation with Adam and Eve, which was also a very long time before anyone knew about the rivers Tigris and Euphrates. And of course, these high cultures existed thousands of years before the birth of the Christians' Jesus Christ or the Moslem's Allah.

What else do we find in our examination of the origins of the teachings that created the so-called Western religions—Judaism, Christianity, and Islam? We discover that thousands of years before the birth of the first Haribu, Abraham, African high-culture civilizations had already reached their zenith, and that the Africans had already given names to the planets and the stars in the universe. This took place as civilization moved outward from east-central Alkebu-Lan into Kush, Nubia, Punt, Kimit, and other areas at the north; Zimbabwe, Monomotapa, the island of Hova (Merina, Dauphine, Madagascar, or Malagasy Republic), etc., at the south; and Kongo, Ghana, Sahara, etc., to the west. Africans had already developed pharmacology and the related disciplines necessary for embalming their dead for entry into the Nether World—whence the terms "heaven" and "hell" originated. They had produced their four most important pyramid-builders; Kjoser (Zozer), Khufu (Cheops), Makh-har-ra (Mycerinus), and Khafra (Chephram). No Hebrew helped to build any of the pyramids; Hebrews were not in existence anywhere in the world, much less having entered Egypt and subsequently been "enslaved on the building of the pyramids." We know nothing of Abraham until *c.*1640 or 1675 B.C.E. at the earliest, and by then all of the major pyramids had been built. For example, the pharaoh * Djoser (whom the Greeks renamed Zozer), the third pharaoh of the first dynasty who reigned from *c.*2870 to 2850 B.C.E., had already provided the materials necessary for Inhotep (the great indigenous African architect and physician, who predated Hippocrates by more than two thousand years) to design and build the Step Pyramid of Saqqara. There were no Hebrews in existence at that

---

* Let it be clearly understood that the word pharaoh as stated here and elsewhere means *king* or *queen,* and one must specify which pharaoh is being referred to in any given situation. It is also necessary to establish the date and dynasty in which the pharaoh lived or reigned in order to avoid the utter confusion such omissions have engendered in the present sacred scriptures. For example, there were many pharaohs named Rameses. From Rameses I through Rameses XIII, there were thirteen different Ramessides.

time, for there was no Abraham. His great-great-grand-mother, ten times removed, was not even born. Pharaoh Khufu, whom the Greeks renamed Cheops, reigned after Djoser. He built the great pyramid and some historians attributed the pyramid Akhet Khufu (the so-called Sphinx of Ghizeh) to him. He was followed by Pharaoh Mah-Khan-rah (Mycerinus), who built another major pyramid. And then came the last of the great pyramid builders, Khafra, whom the Greeks renamed Cephram, or Cheprain. Up to this period in history the first Haribu was not yet born. There were no Adam and Eve yet. When the Africans of the Nile valleys, Blue and White, were building their great pyramids, the existence of a Haribu people was unknown. Thus when the Africans started to embalm their dead and develop the science of pharmacology to make what is today called a mummy, there was still no Abraham. When the Africans built their first canal—not that which is presently called Suez, but their earliest one, running west to east instead of the present south to north—there still was no Abraham. When the Pyramid Texts (writings on the pyramid walls) and the Coffin Texts (writings on and in the coffin of the pharaoh) began to appear, still there was no Abraham—the first Haribu.

African Origins of Judaism, Christianity, and Islam

Dr. Yosef ben-Jochannan

The Hebrew religion did not begin with the first Hebrew —Abraham—around 1640 B.C. Neither did the Hebrew religion, or mankind, begin with anyone named Adam or Eve. The myth of the temptation and fall of Adam and Eve in the Garden of Eden is inconsistent with the theological Mysteries System of the African people out of which Judaism originated. Let us start, then, with a realistic analysis of our African theology.

As we continue the examination of our African heritage with respect to the creation and development of the so-called Western religions (Judaism, Christianity, Islam), we must return to our ancient Coffin Texts—specifically those which we call today the Negative Confessions. For we are now approaching the true beginning of Judaism, the Hebrew religion. It is the Coffin Texts, in what is called the "Osirian Drama," that contain the original works in which the Hebrew Ten Commandments had their origin. In the Osirian Drama no God at Mount Sinai is described giving the 147 Negative Confessions or any tablet to anyone. The Negative Confessions, a set of answers to "Commandments" established by the indigenous Africans in the name of their god, Ra, and other gods, more than four thousand years before the Hebrew Torah, totaled 147 laws. They are called Negative because all of them begin clauses of the formula "I have not committed murder"; "I have not stolen from any man"; "I have not coveted my neighbor," etc. All the Negative Confessions were written by African priests of the Osirica lodges—the mother of them being the Grand Lodge of Luxor. They were passed down orally to the lesser or subordinate lodges of Asia and Europe, including the lodge at Mt. Carmel where Moses, Solomon, and Jesus Christ were initiated. The Confessions were required to be made by the dead, after a dead person had "risen and begun his judgment before the Gods in order to enter the abode and sanctuary of the Gods" (today's so-called heaven). The Confessions were also necessary for the "weighing of the candidate's heart in the judgment scale, which had to balance with a feather." I suggest that you read the *Book of the Dead*. This book is an outstanding translation (hieroglyph into English) of the original Africans' Coffin and Pyramid texts. It is the best one of its kind by far. Its editor was Dr. Ernest A. Wallis Budge. He also compiled another major work that is related to the *Book of the Dead*, entitled *Osiris*. Suggested also for further reading on this phase of my lecture are the following works: Homer W. Smith, *Man and His Gods;* Sir James Frazier, *The Golden Bough;* Sir Geoffrey Higgins, *Anacalypsis* (two volumes); Yosef ben-Jochannan, *African Origins of the Major "Western Religions,"* and *Black Man of the Nile;* Dr. Albert Churchward, *The Origin of Freemasonry, Signs and Symbols of Primordial Man, Origin and Evolution of the Human Race,* and *Arcana of Freemasonry;* George G. M. James, *Stolen Legacy;* Frankfort's *Before Philosophy;* Kleiner's *History of Philosophy;* and Rudick's *History of Philosophy.* It is to be noted that all of these works also include references to other materials relevant to this subject. We cannot forget the work of the

Ionian Herodotus of Greek citizenship, *The Histories*, in which he describes the physical identity of the Africans he lived with and studied under—the descendants of those who were responsible for man's original concepts and theories of religion. He described them thus: "The Colchians, Ethiopians, and Egyptians have thick lips, broad nose, woolly hair, and they are burnt of skin." It is in this same light that we notice that King Solomon of Israel did not write the so-called Proverbs. He plagiarized them, having co-opted them from the writings of Pharaoh Amen-e-ope. One can see the exact quotations, word for word, that Solomon copied. Here we can note the importance of the dating process established by the high priest Manetho in his division of Egyptian pharaonic history into dynasties. For as a result of this dating procedure, we can tell that King Solomon mounted the throne of Israel in the year *c.* 750 B.C. But Pharaoh Amen-e-ope lived in the year *c.* 1290 B.C., more than five hundred years before King Solomon was born. Thus we see that Hebrewism or Judaism, call it whatever you want, is an African religion. But where in the indigenous African culture did it originate? What is its background?

We will note, as this lecture continues, that Judaism came from the worship of the god Ra (the Sun worship), whom the Africans worshiped prior to the birth of Abraham and the concept of his God *Yaweh*. Do not tell me about Moses being the first to deliver the "unitarian principle of one God." How can one say that Moses, Abraham, or any other Hebrew introduced monotheism (the unitarian principle)? The most distinguished Pharaoh, Akhenaten (Ikhnaton, Iknaton, Amenhotep IV) died over two generations (1352 B.C.E.) before the birth of Moses (*c.*1330 B.C.) and Akhenaten spoke of "one God" (Amen-Ra) "above all other Gods," the same God in whose honor most prayers end "Amen." It is because of such facts as these that I have actively withdrawn from Western Anglicized and Greek-promoted "Judaism." I no longer identify myself as a Hebrew or Jew. I am a man, a *Black* man, African-American now, one who can support any Black-oriented religion. This I have done in order to share history with all-Black co-religionists, and in order to be free and honest with my Black brethren. For in order to deal honestly with all religions the historian should remove himself from identification with any particular religion and remain a historian only for the purpose of service to all who need it.

I say further, in dealing with this issue of the Hebrews, and particularly with the role of Moses, we must first examine why Moses is said to be "Black," Judaism is Black, and the Hebrews are Black. Let us say that Abraham was white, pink, green, or technicolored when he arrived in Egypt (remembering that Egypt is still in Africa). If Abraham was any of these colors other than Black, and he came into Egypt with seven people (his wife and other members of his immediate family), and they lived in this Black country in slavery for over four hundred years, African males would have in no way allowed seven people to multiply untouched; neither would any other group of people have allowed it to happen that way. We see the same course followed by the Europeans of the United States in relationship to their African slaves; we, all of us here, being the living proof. It is obvious that most of those original Hebrew women had to have had sexual cohabitation with their African male enslavers, if the story is at all true. How, then, after being subjected to more than four hundred years of raping, could the Hebrews have remained pure anything, which they may have been when they first entered Africa? If they were not Black before they entered, they certainly were when they left. By these facts alone, today we do not have to wonder whether they are Black or not. For by the time they left they must have resembled the ace of spades—just like the description Herodotus gave in his *Histories*,

Book II, in *c.*450-457 B.C. with respect to the Colchians, Egyptians and Ethiopians.

Let us examine the issue of the color of Moses. The story goes that *Moses was born.* We have not had the privilege of knowing much more about his childhood. We also know very little about his parents' background. He was already an old man before any detail of his life is told. In other words, he just got born. Most of the religious characters just got born by remote control also. We know that Moses' birth took place during the reign of Pharaoh Haremhab. This we have been able to establish because we know that Moses was a ninety-five-year-old man when he started to make plans for his exodus to Mount Sinai. If you add ninety-five years to *c.*1232 B.C. (the year Rameses II died), you have *c.*1327 B.C. Why 1232 B.C.? Because Rameses II was the pharaoh of Egypt, Africa, who supposedly chased Moses all over the Egyptian desert to avenge his soldier whom Moses killed. This calculation would set the birth of Moses at least during the reign of Pharaoh Haremhab (1340-1320 B.C.) He had to be born during the reign of one or the other. We may say it is either one, for the sake of this discussion, and there will be no major changes in the facts. Moses, an indigenous African of Egypt (a "soul brother"), is first mentioned *floating down the Nile River.* One must wonder if it is the same Nile River that receives its main sources of water from Lake Tana in Ethiopia— the Blue Nile with its rapids—and the White Nile from Mwanza Nyanza ("Lake Victoria") at Uganda, Kenya and Tanganyika, which is rougher yet. The Nile River, after the meeting of the Blue and White tributaries, becomes even rougher as one passes the first cataract in Sudan—ancient Nubia. But Moses is described in the Book of Exodus as in a *bulrush basket* or *bark* floating down this treacherous river. Now in the first place, how did the daughter of the pharaoh (Haremhab or Seti I) know that

Moses was Jewish? No star of David was stamped on his little stomach or any other part of his body as a means of his Jewish identification. The only proof they had was that he was an African of Egypt, and this did not have to be so.

Moses grew up among the royal class in the Mysteries System of his fellow Africans of Egypt. This System was the university that the Africans had developed in Egypt thousands of years before the time of Moses' birth. In this System Moses grew up and was educated, having been initiated in the subordinate lodge at Thebes and received his advance degrees at the Grand Lodge at Luxor. He moved up in the government. He was brought up as a member of the pharaoh's cabinet. He was a member of the royal family. And if he did anything as they said he did, he was a good man who probably did not like what was going on among his fellow Africans of Kimit and decided to start an insurrection. He killed the military representative (a soldier or guard) of Pharaoh Rameses II. One can just hear Rameses II saying, "Moses, I am going to kill you." Moses started to run. This is the beginning of the so-called exodus, the entire drama in capsule form. Moses ran and ran until he reached a well. At the well a woman named Zipporah was drawing water. Moses helped Zipporah and she went back to the house of her father (the chief priest of the Midianites). And the priest said to his daughter, Zipporah, "How did you get back so quickly?" And she said to her father, "An Egyptian helped me." She could not tell that Moses was a Hebrew or whether he was a worshiper of the god Ra or Jwh (Jehovah). Moses looked like any other indigenous Egyptian you see in the Detroits or Harlems of the United States of America, a soul brother. He looked like any Egyptian you see sitting in this auditorium now. This is what he, Moses, looked like. The proof is that Zipporah did not say "a Jew"; neither did she say "a Hebrew"; nor did she say "a Semite." She said, "An Egyptian helped me."

As we review the history—and we are not yet at Mount Sinai—Moses has already been charged with murder. Aaron, Moses' brother, started out by stealing from the pharaoh's treasury. But Aaron knew that there was a law against theft in Egypt. There were laws existing against all sorts of acts, as shown in the Negative Confessions of the Hymns of Osiris. These laws were commonly enforced in Egypt, Ethiopia, Nubia, Merowe, Bunyoro, and other nations along the more than 4,100-mile-long Nile Valley. Laws of this nature also existed in Numidia, Khart-Haddas (which later became Carthage), and other northwestern African nations. And in Punt (which is today called Somaliland), such laws were also known.

If we look at the Hebrews, who were allegedly fleeing slavery in Egypt, we find them stopping to purchase slaves of their own before they were able to reach Mount Sinai. We also see them later, during the reign of King Saul, setting a stage of genocide as they ravaged the land of the Moabites, Hittites, Zebusites, Amalakites, Pezzarites, and others too weak to withstand their armed might, according to the Book of Exodus. These attacks they later attributed to directives from their own God—Yaweh or Jehovah. Yet when they were being driven out of Egypt by their fellow Africans of the god Ra (Black, Negro, Bantu, etc.), that was not by the command of God. Why, then, do we not look at King Saul's dialogue with his generals in the Torah in the same light as we look at those who similarly acted as Saul, but were enemies of the Hebrews? One can only paraphrase the Saul drama with his generals. Thus: "Have you defeated them? Have you liquidated them all? Yes, my master, we have killed them all. Did you leave anything living? Yes, my master, What? Their dogs, etc. Go back. Kill them. They, too, are Zebusites, Hittites, Amalakites, Moabites, etc. Kill all of them."

The Hebrews or Jews were now African-Asian people,

black-brown combinations and variations at least. They
had become the terror of their neighbors. They, too, now
owned slaves; some they bought while fleeing Egypt,
others they accumulated from their conquest of many nations. We also find the same type of myth in the story
about the Hebrew or Jewish girl, Mary, as we come to
Jesus Christ and his "miraculous virgin birth." But there,
in Asia, not Europe, Christianity was not yet a religion
where people prayed to anyone named Jesus Christ. We
must return to Egypt. For it was in Egypt that the
Christian Church also started. Pantheus, the first bishop
of the North African Church, and Bishop Origen, the
first hermit who went into the Egyptian desert (then
called Zaara, today's Sahara) and there "established the
first monastery for hermits" (hermitic living), were only
two of the many Africans who established the Christian
Church. But at this earliest beginning the Church was
called "the Brethren." That was also the followers' name
—Brethren. And the followers of Jesus Christ (the name
the Christians also called themselves) assembled in memory
of their prophet and teacher who had gone on, not of
God. Jesus Christ was not yet proclaimed a god. Such
proclamation followed his death by hundreds of years.
At this same period, all the books were still in the Hebrew
Torah, and the New Testament was not tampered with.
None had been taken out yet. The Nicene conference
was called for the purpose of removing books from the
Holy Bible that the new rulers of Christendom, the
European conquerors and the Holy Roman Church of
Rome, did not agree with.

One must remember, however, that it was the Africans
of the North African Church (which had grown astonish-
ingly) that began Christendom's popularity. The Brethren
had adopted a new name—Copts. And it had spread into
neighboring Libya, and from Libya into Carthage (for-
merly Khart-Haddas or "new town") and Numidia—
from the extreme eastern limit of North Africa to the

extreme western limit. In Carthage (in today's Tunisia) and Numidia (today's Morocco) among the Africans, the three "greatest fathers of the Christian church"—Tertullian, St. Cyprian (bishop of Carthage), and St. Augustine (bishop of Hippo-Rigus)—were born. St. Augustine, the most noted of the three, was the genius who wrote *The City of God* and *On Christian Doctrine*, two of thirty-eight major works that remain to the present day "Christendom's most sacred teachings, dogmas, and truths." One can safely say, as a result of the historic truths before us, that were it not for these Africans, and others who preceded them in the North African Church and in the original Brethren, there would be no Christianity of the magnitude it is today. It is even these Africans who made Jesus Christ's mother, Mary, the popular "virgin" figure she is today among the adherents of Christianity. For in fact, was it not St. Augustine who emphasized changing the words of the Vulgate Bible which read "to a woman a child would be born," and revise it to read "to a virgin a child would be born"? And even with this new version of Christ's birth, the North African Church—which began when there was no Roman Church—prospered. Rome was still worshiping its "divine emperor" Constantine "the Great," while Africa was developing, practicing, and proselytizing its Christianity.

As I stand here before you at the Shrine of the Black Madonna, I do not say you should not have a Christian religion. All I am saying is, Why have you waited so long to return Christianity to its original African perspectives? I am further saying to you that the Black Madonna, the Mother of Jesus Christ, is nothing more than an adaptation of the Africans' *symbol of fertility*, as depicted by the Egyptian statue of Isis and Osiris—the god and goddess of fertility of the Nile Valley high-culture that predated Mary and Jesus by thousands of years. This point I shall elaborate on later in this lecture. Even Christ's birth on December 25 is nothing more than the celebration of the winter solstice which the Egyptians and all other African people along the Nile River Valley and Great Lakes regions celebrated. This they did even before the dawn of Judaism—the mother of Christianity. I state further that history reminds us that the Sphinx of Ghizeh, symbol of man's mediating the supreme "I Am"—the Unknown One—was and still is African. The picture of the said god, which European and European-American "educators" have held from you for so long, a picture painted at the site of the Sphinx of Ghizeh by Baron Vivant Denon in A.D. 1789, as it appears in my book *Black Man of the Nile* and in other works, will show you how its African features dominated its other characteristics for thousands of years before Napoleon Bonaparte's soldiers blew its nose and lips off with cannon fire because they did not like its "Negroid looks." (See pages 77, 79, and 80 of *Black Man of the Nile* by Yosef ben-Jochannan, Alkebu-Lan Books Associates, New York, 1970).

Major questions usually follow this type of information. Why are these facts not revealed in our major universities? Why do divinity schools ignore them? Do the educators in our institutions of higher learning know them? The answer to all three questions is, Those who know keep them from their students and the general public. Unfortunately, very few Black people and Black universities know these facts. Yet thousands emerged from these institutions with their Ph.D.'s, Litt.D.'s, etc., without ever once hearing these truths.

We now come to some aspects of the origins of the religion of Islam. Most of us have heard many Moslems say that "Mohamet Abdullah was the Holy Prophet of Allah." But those preaching about Mohamet conveniently fail to mention Mohamet's mentor, the Ethiopian Hadzart-Bilal ibn Rhabad. But who was the African called only Bilal? What role did he play with Mohamet? What type of mentor to Mohamet was he? History tells us that the prophet Mohamet was illiterate and could not read the

Hebrew Torah or Christian Bible from whence the Koran is derived. That it was Bilal, an African slave from Ethiopia who had to read and translate them for Mohamet; that Mohamet's origin was as a camel driver, a member of the Koreish tribe; that he was driven out of Mecca and had to flee for his life to Medina—all of which took place in the year 622 of the Christian Era (C.E. or A.D.), where Mohamet later established at the Oasis of Yathrib, the religion of Islam. With this date begins the Moslem calendar—the year one after the Hegira (LAH or AH 1).

With Mohamet always was his most trusted companion, Bilal. All through Mohamet's trials of his faith Bilal was at his side. When his little band of faithful was about to be liquidated by forces from Mecca, Bilal secured help from the emperor of Ethiopia. Hadzart-Bilal ibn Rhabad was treasurer, ambassador, and head of state embassies of Islam. And it was Bilal who wrote the entire *"heavenly scene"* of the Holy Koran. Abu Bekr and Omar the Great, both of whom followed the holy prophet Mohamet as religious leaders of Islam, also looked to Hadzart-Bilal ibn Rhabad for guidance and made no decision relative to the state of Islam without first consulting Bilal. It was the prophet Mohamet who once said, "I am not Islam. He (Bilal) is Islam. He is the writer." Bilal was followed by many other great African and African-Asian writers such as Al Jahiz and Ibrahim Al Mahdi. Islam even had Africans who led the Bendi Soleim people from Arabia that swept over North Africa in the year 640 of the Christian Era (A.D.), or the year 18 after the Hegira (AH)

What do these facts prove? Besides many other things, they prove that the Black man has nothing to fear. That the Black man is the one who was most responsible for so-called Greek philosophy, which is in itself a misnomer. For that which is so entitled we know is in fact basically Egyptian philosophy. This we know because most of what was produced as Greek philosophy has been proven to be of African origin as principles and concepts that

predated the first so-called Greek philosophers. We have
no records of any Greek philosophy until about 600 B.C.
at the earliest, which was thousands of years after the
Nile Valley Africans had already produced their major
philosophical treatises, recorded in their many papyri.
Even eight so-called Ionic (Greek) philosophers, including Thales and Socrates, were not yet born. And of course,
this was hundreds of years before the so-called Greek
philosophers were punished by their own Greek State.
For what? For "teaching foreign philosophy and corrupting the minds of the young with strange gods." The
exact charge against Socrates was presented by Aris-
tophanes. If Socrates was "corrupting the minds of the
young" by teaching the philosophic concepts and disciplines he and others got from Egypt, how could they
have been teaching Greek philosophy when they were
persecuted and prosecuted? Were they not teaching what
they had studied in Egypt, or learned from others who
did? The same holds true for those who did not go to
Egypt but to Ionia—a colony of Egypt at the time. The
Greeks' dilemma was shared by Jesus Christ himself, as
well as Solomon, both of whom had to go to the subordinate lodge at Mt. Carmel and to Egypt's Grand Lodge
at Luxor for their education. I submit that it was not
until 332 B.C., when Alexander the Great (the son of
Philip of Macedon) entered Africa with Aristotle, after
the invasion of Egypt, that the Greeks really acquired a
substantial "philosophy"—African philosophy. At the
time, the Persians were ruling Egypt under the command
of the descendants of Darius I. It was from the Persians
that the Greeks took possession of Egypt, the Africans
having been deposed by the Persians under the general-
ship of Cambyses in 525 B.C. The Egypt the Persians captured had already produced the mighty Queen Hatshepsut,
the only Egyptian queen who traveled down to Punt (or
Puanit) to return a state visit and to purchase myrrh,
elephants, and other products. Egypt had produced Im-
hotep, "the first great physician known to man." He was

such a great physician he was called "the god of medicine" by the ancients after his lifetime. He lived in *c.*1300 B.C., which is thousands of years before the Greeks' Hippocrates was even born; yet this Greek was later to be called "the father of medicine." "Father" of whose "*medicine*"? European "medicine."

Strange as it may sound, the more we examine Greek history, the more it reveals that many Greek citizens were not in fact Greeks. Even Herodotus was not a Greek. Herodotus was an Ionian by birth and had gone to Greece after receiving his education in Egypt. We are to find that Aristotle himself, after seizing and sacking the Grand Lodge of Luxor, the Grand Lodge of Thebes, the library at Alexandria, and then importing Greek students into Kimit (Egypt), forced the surviving Egyptian priests to teach them while at the same time barring Africans from their own studies—including philosophy, medicine, and history. This was the method of destruction employed by the Greeks in their final co-option of things African. It is in this manner that the Africans lost control of Egypt. The Greeks dominated Egyptian life until their own destruction by the Romans in 47 B.C., the Romans subsequently being destroyed themselves by the Arabs from Arabia in A.D. 640 or 18 AH.

Let us then say that when we speak of Christianity and the Europeans and what both have done to Africa and the Africans during the slave trade, do not let us forget the Arabs and other Moslems and what they, too, did to the Africans of East, North, and West Africa with their slave trade more than two hundred years before the European Christians came and did the same.

Let me say in closing, before you ask your questions, that I do not need to deal with African-American history. You can get this in thousands of mass-produced books. But always remember this. Even on the throne of England you sit today. On the throne of Sweden you sit today. And on the throne of France you also sit. I will qualify these points and stop. There was a man called Alessandro de' Medici, the reigning duke of Florence. He was the son of Cardinal Constantine, who later became Pope Constantine, and an African woman by the name of Anna. De' Medici had fourteen children. Thirteen of them became members of royal families of Europe and England. One of his daughters became the wife of the Emperor of Austria, and later became the ruling head of the House of Hesse in Germany—the mother of George III. George III was the great-grandfather of the present Queen of England, Elizabeth. That makes her a "nigger queen." Let us go to Sweden, the whitest of the whites, the fairest of the blonds. There was a man called Count Bernadotte. He was of French and Haitian-African parentage. He was a contemporary of Alexander Dumas I, there being three of them—Dumas first, second, and third. All three were also of African origin: the duelist (swordsman), the playwright, and the theatrical writer. Dumas and Bernadotte were Emperor Napoleon Bonaparte's best generals. But Count Bernadotte was sent to Sweden to represent Napoleon as his ambassador. The Swedes, being afraid of Napoleon, and their King having no heir, convinced the Swedish parliament to adopt Bernadotte so that he could defend them against Emperor Napoleon. So it was done. And when the King died, the parliament voted Bernadotte their king. That line of African-Swedes continues to rule on the Swedish throne to this very day in 1970 C.E. Peace. Shalom. Aalaam Alechem. This was but a peek into "Black studies"—more appropriately, our *African*, African-American, African-Asian, and African-Caribbean heritage.

> All Faith is *false*, all Faith is *true*.
> *Truth* is the shattered mirror strewn
> In myriad bits; *while each believes*
> His little bit the whole to own.*

* From the *Kasidah of Haji Abu el-Yezdi*, translated from Arabic to English by Sir Richard F. Burton.

The following works are suggested for your reading pleasure.

Adamson, R. *The Development of Greek Philosophy* (London, 1908).

Arnold, T. *The Teaching of Islam* (London, 1913).

Beir, Ulli (ed.). *The Origin of Life and Death:* African Creation Myths (London, 1966).

ben-Jochannan, Yosef. *African Origins of the Major "Western Religions"* (N.Y., 1970), *Black Man of the Nile* (N.Y., 1970).

The Bible.

Breasted, James H. *The Dawn of Conscience* (N.Y., 1933), *The Development of Religion and Thought in Ancient Egypt* (N.Y. 1912), *Ancient Records of Egypt: The Historical Documents* (N.Y., 1905).

Burnet, J. *Greek Philosophers*, Part I: Thales to Plato (N.Y., 1966).

Caton-Thompson, Gertrude. *The Zimbabwe Culture* (London, 1931).

Churchward, Albert. *Signs and Symbols of Primordial Man* (London, 1920), *Origin and Evolution of the Human Race* (London, 1921), *Origin and Evolution of Religion* (London, 1920), *Arcana of Freemasonry* (London, 1915).

Cook, S. A. *The Religion of Palestine in the Light of Archaeology* (N.Y., 1930).

Erskine, Mrs. Stuart. *The Vanished Cities of Northern Africa* (London, 1927), *Vanished Civilizations* (date unknown).

Evans-Pritchard, E. E. *Theories of Primitive Religion* (N.Y., 1967).

Frazier, James. *The Golden Bough* (N.Y., 1922), *Passages of the Bible* (N.Y., 1922).

Graves, R. and R. Patai. *Hebrew Myths* (N.Y., 1964).

Heliodorus. *Ethiopian History* Under Downe (London, 1857, 1895).

Herodotus. *The Histories* (translated by Aubrey de Selincourt, N.Y., 1954).

Herskovitz, Melville. Are the Jews a Race?

Higgins, Geoffrey. *Anacalypsis*, Vols. I, II (London, 1840), *The Celtic Druids* (London, 1892).

Jackson, J. and G. Huggins. *An Introduction to African Civilizations* (N.Y., 1937).

James. G. G. M. *Stolen Legacy* (N.Y., 1954).

Johnson, A. R. *The Cultic Prophet in Ancient Israel* (N.Y., 1962).

The Koran.

Malinkowski, L. *Magic, Science and Religion* (London, 1930).

Maspero, G. C. C. *Dawn of Civilisation* (N.Y., 1922).

Meek, T. J. *Hebrew Origins* (N.Y., 1960).

Nkeitia, A. *Art, Ritual and Myths in American Negro Studies* (Ghana, 1966).

Osterly and Robinson. *A History of Israel* (N.Y., 1934).

Poets. *Egypt and the Old Testament* (N.Y., 1922).

Robertson, A. *Origins of Christianity* (N.Y., 1962).

Rogers, J. A. *World's Great Men of Color*, Vols. I, II (N.Y., 1954).

Schofield, J. N. *Historical Background of the Bible* (N.Y., 1938).

Snowden, Frank M., Jr. *Blacks in Antiquity* (Boston, 1970).

Smith, Elliot. *Human History* (London, 1934).

Smith, Homer W. *Man and His Gods* (Boston, 1953).

Steindorff, G. and K. C. Seete. *When Egypt Ruled the East* (Chicago, 1942).

Talbon, P. A. *Nigerian Fertility Cults* (London, 1927).

Tor, Andrea. *Mohammed: The Man and His Faith* (London, 1936).

The Torah.

Wallis Budge, E. A. *The Gods of the Egyptians* (N.Y., 1969), *Osiris* (New York, 1940), *Book of the Dead* with facsimile of the Papyrus of Ani (London, 1894), *From Fetish to God in Ancient Egypt* (London, 1934).

Wheless, J. *Is It God's Word?* (N.Y., 1926), *Forgery in Christianity* (N.Y., 1930).

Werner, A. *Myths and Legends of the Bantu* (N.Y., 1933).

Williamson, S. G. *Akan Religion and Christianity:* A Comparative Study of the Impact of Two Religions (Edited by K. A. Dickson, N.Y., 1965).